D0661743

Mudbaths and Bloodbaths

The Inside Story of the Bears-Packers Rivalry

Gary D'Amato and Cliff Christl

PRAIRIE OAK PRESS
Madison, Wisconsin

First edition, first printing

Prairie Oak Press
821 Prospect Place
Madison, Wisconsin 53703

Typeset by Quick Quality Press, Madison, Wisconsin
Printed in the United States of America by BookCrafters, Chelsea, Michigan
Cover design by Bob Helf

Library of Congress Cataloging-in-Publication Data

D'Amato, Gary, 1956-
    Mudbaths and bloodbaths: the inside story of the Bears-Packers rivalry / Gary D'Amato and Cliff Christl. -- 1st ed.
            p.   cm.
    Includes bibliographical references and index.
    ISBN 1-879483-41-6 (cloth: alk. paper). -- ISBN 1-879483-44-0 (paper: alk. paper)
    1. Green Bay Packers (Football team)--History. 2. Chicago Bears (Football team)--History. 3. Competition (Psychology) I. Christl, Cliff. II. Title.
GV956.G7D35 1997
796.332'64'0973--dc21   97-27098
                                                                    CIP

To our wives, Dee Dee D'Amato and Shirley Christl, for their love and support, particularly during this project; and our kids—Dean D'Amato, Nicole D'Amato, Kelly Christl and Cassie Christl—for being who they are and what they are.

Contents

Foreword

I swore I once covered a Bears-Packers pre-season game won by the Packers, 2-0. In my mind's eye, I could see Bears quarterback Bobby Douglass running out of the end zone for a safety in Milwaukee County Stadium because he had lost track of where he was.

Later research determined I actually had covered a Bears-Packers pre-season game won by the Bears, 2-0. It was Packers quarterback Frank Patrick who ran out of the end zone in Milwaukee County Stadium because he had lost track of where he was.

As I recall, it was a dark and rainy night that obviously contributed to clouding my memory. Such is the nature of the Bears-Packers rivalry, or as Wisconsinites prefer, the Packers-Bears rivalry. It is so old and full of memories that we lose track of where we are.

So when Cliff Christl and Gary D'Amato told me they were writing this book, I was grateful beyond the words I now write to express it. For so many of us from Wisconsin or Illinois or anywhere who follow pro football, the Bears and Packers are more a part of our lives than we realize, or at least sometimes care to admit.

A disclaimer. Just because I have reported for the *Chicago Tribune* since 1967 doesn't mean I'm a Bear fan. Or a Packer fan. I grew up in Ohio, where I was a fan of the Cleveland Browns, which means I have seen the best and worst of what the NFL offers. As a reporter, I am no longer a fan, which doesn't mean I have forgotten what a fan is.

Packers-Bears is the best, unrivaled in NFL history and rivaled in my experience only by Ohio State-Michigan. As a Buckeye, I love the story of Woody Hayes running out of gas in Michigan and pushing his car across the state line to Ohio so he wouldn't have to pay state taxes to support anything Maize or Blue. Apocryphal or not, it can be easily applied to Bears-Packers sentiment.

When my son was a toddler, we went on vacation to Wisconsin. We were sitting in a bar and were having trouble gaining the attention of the bartender. Right away, we knew something was terribly amiss. After pondering why we were being ignored, it suddenly struck my wife. Our son was wearing a Bears sweatshirt. Since he was barely old enough to walk, his attire obviously wasn't his own choice. It's just that his parents were barely smart enough to see that such an innocent selection was thoughtless in more ways than one. It was an affront tantamount to wearing a bikini in church.

Remaining neutral among such interstate tension is not an easy task. Unfortunately, I can't buy neutral license plates. Invariably, I feel self-conscious caught in traffic on Oneida Street in Green Bay. Once, when verbally accosted by a cheesehead a few blocks from Lambeau Field, I stifled the urge to ask how he knew I was from Illinois so I could feign surprise at his ability to read.

But trust me, this is not personal. My daughter and son-in-law live in Wisconsin. My son and daughter-in-law live in Illinois. My wife and I practically straddle the state line and we buy our gasoline on both sides. I took no pleasure from the 61-7 Bears romp in 1980, and I take no umbrage when Brett Favre throws eight touchdown passes whenever he sees a Bears uniform. Rather, I take great delight in the marvelous stories that frame this oldest of all NFL events.

Carolina and Jacksonville could play each other for the next one hundred years and never approach the history. Late-night hallway trumpet blasts to keep the Bears sleepless in places like the Northland Hotel simply are no longer possible in today's sterile, predictable NFL environment. Every change in the game parallels the Bears-Packers story because the Bears and Packers *are* NFL history. For that reason, this is a book that appeals to students of any rivalry or any sport, not just Bear or Packer partisans. It can actually be enjoyed by readers who claim to have no personal stake, which includes myself and the other three neutral observers residing in Wisconsin and Illinois.

My fear is for the future. What this book reinforces in my mind is how the essence of NFL popularity lies not so much with the players or coaches as with the fans. The game itself becomes important and interesting and entertaining only to the extent that the fans allow it to gain entrance into their lives and capture their imaginations. The players, even the coaches, must be taught the significance of the Bears-Packers rivalry.

Most of the participants come with no background or feeling to sustain any meaning of their own. They must learn and absorb from the fans. I have to wonder how long fans can remain loyal and passionate when Jim McMahon and Steve McMichael can not only play for both teams, but be heartily cheered by both. Deep appreciation must be extended Forrest Gregg and Mike Ditka, who drew on their own emotional playing experience to rekindle the true nature of this conflict.

Perhaps a league rule to prevent free agent crossing of adjacent state lines would preserve that sense of separation necessary to the perpetuation of any real feud. I mean, it's bad enough to have Ditka as a Saint, for heaven's sake. To think that under today's trends he could have actually played as a Packer is enough to ruin the whole idea of interstate hate.

Then again, the Packers-Bears rivalry seems to have the resilience to endure anything, much like the hardy citizens of both states. And often, it is difficult to differentiate the players, anyway. Ultimately, it might not matter. Bobby Douglass did end up playing for the Packers and Frank Patrick certainly might have ended up playing for the Bears considering all the quarterbacks I recall traipsing through Chicago with one mission in mind. When the latest, Rick Mirer, was introduced with great fanfare, the very first question he heard was how he planned to beat the Pack.

But if the Douglasses and Patricks have become too interchangeable in your minds for comfort, this book will help sort them all out.

Don Pierson

Acknowledgments

To all the players, coaches and club officials—both past and present—who over the past seventy-seven years have helped make the Bears-Packers rivalry one of the most special in all of sport; and particularly to those 146 who shared their time with us.

Also to Pete Fierle of the Pro Football Hall of Fame for his research assistance; and Bryan Harlan of the Chicago Bears, Mark Schiefelbein of the Green Bay Packers, and Frank Woschitz of the NFL Players Association for helping us track down former players.

Mudbaths and Bloodbaths

Chapter 1

Rage, Roots, and Revelry

Forrest Gregg wasn't merely angry.

Angry doesn't quite describe the bonfire of rage that burned within the Green Bay Packers coach. It doesn't do justice to the bitter frustration that settled in his gut like a shot of acid. It doesn't reflect the size of the dents in his ego and pride.

No, this was a different emotion, darker and meaner, triggered by a profound disdain for the Chicago Bears and their coach, Mike Ditka.

Two hours earlier, on the Sunday of Thanksgiving weekend in 1987, the Bears had beaten the Packers, 23-10, on a cold, rainy, altogether miserable afternoon at Soldier Field in Chicago. The Packers had turned in a turkey of a performance, underscored by place-kicker Max Zendejas' three missed field goal attempts.

The outcome was hardly shocking. In the mid- to late-1980s, Chicago was clearly the superior team, with more talent than Green Bay at virtually every position. The Bears had won Super Bowl XX two seasons earlier, and their victory that day was their sixth straight over the Packers.

Still, every loss to Ditka's Bears left a sour taste in Gregg's mouth.

Ditka was Chicago through and through. He was tough. He was hard. He was arrogant. He was the sort of man who whipped your ass, then lit a cigar and blew smoke in your face. Gregg was no less competitive. He, too, was a hard-driving, no-nonsense coach. And his inability to beat the Bears and Ditka grated on him to no end.

The Packers hadn't topped the .500 mark in Gregg's first three years as head coach, and this year they were on their way to a 5-9-1 record in his final season with the team.

It had been so different in the 1960s, when Gregg was a star tackle on Vince Lombardi's perennial powerhouse Packers and Ditka was a rough-and-tumble tight end for the arch-rival Bears, coached then by the legendary George "Papa Bear" Halas. Gregg had mostly had the upper hand in those days. Now, it was Ditka's turn to crow.

So Gregg was in a dark mood as his players boarded the three buses that would transport them from Soldier Field to O'Hare International Airport for the flight back to Green Bay. All he wanted to do was get out of Chicago. It wouldn't be that easy.

The Sunday of Thanksgiving weekend is one of the biggest days of the Christmas shopping season. Thousands of shoppers, combined with the usual throng of tourists and more than sixty thousand fans leaving Soldier Field, had created gridlock on this dreary, drizzly day in downtown Chicago.

The Packers' buses inched west on one-way Ontario Street in bumper-to-bumper traffic and eventually came to a standstill directly outside Ditka's, a restaurant and bar in which the Bears' coach owned a part interest at the time.

It was irony of the highest order.

"I mean, we sat there for twenty minutes without moving," said Tom Kaminski, a Milwaukee-based travel agent who handled the Packers' travel from 1962 through 1994. "There were people going into Ditka's restaurant with their Bears signs, yelling and laughing. They could see the buses, and they were flipping their (middle) fingers."

Gregg, who was seated in the front row of the lead bus with his wife, Barbara, did a slow burn. After several long minutes, Kaminski went looking for a police car to escort the buses, but had no luck. There was nothing to be done but sit and wait.

"The more people who went in and out of Ditka's, the more you could see Forrest turning red," Kaminski said. "You could see his blood pressure was about to erupt."

As the anger welled up inside, Gregg cut a pose that was familiar to those who had witnessed his tempestuous, emotional swings as coach of the Packers. His eyebrows twitched. His nostrils flared. The veins in his neck bulged and his face reddened.

Finally, his legendary temper got the best of him and he snapped. "Of all the goddamn places," he snarled. Then, turning to the helpless bus driver, he hissed, "Get us the hell out of here. Do something!"

The players shifted uneasily in their seats, glancing at one another, staring blankly out the windows, wishing they were somewhere—anywhere—else. No one dared say a word. An uncomfortable silence settled over the bus, punctuated only by Gregg's intermittent profanity-laced outbursts.

"Man, he went ballistic," said Packers defensive end Ezra Johnson, who was seated behind his agitated coach. "But that was him. He could get worked up about anything."

Gregg yelled at the bus driver, he berated Kaminski, he cursed the Bears' fans.

"He would quiet down for a while, and the worst part of it was, it was raining and it got kind of humid on the bus," Kaminski said. "The only noise you could hear was that windshield wiper: 'Whack, whack, whack.'

"Then another group of four or five people would go into Ditka's, and it would just fire him up again. He would yell some more, but I didn't know what the hell he wanted me to do. Pick up the bus and carry it?"

Today, both coaches downplay the intensity of their personal feud. But they made few attempts to hide their feelings in the 1980s. Their mutual disdain was genuine, it was palpable, and it was evident in the war-like, take-no-prisoners mentality their teams took into the games.

But by no means was their approach to the rivalry an aberration. Rather, it epitomized the bitterness, the raw emotion, and the unwavering loyalty that have been tenets of the series since the dawn of the National Football League.

Arguably, Bears vs. Packers has produced more vitriol, more tradition, and a greater number of savagely contested games than any other rivalry in American sport. No two football teams, on any level, have played one another as often as the Bears have played the Packers. The National Football Conference Central Division foes had met—going into the 1997 season—152 times since 1921, shortly after the birth of the NFL. They also had met once in post-season play and twenty-two times in exhibitions.

"If you say NFL rivalry, two teams, it would be the Bears and the Packers," said John Madden, the NFL analyst for the Fox television network and former head coach of the Oakland Raiders. "I have a picture in my office of Vince Lombardi and George Halas. They're standing in Wrigley Field before a game. That kind of reminds me, not only of the Bear-Packer rivalry, but of football. As an ex-football coach and traditionalist, I just look at that picture and those two men standing there and I say, 'Hell, this is what it's all about.'

"When I think of the rivalry, I think of the Lombardi Packers and the Monsters of the Midway. Just football. Central Division football. Black and blue. And all those things that football used to be, that it's not anymore."

The Chicago Bears and Green Bay Packers are without question the two most storied franchises in pro football.

The Bears trace their roots to 1920, when they were established as the Decatur Staleys and became charter members of the American Professional Football Association. The team moved to Chicago in 1921 and adopted the nickname Bears the following year. The Packers were founded in 1919 and two years later joined the APFA, then in its second year of existence.

In 1922, the APFA changed its name to the National Football League. The league had eighteen franchises at the time, mostly in small Midwestern cities, and only three have survived: the Cardinals, who have since moved from Chicago to St. Louis to Phoenix; and the Bears and Packers. Given the history and stability of the Chicago and Green Bay franchises, it's obvious why the rivalry between them is something special.

"The Packers and Bears is the older definition of pro football," said David Halberstam, Pulitzer Prize-winning journalist and author of several acclaimed sports books. "It dates to a time when the NFL wasn't slick or fancy, before the big salaries and the television cameras arrived. These two teams ground it out. They reflected the culture of the area, the children of immigrants who were trying to get a better deal in life.

"You think of it as the sort of prairie years unvarnished. Pro football had almost no medical facilities. The players were lucky to get cold showers after the game. They washed their own uniforms, that sort of thing."

To this day, it is a rivalry that evokes images of hard-nosed, blue-collar football. But there is so much more to its appeal. It's about dynasties and great teams. The Packers have won twelve NFL championships, more than any other franchise. The Bears have won nine, second most in the league.

It's about Lambeau Field and Soldier Field, arguably the two most hallowed stadiums in the NFL.

It's about the legendary players who have lent it their grace and prowess over a span of more than seventy-five years. Johnny Blood

McNally. Red Grange. Don Hutson. Sid Luckman. Bart Starr. Paul Hornung. Gale Sayers. Walter Payton. Brett Favre.

It's even more so about a small pantheon of players with hard-edged
names who were seemingly destined at birth to be a part of it. Brute
Trafton. Bronko Nagurski. Clarke Hinkle. Bulldog Turner. Ray Nitschke.
Dick Butkus. Mike Ditka.

Between them, the Bears and Packers have sent forty-two players and
coaches to the Pro Football Hall of Fame in Canton, Ohio, led by Halas
and Packers founder Earl "Curly" Lambeau in the initial class of 1963.
The Bears lead all teams with twenty-three inductees and the Packers are
second with nineteen. In addition, eleven other inductees spent at least a
brief portion of their careers with either the Bears or Packers.

"You have so many great players on both sides," said Dick Schaap,
the author and Emmy-winning television essayist. "I mean, if you want
to draw a picture of football, you just draw Ray Nitschke's face and Dick
Butkus' face. That tells you all you have to know about the game."

The teams played for the first time on November 27, 1921, in
Chicago. The Staleys, as they were known then, beat the Packers, 20-0,
before a reported seven thousand fans at Cubs Park, now Wrigley Field.
The teams didn't meet in 1922, then played for the first time in Green
Bay on October 14, 1923. A crowd of 4,451 watched at Bellevue Park,
an old baseball grounds that served as the Packers' home for two seasons, as the Bears won again, 3-0.

Since 1925, the Packers and Bears have met at least twice annually,
with the exception of the shortened 1982 season, when a two-month players strike wiped out both scheduled games.

There have been mudbaths. There have been bloodbaths.

There have been games played in monsoon rains and white-out bliz-
zards, in biting below-zero wind chills and on idyllic autumn days. There
have been games spiced with crushing tackles and charges of cheap shots,
as well as crippling injuries and nasty, sometimes even bizarre, confrontations.

It is clearly a rivalry of the ages, one that has stood the test of time
like few others in American sport.

In fact, if rivalries could be rated by assigning points in pertinent cat-
egories—such as tradition, fan involvement, continuity, and memorable
games and plays—Bears vs. Packers might come out on top.

Before we examine the dynamics of Bears vs. Packers, a word about rivalries: they are not to be confused with matchups. Rivalries are about turf, in a societal sense, and generally need time to ferment. Matchups need only a temporary sense of occasion and urgency.

Going back to the late 1800s, and continuing through the first half of this century, true rivalry games were the essence of sports in this country. They involved, by necessity, teams from the same geographic region, because jet travel and freeway systems were merely futuristic concepts. So the games that stoked the greatest interest were those that matched teams closest in proximity. State university vs. the state university across the border. Town team vs. the town team down the road. The high school on one side of the river vs. the high school on the other side.

Lafayette and Lehigh, two schools in eastern Pennsylvania, began in 1884 what is today the most frequent and longest uninterrupted rivalry in college football. Ten years later, Marinette and Menomonie, twin cities separated by the Wisconsin-Michigan border, began the nation's oldest interstate high school rivalry. On the sandlots of eastern Ohio, a rivalry between the Canton Bulldogs and Massillon Tigers, two professional football teams, pre-dated the NFL.

The charm of these games was that they involved not only teams, but entire communities. No trophy, no matter how big, can take the place of civic pride. Trophies gather dust; bragging rights do not.

Unfortunately, moreso now than ever, our games are about trophies.

"Rivalries used to be more regional, so I think they meant a great deal more than they do now," said Frank Deford, widely acclaimed author and sports journalist. "We have become much more national in our outlook, so we tend to look simply at the top two teams, whoever that may be at the moment. What we've always referred to as traditional rivalries simply don't count as much anymore."

Halberstam made a similar point with a personal anecdote.

"I'm sixty-two years old," he said. "I grew up when all my family lived within one hundred miles of each other. Aunts, uncles, cousins. We were basically all living in the Naugatuck Valley of Connecticut. Now, our children are scattered all over the country. So when you talk about rivalries, who is from where? It's harder to sustain."

In the Roaring '20s, when the Bears-Packers rivalry was born, the ultimate sporting event in the country may well have been the ultimate rivalry game of the times: Army vs. Navy. The late Grantland Rice, legendary sportswriter, stated in 1925 that the Army-Navy game exceeded all other major sporting events in terms of significance. The passion and pageantry, he said, set it apart from the World Series, the Kentucky Derby, or a heavyweight championship fight.

"In the way of drama, action, color, dash, crowds, noise, music, competition, thrills, excitement, cheering, and a whirling kaleidoscope of medley for the eye and the ear, the Army-Navy football game now steps forward as the greatest of all spectacles, the best of all shows, the most vivid, and the most spectacular ensemble in the world of sports," Rice wrote.

The Bears and Packers, at the time, were still young rivals, playing in virtual obscurity in a fledgling league. Fans in northern Illinois and most of Wisconsin had started to warm to the rivalry, but hardly anyone outside those two areas cared, or even noticed. From the late 1920s into the early 1940s, when the Bears and Packers played more meaningful games than at any other time in their history, the rivalry attracted little attention outside the Midwest. Moreover, pro football had yet to be embraced by the sporting public. It had a bawdy image and still often played to paltry crowds in small, primitive stadiums.

To fully appreciate the regional appeal of the Bears-Packers rivalry then, and also the limited interest in pro football, consider what happened in 1941 when the Bears and Packers tied for the NFL's Western Division championship. On December 14, seven days after the bombing of Pearl Harbor, the teams drew an overflow crowd of 43,425 to their playoff game in Wrigley Field. The following Sunday, the triumphant Bears played host to the New York Giants in the NFL championship game. The attendance that day was a mere 13,341.

Before too long, however, the landscape of sport would change, and so, too, would people's habits.

The 1950s ushered in the age of television and a new perspective on leisure activities. People's horizons broadened. Their interest in sports became less provincial and more national in scope. Interest in pro football mushroomed to the point where it became America's most popular spectator sport.

The term rivalry took on a whole new meaning.

Perhaps the first memorable rivalry fostered largely by television was Arnold Palmer vs. Jack Nicklaus. As a nation, we had taken notice of similar rivalries in the past—Dempsey vs. Tunney and Hogan vs. Snead, to cite two examples—but the images of Palmer as a charismatic, go-for-broke commoner and Nicklaus as a bland but immensely talented youngster, were not just imprinted in the minds of newspaper readers, they were brought to life in living rooms across the country.

Television continued to turn other personal battles into huge rivalries over the next two decades, in part because individual sports—namely boxing, golf, and tennis—were among the first to be broadcast nationally. Billie Jean King vs. Chris Evert, Jimmy Connors vs. John McEnroe, and Muhammad Ali vs. Joe Frazier were examples of rivalries, in the broadest sense of the term, created largely by free or closed-circuit television.

Television had a different sort of impact on pro football. In the beginning, almost all pro football broadcasts were carried on a regional basis. So early TV fostered traditional rivalries—Bears vs. Packers, Cleveland Browns vs. Pittsburgh Steelers, New York Giants vs. Washington Redskins, among others—but showcased them to a limited audience.

Then, as interest in pro football escalated through the 1960s, television, either directly or indirectly, brought about the formation of the American Football League, expansion, expanded playoffs, Sunday afternoon doubleheaders, the Super Bowl, and Monday night football. Those developments, in turn, created competition between the networks and sharply increased the financial stakes.

Forced to resort to self-serving hype and promotional overkill to attract a national audience and win the all-important ratings wars, the networks, in essence, created a whole new wave of what they passed off as rivalries. In actuality, they were merely pivotal matchups. Whenever two teams emerged as powers within either the National Football Conference or American Football Conference, their battles were pitched to the public as football's version of Armageddon. What television essentially did was stop cultivating traditional rivalries, if the two teams weren't involved in showdown games, and started creating its own.

In the 1970s and 1980s, two of the more ballyhooed matchups were Dallas vs. Washington and Oakland vs. Pittsburgh. The most hyped contest of the 1990s has been Dallas vs. San Francisco.

The Bears-Packers rivalry, by comparison, has received limited national attention since the early 1960s, largely because the two teams have played few meaningful games. Since 1970, each franchise has won a Super Bowl, but together they also have experienced some of the sorriest seasons in their histories. And when one team was winning, the other invariably was losing. From 1963 until 1993, the Bears and Packers never played a game in the second half of the season when both teams had winning records.

Nonetheless, the rivalry has lost neither its fervor nor its place in history. It has ebbed and flowed, but always retained its relevance with the players and fans. And it has had its occasional moments in the national spotlight.

So what is the number one rivalry in sports today? Some might nominate Army-Navy, in large part because no other game may mean as much to the participants. But with apologies to Grantland Rice, that game long ago faded from the national consciousness.

Many college football fans might argue that Auburn-Alabama, Michigan-Ohio State, Texas-Oklahoma, or some other heated intra- or interstate rivalry belongs at the top of the list. More than twenty-five regional college football rivalries date to the 19th century. Yet another collegiate rivalry, Notre Dame vs. Southern California, which dates to 1926, has a rare intersectional flavor to it.

But none of those rivalries has the national appeal and the marketing arm of the National Football League on its side.

North Carolina vs. Duke in college basketball also could be tossed into the debate. Not only is that rivalry steeped in tradition, but it matches two neighboring programs that have maintained a rare and combined standard of excellence for years.

Baseball, too, has its rivalries. The New York Yankees vs. the Boston Red Sox stirs passions in millions of fans along the Eastern seaboard. The Chicago Cubs vs. the St. Louis Cardinals does the same in the Midwest. But what was once baseball's fiercest rivalry—the Dodgers vs. the Giants—lost something when the teams moved to the West Coast and found themselves separated by hundreds of miles of freeway, rather than the subway that ran from Brooklyn to Manhattan.

In the National Basketball Association, the best rivalries have tended to revolve around individual stars, such as Wilt Chamberlain vs. Bill Russell or Larry Bird vs. Magic Johnson, and as such are cyclical. Another strike against the NBA is that only three of its teams have retained the same identity since 1960: the Boston Celtics, Detroit Pistons, and New York Knickerbockers.

Moreover, baseball teams play 162 regular-season games, and NBA teams play 82. The sense of occasion is missing that exists in pro and college football.

"As a general rule, I think football lends itself more to rivalries because of the nature of the event," Deford said. "Not necessarily of the game itself, but of the event. It's scheduled on a weekend. You look ahead to it. You plan for it. You bring a date. The whole thing. There are marching bands, et cetera. You don't have that in other sports.

"It's very much a part of the culture—a football game—in a way that other sports aren't."

There are few compelling individual matchups today, either. Golf and tennis have become diluted with too many players of comparable ability. The phenomenal success of golfer Tiger Woods underscores that fact. Boxing has lost both its luster and credibility with the American public.

What about other pro football rivalries?

Dallas vs. San Francisco may be the most hyped contest of the 1990s, but the teams had met just twenty-six times, including seven playoff games, as of the end of the 1996 season.

Fans of the Kansas City Chiefs and Oakland Raiders might argue that their rivalry is king, but those teams had played fewer than half as many times as the Bears and Packers: just seventy-three games, plus three others in the post-season, over thirty-seven years.

The New York Giants have had long-standing battles with the Washington Redskins and Philadelphia Eagles. And, besides the Bears and Packers, there are several other tradition-bound, border-state rivalries in the NFC Central Division: Chicago vs. Detroit, Green Bay vs. Minnesota, Detroit vs. Green Bay. But, again, the Bears-Packers rivalry has several more years of history on its side. The Bears and Packers first played almost a decade before the oldest of those other NFC Central rivalries, and some forty years before the youngest of them.

"Historically, I don't know how you could find a rivalry that compares with Packers-Bears," said Paul Zimmerman, senior pro football writer for *Sports Illustrated.* "I'm an old AFL man, so there are some of those rivalries that are interesting to me. But, in all fairness, you can't say in historical significance they match the Packers-Bears."

Undoubtedly, when it comes to rivalries in all of sport, the Bears-Packers game belongs on a pedestal. Whether it occupies the spot at the top of the list is open to debate, but there are those who will convincingly argue the cause.

"I would say it's incomparable," said Bill Gleason, a sportswriter in Chicago since 1941. "Those are the teams that people who didn't have a college alma mater became very much involved with. The Bears-Packers rivalry, when it's at its zenith, there is nothing else like it."

Ron Wolf, general manager of the Packers, came to Green Bay in November, 1991, after stints with the Raiders, Tampa Bay, and New York Jets. A native of south central Pennsylvania, he admitted he had no idea how big the rivalry actually was until he got there.

"It's enormous," said Wolf. "I can't begin to describe what the feeling is for someone who is not accustomed to such a setting when he becomes a member of the Green Bay Packers and you're going to play the Chicago Bears. How really important that game is. I guess I'd liken it to when I was growing up as a kid and we had Army-Navy.

"You could be zero-and-whatever, but if you beat the Bears twice, that accounts for a lot. I realize that is a simplification. But it's a huge rivalry. Really and truly, this is what football is all about. It's a shame the nation doesn't know about this rivalry. Maybe it does.

"But I don't believe that until you become a part of it and live through it, you can realize what it's like."

It's a theme that is repeated over and over by coaches and players who come to the respective organizations from other teams or areas of the country.

Larry McCarren knew about the Bears-Packers rivalry because he was raised in Park Forest, Illinois, and attended the University of Illinois. But when McCarren joined the Packers as a rookie center in 1973, he found out just what the game meant to the veteran players. McCarren now works for a Green Bay television station and does radio commentary for Packers broadcasts.

"When I first got here, Bob Brown gathered all the young guys together and explained to them: 'This is Bear week,'" said McCarren. "I was expecting something mystical to come down from up high, but he explained: 'This is Bear week, so there is no bullshit this week. You really get wired tight for this one.' That was the first time, I guess, that I realized this was something special."

Two decades later, defensive end Alonzo Spellman had a nearly identical experience when he joined the Bears as a rookie out of Ohio State University.

"My first year here, I noticed that the whole attitude around camp changed during Packer week," said Spellman, a first-round draft choice in 1992. "You're in a serious state of mind all season, but Packer week— I mean, Steve McMichael, he'd go into a shell. You couldn't really talk to him that week. Richard Dent, the same thing. William Perry, the same way.

"You don't come in asking questions, like, 'Why are you in this zone right now?' Just like you don't ask a guy why he was in jail. You just kind of realize that this game means a whole lot more than just a division game."

Packers coach Mike Holmgren, who came from the San Francisco 49ers organization, and Bears coach Dave Wannstedt, who arrived from the Dallas Cowboys, both were surprised by the amount of animosity and contempt that their respective teams' fans held for the opponent. They learned very quickly that Bears vs. Packers was not just another game.

"I don't think it takes a coach long before it hits home, just because of what the fans tell him," said Bob Harlan, president of the Packers. "Whether he's making a speaking appearance or from his mail, he gets, 'You gotta beat the Bears. This is *the* rivalry.' Mike Holmgren said it took him a very short period of time to realize how important the rivalry was. He got letters when he first got here that said, 'Congratulations, coach, wish you well.' And the last line was, 'Make sure you beat the Bears.'"

Said Holmgren, with a wry smile: "The players have always understood the rivalry. I've emphasized the point, because it was emphasized to me when I got here by all the little old ladies at the supermarket."

Dave Wannstedt had a similar experience when he replaced Ditka as the Bears' head coach in 1993.

"Oh yeah, I have grasped what it means to the fans," said Wannstedt, whose office wall features the same Lombardi-Halas photograph of which Madden spoke so reverently. "I know how important it is to them. God, half the people who are season ticket-holders here, if they're going to go to one road game, it's going to be Green Bay. And vice versa.

"I know how our fans feel. I've got an appreciation for that."

By definition, if you are a Chicago Bears fan, then you detest the Green Bay Packers and their loyal cheeseheads. And if you are a Green

Bay Packers fan, you hate the Bears with a passion normally reserved for wartime enemies. There is no in-between, no gray area, no blurring of the lines. This is sports' version of the Hatfields and McCoys, a feud that goes back generations.

"I think there is truly hatred," Wolf said. "It's very, very important to the people involved. To the people up here, this is as big a game as there is on our schedule."

The phenomenon has at its roots unique geographical dynamics. Chicago and Green Bay are separated by two hundred miles of Lake Michigan shoreline, the Wisconsin-Illinois border, and a cultural gulf. And so, there is the biggest city in the Midwest vs. smallest city in the NFL; urban sprawl vs. small-town comfort; gourmet restaurants and theater vs. fish fries and corner taverns.

Each has what the other does not. People from Wisconsin shop on Michigan Avenue in Chicago, visit the city's museums, and marvel at the view from the top of the Sears Tower. Meanwhile, people from Illinois vacation in Wisconsin's Door County, dock their sailboats at marinas in cities north of the state border, and fish on Wisconsin's pristine lakes.

Jealousy, loyalty, and resentment get thrown into the mix. Chicagoans tend to look down their noses and poke fun at their neighbors to the north; Wisconsinites get defensive about their Dairy State image.

Michael Bauman, a sports columnist for the *Milwaukee Journal Sentinel*, expressed what many Packers fans think when he wrote in October, 1991: "We understand that a portion of our state's tourist economy consists of dollars from Illinois people, particularly those from the Chicago area. We wish that there was a way that they could just send us the money without showing up themselves. . . . They come up here, pollute the environment, and call us hicks and cheeseheads. They are condescending and arrogant. And those are two of their better qualities."

Wolf recalled, with some bitterness, the lead to a column written by the acerbic Bernie Lincicome of the *Chicago Tribune* in 1993. Lincicome had attended a Halloween weekend game at Lambeau Field in which spectators were given Mike Holmgren masks as they entered the stadium. Lincicome wrote that the gesture "was thoroughly redundant. Everyone in Green Bay already looks exactly like the Packers coach, although, to be fair, not all the women have as prominent a mustache."

These written and verbal exchanges, while common and usually harmless, at times stick in the craw of those involved.

"You've got this little community," said Wolf, "that everyone is taking potshots at versus the big city, you know, the know-it-all guys, the guys whose shit doesn't stink. They're very sophisticated, and that's what they show you. I subscribe to the *Chicago Tribune* and any time they can, they take a shot at us here. They had a Sunday feature on travel and what it's like to be a cheesehead. So they're constantly throwing this up in our face and, right now, we're kicking sand back and that's what makes it more exciting for me."

Of course, Packers fans aren't exactly innocent bystanders in this rivalry. They fire back at the Bears' fans with their own unique salvos. The "Happy Schnapps Combo," a popular Wisconsin polka band, plays a song titled "The Bears Still Suck Polka" that never fails to bring down the house. The song was written by the late Jim Krueger, a native of Manitowoc who toured for years with Dave Mason and also wrote Mason's hit pop song, "We Just Disagree."

"It was an instant hit," Rich Krueger, Jim's brother, said of the Bears polka. "It started out as just a bunch of goofing around, but people ate it up so we kept going along with it."

The song was written in 1991 when Ditka was still coaching the Bears and well before Jim McMahon had joined the Packers as a backup quarterback. The first two verses follow:

How many times must we take this disgrace?
Another Bears fan throwing insults in our face
The Packers are the greatest team to ever play the game
Even if from time to time they get a little lame
How could you ever love a team with Jim McMahon?
Not even Porky Pig was as big a ham
They got a reputation that's mostly based on luck.

If you drive to Soldier Field, they make you pay a toll
For cripes sake, they only won one lousy Super Bowl
They make fun of Wisconsin, but we don't get upset
Where do you think they're all headed every chance they get?
We don't really hold a grudge, 'cause this is all in fun
As far as football rivalries, we're both No. 1
Still, we wouldn't mind seeing Ditka run over by a truck.

The sing-along chorus after each verse is as follows:

The Bears still suck.
The Bears still suck. The Bears still suck.
The Bears still suck. The Bears still suck.
They really, really, really, really, really, really suck.
Yeah, the Bears still suck.

The fans, more than anyone else, have kept the fires of this rivalry burning. Starting with the first game, more than seventy-five years ago, and continuing to the dawn of the 21st century, the fans have gone to unusual, unprecedented, and occasionally unsportsmanlike extremes to display their loyalties.

In 1921, Chicago, the heavily industrialized "City of Big Shoulders," was the nation's second-largest city with a population of 2.7 million. Green Bay was a nondescript but hard-working paper mill town on the mouth of the Fox River, in the middle of nowhere, with no identity save for its local football team. Population: 31,017. Their proximity, along with the David vs. Goliath angle, made the rivalry a natural from the beginning.

"Once again, you've got the little city, the smallest city in professional sports," said Gleason, who has covered the Bears for more than forty years. "There is drama and romance in this thing."

Understandably, Packers fans were first to pour their emotions into the rivalry. Although negotiations for the first game weren't completed until the week before it was played, in late November, 1921, an estimated three hundred fans each paid $11.52 to ride a special excursion train from Green Bay to Chicago the day of the game. They were spurred to a degree by a "pep talk" in the *Green Bay Press-Gazette*, that read, in part: "Although Green Bay is the smallest city in the professional league, it is only a step away from the top of the heap. Support means a whole lot in a football game."

The three hundred fans were accompanied by the Lumberjack Band, twenty-two units strong and headed by George DeLair, a popular Green Bay restauranteur. The band members had gone to Chicago for the first time just the week before for a Packers-Cardinals game and were so well-received that they decided to make a return trip. They left on the midnight train and arrived in Chicago's Loop early Sunday morning.

Dressed in corduroy pants, lumberjack shirts and mackinaws, hunting caps and high boots, they marched first to the Stratford Hotel, where the Packers were headquartered, to hold a small celebration. After leaving the Stratford, which was located at Michigan Avenue and Jackson Boulevard, they paraded through downtown, marching in and out of a series of other hotel lobbies, raising a musical storm before they were halted by the police for not having a parade permit. They performed again between halves of the game and broke into a rendition of "On Wisconsin" when it ended.

"I will never forget it," Ernie Stiller, one of the band members, told the *Press-Gazette* almost forty years later. "The ride to Chicago was a nightmare. Then came the parade from the station and the run-in with the police, which was soon smoothed over. We marched into several of the Loop hotels and spread the Green Bay football gospel all around."

Ed Smith, dean of Chicago sportswriters, was quoted as saying, "Never in my experience have I witnessed a better display of spirit. I take my hat off to Green Bay. It was splendid."

Those fans who couldn't make the trip to Chicago were able to follow the game via telegraph wire at Green Bay's Turner Hall, which was located at the corner of Walnut and Monroe streets. Within two seconds after each play, a local announcer read a message off the wire, informing a packed house how much yardage had been gained on the previous play and the position of the ball.

Two years later, the Bears invaded Green Bay for the first time. Reserved tickets were put on sale the Wednesday before the game and sold out in six hours. On Sunday, the game drew 4,451 fans, the largest crowd that had attended a sporting event in northeastern Wisconsin and about one thousand more than capacity at Bellevue Park.

A rivalry had taken root. Rituals had begun that would be practiced for years. A Bears-Packers game already had become an event, not just another game.

The special trains out of Green Bay would carry more than one thousand fans to Chicago by the end of the 1920s and continue to provide service into the 1960s. The play-by-play transmission from Chicago would become increasingly sophisticated. A Grid-O-Graph was introduced at Turner Hall in 1924 to display the spot of the ball after each play. Within a few years, the board was being displayed in larger quarters, at the Columbus Club auditorium, where a Vita-Vox public address system also was hooked up to give fans interesting sidelights of the game. In 1930, moving pictures of the first of two games at Wrigley Field were shown the next day at Green Bay's Fox Theater, located on Washington Street. The second game played at Wrigley in 1930 marked the first time a Packers-Bears game was broadcast back to Green Bay over the radio.

The Catholic churches in Green Bay recognized in short time what kind of impact the rivalry had on people's lives. By 1928, St. Mary's parish had scheduled a special mass at 5:15 Sunday morning, so fans could catch the early train to Chicago.

George W. Calhoun, a former sports editor of the *Press-Gazette*, was the man who called the first meeting of the Packers in 1919. He also was the first to cover the Packers for the newspaper and served as the team's first publicity director. For years, he acted as team secretary, and he even passed a hat in the stands in the club's early days to help keep it afloat.

The following is an excerpt from a story Calhoun wrote for the *Press-Gazette* in 1962:

"The Chicago excursions were always humdingers to one who traveled with the Bays for over a quarter of a century. Fond memories exist over the four-dollar round-trip fares on both railroads; early services in the churches so the fans could catch the 7:00 A.M. Sunday trains; and, last but not least, red fire along the railroad tracks as we were riding home, and the crowds at the stations joyful with victory. It was a great life!"

It was a great life. Those words illustrate the point that Bears-Packers games were events that held real meaning for the thousands who actively participated as fans.

When the Packers played host to the Bears early in the 1929 season, a crowd of thirteen thousand jammed into City Stadium, located behind Green Bay East High School. The eager spectators filled every seat in the stands and lined the open areas around the field. Those unwilling or unable to pay the ten-dollar scalper fees found other perches. "Every tree in the vicinity of the park was filled with boys and men two hours before the game started," the *Press-Gazette* reported the next day. "Many of the boys brought sandwiches, which they munched as they waited for the game to start."

Later that year, after the Packers clinched their first NFL championship against the Bears at Wrigley Field, a crowd estimated at twenty thousand greeted them at the Chicago & North Western depot upon their arrival home. In 1938, the Packers received ninety-two telegrams at

Chicago's Knickerbocker Hotel the night before the game, all from fans back home. Curly Lambeau read them to the team as part of his pre-game pep talk.

It wasn't just the people of Green Bay, either, who had gone mad over the rivalry. The Packers' fan base already had spread across the state and throughout Michigan's Upper Peninsula.

When the Packers played host to the Bears in Green Bay in 1931, two years before they started playing home games in Milwaukee, Billy Sixty reported in *The Milwaukee Journal* that eight hundred fans from his city would be attending the game and hundreds more would like to, but couldn't get tickets. "You'd think these Packers were Milwaukee's team," Sixty wrote. "Never seen anything like it in my life. Evidently the depression hasn't hit the pockets of the professional football fans who follow the fortunes of that great Packer team."

Later that same year, when airplanes were still a novelty, two dozen fans from Wisconsin Rapids arranged to fly to Chicago for the first of two late-season games at Wrigley Field. A group of fans from Sheboygan took part in some pre-game high jinks before the 1938 game at City Stadium. "The Royal Order of Pisces from Sheboygan chartered their own bus and clad in fur coats of questionable quality and pith helmets ran through a little signal drill of their own before the game," the *Press-Gazette* reported. "A beer bottle served as their football."

By 1941, as many as four special trains, sponsored by local bars, were taking fans to the game in Chicago. In early November, 1944, at the height of World War II, some 2,500 Packers fans traveled to Wrigley Field, only to see their team lose for the first time that season.

Following the war, the Packers fell on hard times, both fiscally and on the field. Civic leaders, urgently looking for ways to drum up interest and save the franchise, started scheduling send-off and welcome-home parties before the Bears game. From 1948 through most of the 1950s, on the Saturday before the Packers played in Chicago, hundreds, sometimes thousands, of fans would gather at the train depot to try and lift the players' morale. The Packers band would march through downtown on its way to the depot; local officials would give brief speeches on the station platform; and a local radio station would offer live broadcasts of the festivities. The welcome-home ceremonies, even given the well-documented and loyal support of the Packers' fans, went above and beyond the call of duty.

In 1952, after the Packers had scored a 41-28 victory at Wrigley Field to improve their record to a mere 4-3, they were greeted by approximately six thousand fans at the North Western depot. The fans had to brave 23-degree temperatures until almost midnight because the train was more than an hour late.

Even after defeats, it wasn't unusual for large throngs of fans to greet the team. In the early hours of Monday morning, following a 24-3 loss to the Bears in November, 1949, a large gathering of fans awaited the Packers' arrival at the old Milwaukee Road depot on Washington Street. When the players stepped from the train, the fans rushed toward star half-back Tony Canadeo, hoisted him on their shoulders, and carried him off the platform.

Paul Mazzoleni, who was born in 1913 and served as a Packers water boy as an eight-year-old in 1921, remembered those heady days with a smile.

"It was just a wonderful time," Mazzoleni said. "We'd leave the Chicago & North Western depot at six or seven in the morning. We'd have ten or eleven cars filled up. Then we'd make one or two stops down in the (Fox River) valley and we'd wind up with about fifteen cars filled. And there was one car just for drinking. It was a bar car. The liquor would flow just like rain.

"We'd get back to Green Bay late at night and you talk about Packer fever. When we got home, there'd be three to five thousand people there at the railroad station, waiting to see the Packers."

The women of Green Bay also had their own rituals that centered around the Packers-Bears weekend. Because the game often was played in mid- to late-September in the 1950s and early 1960s, it unofficially ushered in the city's fall fashion season. Women would wear fabulous hats and furs, as well as heels, even to the games at rickety old City Stadium.

The tradition also continued for several years after the Packers moved into their present stadium in 1957. Charles Hanaway, born in 1908 and, prior to his retirement, a lawyer in Green Bay for sixty years, remembers well one of the first Packers-Bears games played there.

"I remember I handled a case for a lady," said Hanaway. "It was a personal injury case. She won a chunk of money and she bought the most beautiful fur coat that you'd ever want to see. The first Packer game was sometime in September and it was about a hundred degrees in the shade. She and her husband had seats on the 50-yard line, down in the second row. And she walked down there in that damn coat in hundred-degree weather."

The Bears did not have the same captive audience in Chicago. Particularly in their early years, they found it tough competing with baseball's Cubs and White Sox, as well as the region's college football teams, for a place in the hearts of Chicago sports fans, not to mention space in the local papers. Thus, it took somewhat longer for the Chicago fans to gain an appreciation for the rivalry. But by 1932, Bears management had arranged for a "football special" train to transport the team's fans from Chicago to Green Bay. The train left Chicago Saturday afternoon with about a hundred people and returned Sunday night; ten dollars covered the round-trip fare—plus hotel, game ticket, and taxi fare to and from City Stadium.

By 1945, the number of fans arriving in Green Bay by train the weekend of the Bears-Packers game numbered more than a thousand. Not all of them were Bears fans; some were Packers fans picked up in Milwaukee and points north, but the railroads were thriving. The Chicago, Milwaukee, St. Paul & Pacific train that left Chicago on Sunday morning in 1945 for the trip to Green Bay included ten coaches, two dining cars, a baggage car, and three sleepers that were used as parlor cars.

In 1957, when new City Stadium, was dedicated, several hundred fans traveled by train from Chicago to Green Bay for the weekend festivities.

"That was a big thrill," Stan Jones, a lineman with the Bears from 1954 to 1965, said of the train rides. "We'd start in downtown Chicago and pick up everybody else in Evanston and along the way. The whole train was nothing but fans. The team was on the last two cars on the train.

"Then, when you got up there, you got off at the railroad station and walked to the Northland Hotel. We didn't have any buses or anything."

When the game was over on Sunday, the players went back to the Northland—in fact, that was where they dressed in the days of old City Stadium—and waited until it was time to catch the train. Then, they'd walk two blocks through downtown and across the Main Street bridge to the North Western depot.

"Everybody in the hotel would be partying until the team got ready to go back," said Jones. "That was a tradition and, hopefully, you won, because if you didn't, you had to walk that gauntlet all the way down the railroad station with all the irate Bears' fans booing you. And we were the last two cars on the train. But if you won, oh! It was a great experience to walk down to that train with all the fans cheering you."

Some disgruntled fans vented their frustrations in other ways, as well. Ed McCaskey, chairman of the board of the Bears, said he remembered an incident in the early 1960s, several years before he joined the organization in a front-office capacity, that involved Halas—his father-in-law—and a boorish fan.

"I don't remember the year. The Packers murdered the Bears. It was like 49-7," said McCaskey, probably referring to the game in Green Bay in 1962. "We got to the railroad station and I was walking down the platform on one side of Halas. Phil Handler, our line coach, was on the other side. Halas had a club bag in his hand. And just as we got to the Bears' car, a guy with a red and black lumberjack shirt, open down the middle with his hair sticking out, came down the stairway of the fans' car and said, 'Hey Halas! Why don't you quit?' With that, George dropped his bag and said, 'I'll show you why, you bum.' Bam! He hit him right on the chin and the guy just collapsed down on the steps of the car. A few people came and dragged him back in and Halas picked up the club bag and went along to our car. At that time, Halas was about sixty-five years old."

Visits to Green Bay offered both the Bears players and their fans a special aura, not found in any other city in the NFL.

Before Green Bay demolished its downtown in the late 1960s and early 1970s to build a shopping mall, activity during a Packers-Bears weekend centered around the Northland Hotel. Located at the corner of Adams and Pine streets, the eight-story Northland, for many years, was the only hotel in Green Bay large enough to accommodate a visiting team. Today, it serves as a home for low-income people in a barren, lifeless downtown. But, back then, it was where people in Green Bay went to have a bite to eat, a drink, even a haircut. And it was surrounded by small shops, restaurants, and taverns that all did a bustling business on the weekend of the Bears game.

"There was something special about the old days," said Jones, who later became an assistant coach in the NFL for twenty-seven years. "It was just like a college football weekend."

Fans and players would mingle in the Northland lobby. The Saturday night before the game would be another New Year's Eve in the neighboring bars. And fans from both sides would prowl the streets looking for mischief and fun.

Before the game in Green Bay in 1969, a brave Bears fans walked into the Lyric Lounge, a piano bar located across from the Northland, and passed out mimeographed copies of the Bears fight song, "Bear Down Chicago Bears."

Packers fans, in turn, were guilty of their own pranks.

"They'd have bands play outside the hotel all night long," said McCaskey. "People would set off the fire alarms. They'd have mass up the street there and you'd hear a priest say, 'We must love our neighbors, except those dirty Bears. We've got to beat them today.' Then, you'd come out of mass and they were selling programs for the game on the church steps."

The festivities in Chicago the weekend of a Bears-Packers game obviously were more spread out, but they, too, had a feverish pitch at times.

In November, 1941, a little more than a month before the breakout of World War II, the Bears and Packers met at Wrigley Field with the NFL's Western Division lead at stake. The game drew a crowd of 46,484, at that time the largest ever to watch a professional football game in the Midwest. The *Chicago Tribune* reported the next day that eleven scalpers had been arrested outside the stadium and that a filling station on Addison Street had "wrecked the tempers of many fans" by doubling its parking rates from seventy-five cents to $1.50.

Twenty-two years later, when the Bears and Packers met again in a November game at Wrigley with the Western Conference lead at stake, fan interest in Chicago was at an unparalleled high. In fact, the game in 1963, when the Bears beat Vince Lombardi's Packers to gain the inside track on the NFL title, may still rank as the most eagerly awaited pro football game in the history of Chicago.

When 1,500 standing-room-only tickets went on sale the Monday before the game, fans started lining up in front of the Bears' downtown office, located at 173 West Madison Street, at 4:30 in the morning, four-and-a-half hours before the doors opened. Scalpers that week demanded what was then the outrageous sum of one hundred dollars a ticket. The morning of the game, several hundred Bears fans took the train from Chicago to Galesburg, Illinois, a 180-mile, three-hour trip, to watch it on TV because all NFL games were blacked out at the time in the home team's market.

Packers fans have been recognized, since the birth of the franchise, as being among the most rabid and loyal in the country. And, in large part, because of the small town vs. big city aspect of the Packers-Bears rivalry, it's understandable why games between the two teams generally have stirred more interest in Green Bay than any other on the Packers' schedule. But Bears fans also derive considerable satisfaction from watching their team beat the Packers.

"It's very simplistic," said John Jurkovic, a nose tackle with the Packers from 1991 to 1995 who was raised in suburban Chicago. "Basically, they're from a small town and they're perceived to be simpletons. When I was growing up, we looked at them like they were backward, like they were stuck in a time warp. You know, farmers. Still stuck in the '60s. Folks from the city, obviously, we're going to mock a town of ninety thousand. Plus, it was the dumb cheeseheads they wore. They had every strike going against them."

Most of the interaction between the fans in the two cities is done in good fun. Verbal exchanges at the games are common and usually harmless. But there also can be an undercurrent of tension in the stands at both Lambeau Field and Soldier Field. And when that tension is fueled by alcohol, it sometimes manifests itself in physical confrontations.

"I've talked to people who have said, 'I'll never go to Soldier Field again with my Packer jacket on for a Packer-Bear game,'" said Bob Harlan. "In fact, I've warned my youngest son. I've said, 'Mike, don't you ever go down there and wear Packer clothes.' You know, you're taking a chance. It's a crowd that is pretty wild.

"And I imagine they feel the same way about us."

Contemporary fans have exchanged vulgar chants. They've pelted each other with snowballs and cheeseballs. They have harassed each other in the parking lots, the bathrooms, and even in the stands. But no fan in more than sixty years has come close to venting his emotions quite the way Emmet Platten did.

On September 20, 1936, Platten, a Green Bay radio personality who stood 6 feet 4 inches and weighed 230 pounds, rushed onto the field at City Stadium after what he felt was a bad call: a penalty that wiped out a Packers touchdown. When Ted Rosequist of the Bears tried to restrain Platten, who was trying to get at the official, Platten punched Rosequist square on the jaw.

The Bears won, 30-3, but coach George Halas, understandably, was left shaking his head at the conduct of the Packers' fans. "One doesn't expect the fans to come down and start swinging," he said in an uncharacteristic understatement.

Certainly not. But when bitter feud mixes with utter frustration, strange things happen. There is only one explanation for Platten's actions, just as there was only one explanation for Forrest Gregg's moment of rage on a stalled team bus some fifty years later.

It's called Bears vs. Packers.

Chapter 2

Papa Bear and Curly

Stan Jones and George "Mugs" Halas Jr. were having dinner in Denver one evening in 1970 when the conversation turned to Vince Lombardi, the legendary Packers coach who had died earlier that year.

Jones, by then an assistant coach with the Denver Broncos, had played offensive and defensive line for the Bears from 1954 to 1965. He had played for Mugs' father, George S. Halas, who viewed the Packers as his mortal enemy.

So when Jones and Mugs talked about Lombardi that night, Jones confessed somewhat sheepishly that, try as he might, he was having a hard time working up warm feelings for the late, great Packers coach.

"I know everybody thinks the world of Vince Lombardi," Jones confided in Mugs, "but it's hard for me, having played for your dad, to feel that way."

Mugs was surprised.

"Geez!" he said. "My dad loved Vince Lombardi!"

Jones wasn't sure he had heard right. He cleared his throat.

"You mean," he asked hesitantly, "your dad actually loved Vince Lombardi?"

"Yeah, sure," Mugs said with a laugh. "My dad thought the world of Vince."

Jones was dumbstruck. He had never heard the old man utter a single positive word about Lombardi. If Halas spoke at all about his counterpart in Green Bay, it was with derision and sarcasm.

"I always thought George Halas hated Vince Lombardi," Jones said. "I really did. He conditioned us to hate Vince Lombardi. I said to Mugs that night, 'You know, he never let on for a minute to his football team that he did anything but hate him.' We'd watch films and we'd see Lombardi standing on the sideline, and Halas would say, 'Look at that son of a bitch.'"

Halas' attitude had rubbed off on Jones and the rest of the Bears. And here was Halas' son, telling Jones that the crusty Bears coach had held Lombardi in high esteem, had even admired him. It didn't add up. It didn't make sense.

On the other hand, knowing George Stanley Halas' modus operandi, it most certainly did. So intense and bitter was the Bears-Packers rivalry that Halas carefully avoided saying anything good about the enemy in front of his team. Long before there were sports psychologists, Halas was an expert in the field. He wasn't about to let his regard for Lombardi soften his players' will to win.

Papa Bear always wanted his teams to play angry, and the angrier they played against the Packers, the better. He saw no reason to change a spicy recipe that had been handed down from player to player, on both teams, since the NFL's infancy in the 1920s. Green Bay had been his number one nemesis then, and he remained paranoid of the Packers organization decades later.

This fear and loathing—and it certainly was not one-sided—dated to the roots of the rivalry, when Halas' Bears battled Packers teams coached by Earl "Curly" Lambeau, another legendary pioneer of the NFL.

"I trace the intensity of this rivalry—and I think anyone would—to those two guys," said Lee Remmel, director of public relations for the Packers since 1974 and a sportswriter for the *Green Bay Press-Gazette* for twenty-nine years before that. "I don't think there's any question that's where it stemmed from: the personalities of Lambeau and Halas.

"They were such incredible competitors. And the thing they wanted more than anything was for the Bears to beat the Packers, and the Packers to beat the Bears. That was more important than winning any other game all year, and the fans felt the same way.

"They never shook hands—never, ever—after a game. There was never that evidence of mutality of respect that there was with Lombardi and Halas."

As we will see, Halas and Lambeau greatly distrusted one another, spied on each other's teams, and had disputes over player signings and other disagreements. As time went on, they developed a mutual grudging respect. And when both were aging icons—notably after Lambeau had retired from coaching—they softened somewhat and established what could be called a friendship.

In 1961, when Lambeau arrived in Chicago without a ticket before a sold-out Bears-Packers game, Halas told the *Chicago Tribune* that his former adversary was assured of a seat, even if it meant finding a spot for him on the Bears' bench. In 1965, Halas served as an honorary pall-bearer at Lambeau's funeral. But throughout the three decades they clashed as coaches, they were too competitive, too vain, and too prideful to acknowledge one another in a positive light, if at all.

Although both Halas and Lambeau wielded great power in the league, they didn't socialize at league meetings, either.

"They weren't exactly bedmates," said Bob Snyder, who played and scouted for Halas, and spent the 1949 season with the Packers as an assistant coach. "They respected each other in every way, but I don't think they ever went out socially."

Furthermore, the bitter rivals refused to speak to one another before games and never recognized one another afterward.

"Shake hands! That would have been a lie," Lambeau once said. "If I lost, I wanted to punch Halas in the nose. If he lost, Halas wanted to punch me."

Yet, it was Halas who in 1956 urged the citizens of Green Bay to build a new stadium that would later be named Lambeau Field. It was the Packers who accepted Halas' IOU when he couldn't cover a $2,500 guarantee after a game at Wrigley Field in 1932, during the Great Depression. And it was the visionary Halas who helped push for the league's sharing of television revenue, without which the small-market Packers almost certainly would not have survived.

The simple explanation for their contradictory behavior is that Halas and Lambeau realized, early on, that they needed each other. All they had to do was total the gate receipts from a Bears-Packers game to understand that theirs was a symbiotic—if not sympathetic—relationship.

"They were smart enough to know that those games put money in the treasuries," said Bill Gleason, longtime Chicago sportswriter. "The thing I liked about it was that they were willing to play, sometimes three games a year, even though a potential loss would be disastrous to their championship hopes. In those days, the box office was everything."

But just because they had a business relationship didn't mean the two men had to like each other.

Sandlot coaches and fine athletes, Halas and Lambeau played in the first game between the teams, a 20-0 victory for Chicago on November 27, 1921.

Halas, the starting right end, returned the very first kickoff twenty yards for the Staleys—who would change their nickname to Bears a year later—and caught a touchdown pass in the fourth quarter. Lambeau was listed as the Packers' quarterback and place-kicker.

Both men continued to play through 1929. In fact, Halas still holds the Bears' record for longest run with an opponent's fumble: ninety-eight yards, on November 4, 1923.

But it was as coaches, team executives, and power brokers in the young NFL that Halas and Lambeau left their indelible marks on the game of professional football.

Born in Green Bay in 1898, Lambeau helped organize the Packers in 1919. A year earlier, he had lettered as a freshman on coach Knute Rockne's first team at Notre Dame. Forced to withdraw from school after the season because of a lingering illness, Lambeau returned home and with the assistance of George Calhoun, sports editor of the *Press-Gazette*, assembled a sandlot football team. The team was christened the Packers and played an independent schedule in 1919 and 1920. In 1921, it joined the American Professional Football Association.

Lambeau coached the Packers for their first twenty-nine seasons in the NFL—the APFA changed its name in 1922—and compiled a sterling 212-106-21 record. His teams won six NFL titles, including three straight in 1929, 1930, and 1931.

Halas was born in Chicago in 1895 and grew up two miles southwest of The Loop. After playing three sports at the University of Illinois, he joined the Navy and played for the Great Lakes Training Station in the 1919 Rose Bowl. Later that year, Halas also played with the New York Yankees, as an outfielder, and with the Hammond Pros, an Indiana-based professional football team.

In 1920, A.E. Staley, owner of a Decatur, Illinois, starch-making company, recruited Halas to work for him and run his semi-pro football team. Halas accepted the offer in March and by August was instrumental in forming what became the National Football League. After the

1920 season, Staley encouraged Halas to take over the team and move it to Chicago.

Halas followed his advice, retaining the nickname Staleys for one more year before changing it to Bears in 1922. He remained actively involved with the franchise until his death on October 31, 1983.

Halas served four ten-year stints as the Bears head coach: 1920 to 1929, 1933 to 1942, 1946 to 1955, and 1958 to 1967. He retired from coaching on May 27, 1968, with a career record of 324-151-31 and eight world championships.

During the 1940s, the Bears reached the height of their power— although Halas was in the service from 1943 through 1945—with four consecutive NFL Western Conference titles, three world championships, and an incredible record of 81-26-3. Halas' championship team in 1940, which crushed the Washington Redskins, 73-0, in the NFL title game, was voted the greatest professional team of all time by the National Academy of Sports Editors in 1963.

The Bears' image as a tough, hard-nosed, blue-collar team stems directly from Halas, who often was described as irascible, flinty, wily, and cranky. He also was a showman, a conman, an innovator, a superb motivator, and a man who absolutely hated to lose.

"He was a fierce competitor," said Ed McCaskey, who married Halas' daughter, Virginia, and succeeded his father-in-law as chairman of the board of the Bears in 1983.

"You must have heard the stories about him reaching out with one foot and tripping guys going down the sideline on kickoffs? That's not an exaggeration. He really did. He'd do anything to win."

The arch-rival Packers, and their strutting coach, Lambeau, almost always brought out the best in Halas. He coached against the Packers seventy-six times and compiled a 42-30-4 record. Lambeau faced the Bears sixty times and had a 21-34-5 record.

"There was a tremendous, tremendous competitiveness between Curly Lambeau and George Halas," said Hall of Fame quarterback Sid Luckman, who played with the Bears from 1939 to 1950. "It continued throughout their whole careers.

"To Halas, that was his number one game. He felt if we could win that game we could go on and win the division and play for the championship. And he was right. He built that up in his own mind and instilled it in the players."

Driven by their obsession to beat each other, both men turned fanatical the week before a Bears-Packers game. In 1946, the *Press-Gazette* reported that on the Thursday before the Packers were to open the season against the Bears, Lambeau put them through a six-hour workout and topped it off with a meeting at night. Halas also regularly altered his routine.

"We practiced twice on Monday, twice on Tuesday, twice on Wednesday, twice on Thursday, twice on Friday," said Bob Snyder, recalling his days as a quarterback for the Bears. "We had meetings every night. We called it 'Green Bay Nut Week.' All the guys bitched, but Halas would just go crazy. Then, I go up to Green Bay as an assistant coach and I'll be goddamned if it wasn't the same thing with Lambeau."

Because Chicago and Green Bay so often contended for the world championship—in the eighteen seasons from 1929 to 1946, the two teams combined to win twelve NFL titles—Halas considered a loss to the Packers to be catastrophic. He often went into fits of rage during and after the games.

"He was up and down the sideline," said Chester "Swede" Johnston, who played with the Packers from 1934 to 1939. "He wore one of those old-time hats, and he'd be jumping and running out on the field. He'd yell the loudest. He was the coach. He was the owner. He was it."

After the Packers won, 7-0, on September 22, 1935, ending a six-game losing streak to the Bears, a report in the *Press-Gazette* described the scene as the Bears' team bus departed old City Stadium and made its way toward downtown Green Bay: "The thundering voice of George Halas could be heard over the din of traffic down Walnut Street. . . . Halas was bitter about the game, and left little doubt about it in the minds of his players—and everyone else within hearing distance."

There was more to Halas than bluster, of course. He wasn't just from the old school. He *was* the old school, and he didn't suffer players who made foolish mistakes, particularly against Green Bay.

Said Bill Bishop, a defensive tackle with the Bears from 1952 to 1960: "I saw Halas cut guys right in the locker room if we lost to Green Bay."

Bishop will never forget Halas' reaction when teammate John Kreamcheck was penalized fifteen yards during a game against the Packers. "Halas was screaming at him," Bishop said. "John was about 6-5, and Halas had his hands around his throat."

Don Kindt, who was one of the Bears' first-round draft choices in 1947 and who played mostly as a defensive back until 1955, also had a close encounter of the physical kind with Halas during a Packers game. Green Bay had scored on a long pass, and an enraged Halas, thinking the touchdown had been Kindt's fault—he wasn't even on the field for the play—stormed up to him and kicked him squarely in the shin. Kindt kicked back, and player and coach had to be separated.

"After the game, he apologized," Kindt said with a grin. "He said he was trying to kick at the grass and he accidentally hit me."

As demonstrative as Halas was, he had an equal in the fiery, flamboyant Lambeau, who was more than capable of matching the Bears' coach tirade for tirade on the sideline.

"And how, he would rant and rave," said John Biolo, a guard for the Packers in 1939 and longtime head of the Packer Alumni Association. "During a game, nobody would want to talk to him. You'd stay as far away as you could on the bench."

After one particularly bitter defeat to the Bears in a battle royal in 1946, rumors circulated that Packers end Carl Mulleneaux had died of injuries suffered in the game. A reporter checked with a hospital in Green Bay and found Mulleneaux very much alive but dreading his return to practice.

"Dead? I'm only in a hospital, and glad of it," Mulleneaux said. "I don't want to be near Lambeau for a week."

Off the field, Lambeau fancied expensive suits, kept himself in superb physical condition, and was a man of considerable charm who attracted plenty of attention from the opposite sex. His first wife divorced him in 1934, after fifteen years of marriage, on grounds of "cruel and inhuman treatment." One year later, Curly married a former Miss California. Their marriage lasted five years. Lambeau married a third time to a former wife of a Hollywood film director and also was divorced a third time.

Lambeau might have been more dashing and sophisticated than Halas, who was raised in Chicago's Bohemian community by immigrant parents, but he, too, could get down and dirty on the football field—especially when the opponent was Halas' Bears.

"I think Curly and Halas were such enemies—maybe I shouldn't say enemies, but they wanted to beat each other so damn badly—that Curly would just go wild before a Bears game," said Dick Wildung, who played tackle for Green Bay from 1946 to 1951 and, again, in 1953.

"The whole week before . . . oh, God! He hated 'em so bad, I think it always hurt us in the game, especially the first game of the season. We never played very well that first Bear game. Later in the season, we'd go down and have a good football game in Chicago.

"I think we'd get too high because Curly was so damn high. Before the game, he was wild. During the game, he was wild. He'd call for somebody to go into the ballgame who was no longer on the football team. He'd lose his cool when he was going to play Halas."

In large part, Lambeau and Halas got worked up for Bears-Packers games because of their implications on the title chase. But, in the beginning, there was another agenda for both coaches, and it was personal.

When Halas moved the franchise to Chicago after the 1920 season, A.E. Staley told him that towns the size of Decatur, which had a population at that time of 43,818, could never support a pro football team.

"Professional teams need a big city base," Staley told Halas, according to the coach's autobiography, *Halas on Halas*. "Chicago is a good sports city. Look at the way the baseball teams in Chicago draw profitable crowds."

With that advice in mind, Halas probably didn't think much of the Packers' chances for survival in the fledgling professional league. In fact, when he agreed to play them for the first time, he didn't do it as a favor. And, certainly, he didn't have a vision that the rivalry would soon flourish like no other in pro football. Halas was simply looking for another opponent to beat so he could stake a claim to the league championship, according to Jack Rudolph, a former Green Bay historian and cohort of George Calhoun.

Halas agreed to play the Packers a mere five days before their first game. The Staleys had beaten the Cleveland Indians on November 20, and were scheduled to play the Buffalo All-Americans on November 24, Thanksgiving Day. Both the Staleys and All-Americans were unbeaten, and Halas, hoping to draw a large crowd to Cubs Park, billed the game as a battle for the national championship.

In reality, there was no binding agreement that assured anything to the winner of the Chicago-Buffalo game. And with no formal league schedule, it behooved both teams to secure as many victories as possible. To make a long story short, the Staleys lost to the All-Americans, 7-6, on Thanksgiving, then beat the Packers three days later. On December 4, in a rematch with the All-Americans, the Staleys won, 10-7.

As a result, Buffalo and Chicago each claimed the championship and each argued its case at a league meeting after the season. Based on the official league standings, Chicago finished 9-1-1 and Buffalo, 9-1-2. While both teams had the same number of wins and losses, the league decided in Halas' favor and awarded the championship to Chicago. Clearly, the victory over the Packers boosted Halas' cause.

The following year, the Bears finished a distant second to the unbeaten Canton Bulldogs and had no reason to play the Packers; nor was Halas inclined to do the Green Bay franchise any favors.

When the Packers found themselves $3,400 in the red in early November, they attempted to schedule the Bears for a game in Green Bay on Thanksgiving Day. Halas rejected their proposal. Negotiations collapsed when he demanded a four-thousand-dollar guarantee, a prohibitive sum in those days.

Halas also may have been guilty of one other dirty deed that jeopardized the existence of the Packers' franchise in the early years of pro football. He has been credited—or charged—with playing an influential role when the Packers were kicked out of the league following the 1921 season for using players who had college eligibility remaining.

Three Notre Dame players—Hartley "Hunk" Anderson, Arthur Garvey, and Fred Larson—played for the Packers in a game against the Racine Legion on December 4, 1921. All three adopted assumed names to protect their amateur status. Anderson had used up his eligibility in football, but was captain of the Notre Dame hockey team. Garvey and Larson were juniors.

The scandal was exposed in mid-December by the *Chicago Tribune*. The paper also urged league president Joe Carr to banish the Packers from pro football "for all time."

Six weeks later, the Packers were expelled and Carr wired the *Tribune* stating that the punishment was a direct result of the paper's coverage of the story. However, the late John Torinus, longtime member of the Packers executive committee and author of a book about the history of the team, said in 1983, at the time of Halas' death, that the *Tribune* didn't stand alone in advocating a harsh penalty.

"Halas was the guy who was really adamant about not using college players and he apparently wanted to make an example of Green Bay," said Torinus.

By the time the 1922 season started, the Packers had been reinstated by the NFL, but Halas had signed Anderson, Garvey, and Larson to play for the Bears.

A year later, Halas and Lambeau had their first public spat over a player. After playing with the Bears in 1922, Joe LaFleur asked for his release so he could play with the Packers. He had business interests in Escanaba, Michigan, and wanted to play closer to home.

Lambeau and Halas wrangled over the matter for a month. LaFleur also traveled to Chicago to plead his case with Halas. But Halas flatly refused to allow LaFleur out of his contract.

It is easy to imagine Lambeau's chip-on-the-shoulder reaction to what he surely perceived to be Halas' air of superiority. And it is easy to imagine Halas' amusement as the Bears won the first three games in the series and didn't give up a single point to the upstart Packers.

But Green Bay wouldn't go away. The Packers beat the Bears for the first time in a regular-season game in 1925, after Lambeau set a precedent by closing practices to the public. By then, the games were drawing standing-room-only crowds to City Stadium in Green Bay; and by the late 1920s, they were starting to draw fifteen thousand fans to Wrigley Field in Chicago.

And those fans had become fiercely involved in the rivalry.

Paul Mazzoleni, who was born in Green Bay in 1913, remembers standing along the mile-long route that the Bears would take from their downtown hotel to City Stadium.

"We used to wait for their bus over on Walnut Street," he said. "We'd yell, 'Go back to Chicago, you bunch of bums.' A lot of people who had their houses there knew the bus was coming by and they'd holler at 'em. There were hardly any cars in those days, so the fans on the west side would walk to the stadium. They were part of the crowd that was jeering them, too. The Bears were our rivals. They were our enemies."

Against that backdrop, as the rivalry heated up and the games became increasingly intense and important, Halas and Lambeau invested their time and energy accordingly. Both prepared meticulously for the encounters and were paranoid of spies watching their pre-game practices.

"Halas used to go crazy the week before we played the Packers," said George Connor, a Pro Football Hall of Famer who played with the Bears from 1948 to 1955. "He'd change defenses. He was worried about spies looking at our practices. Packer week was really something."

The level of distrust was not unwarranted, because neither Halas nor Lambeau was above bending, or breaking, an occasional rule as he saw fit. Neither was overly concerned with whatever loose code of ethics existed in the pro game. As Tony Canadeo, Green Bay's Hall of Fame running back, so succinctly put it, "I wouldn't turn my back on either one of them."

Both men would resort to just about anything to maintain a competitive edge. A case in point was when the Bears signed Joe Savoldi, a fullback from Notre Dame, in 1930. Savoldi withdrew from school on November 17 to avoid expulsion for seeking an annulment of his recent marriage. Two days later, the *Tribune* carried a story that Savoldi was about to sign a contract with the Packers in violation of an NFL rule. The rule stated that no NFL team could sign a player before his college class had graduated. It was a rule that had been adopted by the NFL four years earlier at Halas' urging.

Once the story broke, the Packers stopped pursuing Savoldi rather than run the risk of being punished by the league. Savoldi's class wasn't due to graduate until June, 1931.

Three days later, the Packers learned much to their chagrin that Savoldi had signed with the Bears. Halas justified the signing by stating that Savoldi was no longer a member of any class because, in effect, he had been expelled from school. Once again, Halas had gotten the best of his hated rivals. But whatever satisfaction he derived from his coup was shortlived. After Savoldi made his debut with the Bears five days later, a league committee fined the team one thousand dollars. While the committee didn't nullify the contract, Savoldi played only three games that season, then retired.

The subterfuge between Halas and Lambeau also extended to the playing field. After a 20-17 defeat in a bitterly contested game on November 9, 1947, the Packers complained loudly that their telephones at Wrigley Field were inoperable, preventing the exchange of vital information between line coach Walt Kiesling, who was sitting high in the stands, and the bench. In those days, there was no league rule that called for a team to stop using its phones if the other team's phones were not working. In an account in *The Milwaukee Journal* two days after the game, sportswriter Oliver Kuechle described an angry Kiesling "ripping out the phone, stomping his feet" and returning to the field just in time to see the Bears score their first touchdown.

An equally frustrated Lambeau blamed the silent phones for the Packers' inability to score from the two-yard line.

"That was awful," Lambeau said. "Never heard anything like it. A full sixty minutes without a telephone. And you know what made it worse? They stuck our bench on the east side of the field for the first time, down about the 20-yard line, so we could hardly see a thing that happened on the other end of the field."

George Strickler, who served as the Packers' publicity director from 1947 to 1950 and as sports editor of the *Chicago Tribune* from 1966 to 1969, wrote years later that the Packers sought an explanation for the phone problem from both Halas and Illinois Bell, but never received a satisfactory answer.

"The explanation, duly received in Green Bay after several weeks of investigation, and accompanied by photostatic reports from the telephone company, was that several youngsters playing in the middle of the intersection of Diversey and Clark streets had lifted the lid and frolicked in a manhole," Strickler wrote. "The frolicking had included playfully pulling out a jack, destroying the circuit. It was just coincidental, the report said, that the only phone on the circuit was the one from the press box to the Packer bench."

In late October, 1954, the week before the Packers and Bears met at Wrigley Field, the Packers played a Saturday night game against the Philadelphia Eagles at Connie Mack Stadium. When assistant coaches Tom Hearden and Ray "Scooter" McLean reached the press box just before kickoff, they found Walter Halas, George's brother and the Bears' head scout, as well as some of his aides, sitting next to their telephones.

"The Packer coaches couldn't move since they had to have telephones and the Bear contingent wouldn't move," Art Daley, former sports editor, wrote in the *Press-Gazette*. "Thus, the Bears had a ringside seat to the Packers' inside operation."

Halas also was known to call players who had been cut by the Packers to see if they would divulge any secrets about personnel or strategy.

"He'd try to pump information out of them," said Vito "Babe" Parilli, who played quarterback for the Packers from 1952 to 1953 and again from 1956 to 1958. "I got cut by Lombardi in '59 and I went up to Canada. And George Halas called me. He said he couldn't understand why I got cut. He was giving me all that and asking me about the Packers.

"But, of course, I didn't have too much to say to him. For years, I didn't like the guy. He'd pull every trick in the book."

While acts of espionage apparently were somewhat common, the precautions both organizations took to prevent them sometimes were comical. On the Wednesday before the Bears played the Packers for the second time in 1941, Halas noticed three men outlined against a window in one of the apartments across the street from Wrigley Field. Trainer Andy Lotshaw was sent to investigate and returned with the information: the three men were playing pinochle, and they had invited Lotshaw to join them.

The ever-suspicious Papa Bear extended his distrust even to Lombardi, whom he suspected of bugging the visitors' locker room at Lambeau Field.

"The pre-game talks were always done outside because he was afraid the dressing room was bugged," said Bill Bishop. "He'd take us in the dressing room and pretend like he was talking to us, 'The defense does this, the offense does this.'

"Then we'd go down the ramp and he'd tell us what we were really going to do."

Jerry Kramer, Lombardi's all-pro right guard, witnessed Halas' secretive ways in the 1964 Pro Bowl game, in which Halas coached. The Bears had just won the NFL championship, while the Packers had beaten the Cleveland Browns in the Playoff Bowl, which basically was a consolation game between the runner-up teams in each conference. Kramer and seven teammates flew from Miami to Chicago and then caught a red-eye flight to Los Angeles for the Pro Bowl.

The flight touched down at about 8:00 A.M. and Halas was waiting to escort the Packers to practice that day.

"We were really tired," Kramer said. "I got on the bus and sat about four seats back on the right side and George handed me a playbook. I said, 'I'm not going to do a hell of a lot today, but I might as well look at the playbook.' So I open the playbook, and the first play was red-right-49, which was our sweep. It was exactly our blocking scheme, our color scheme, and our number scheme.

"I turn the page and it's red-left-28. And then a brown-right-37, brown-left-36. I go to the next page, and the next page, and the next page. Shit, they're all our plays.

"So I look up at George. He had been watching me all this time to see my reaction. Now, when you go to the Pro Bowl and get, say, the

Bears' offense and defense, it gives you a little clue the next time you play them. It's like going to school with them for a week.

"So George looks at me and says, 'Jerry, we didn't want you Green Bay boys to get behind, so we put in your offense.' He knew our offense that well. And he wasn't going to give away any of his secrets."

Halas also made sure his players didn't divulge any secrets. They were instructed to avoid all conversation with strangers when they arrived in Green Bay the Saturday before a game.

"He'd say, 'You don't talk to the elevator operator, anybody,'" said Ken Kavanaugh, who played end for the Bears from 1940 to 1941 and again from 1945 to 1950. "He'd say, 'That Lambeau would do anything to beat you. So don't tell anybody anything about what we're going to do or how we're going to do it.'"

At the same time, Halas wasn't the only coach to play the NFL's version of James Bond. Lambeau was just as wary and equally secretive.

Lambeau told his players to avoid unfamiliar faces around Green Bay the week before the Bears game. He was convinced that Halas would send spies up from Chicago to hang around hotel lobbies, the downtown YMCA, and some of Green Bay's watering holes to glean whatever inside information they could get.

"Hell, you couldn't even smile," said Ken Keuper, a halfback with the Packers from 1945 to 1947. "No sir. You'd be uptown—we stayed at the Astor Hotel and Lambeau would walk by going to the Northland Hotel to eat—and we'd be out in front laughing and joking and that, and he'd come across the street and get on you, right there, on the sidewalk."

Fraternization before and even after a game was something else that Halas and Lambeau frowned upon. Dick Schweidler, a back for the Bears, had served in the same Army unit during World War II with Tony Canadeo, Green Bay's star running back. Just before Schweidler was discharged, Canadeo told him, "You son of a gun. You're going to get back just in time for football and here I am, stuck in Germany."

When the Bears played the Packers in the 1946 season opener, Schweidler was surprised to see Canadeo warming up on the field before the game.

"I went over and hollered, 'Tony! How are you?'" Schweidler said. "He said, 'Don't talk to me. Meet me at the hotel after the game.' Well, after the game, I met him in the hotel and he told me Lambeau said, 'I don't want any of this buddy-buddy stuff. You don't even talk to those guys. You'll get a heavy fine if you talk to any Bears before the game.' "

Halas was no different.

"The Packers had an end named Carl Mulleneaux," said Bob Snyder, former Bears quarterback. "We had played in an all-star game together and we opened in Green Bay. I walked out on the field and said, 'Jesus, Carl. How the hell are you?' Somebody kicked me right in the butt. It was Halas. He said, 'Come on Snyd. This is Green Bay.'"

Not only did Halas and Lambeau distrust one another, but they were forever engaging in acts of gamesmanship. Both were masters in the art of psychological warfare, and their dislike for one another often was evident in their pre- and post-game comments.

On November 5, 1939, the Packers completed fifteen passes for 311 yards, unusually high totals in the pre-World War II years. Even though the Bears won, 30-27, Halas complained that the Packers, along with the Detroit Lions, were using illegal plays.

"Permitting the use of illegal plays is the most positive method of destroying professional football," said a typically melodramatic Halas. "The other eight coaches in the National League are just as smart as the two who are deliberately seeking ways of beating the rules. If these two guilty parties are allowed to continue, the other eight will feel privileged to follow suit and before long, professional football will be a dead sport. Such methods not only are a reprehensible practice from a business standpoint, they are a flagrant disregard for all the tenets of sportsmanship."

Lambeau reached the boiling point in record time when informed of Halas' remarks.

"George Halas will apologize or prove those charges," Lambeau fumed. "The Packers have no illegal plays. . . . Furthermore, the Chicago Bears are the last team in the world to talk about unfair tactics on the football field. We have tolerated their rough, dirty play long enough, and now I am going to demand that Halas either apologize for his inferences in yesterday's *Tribune*, or try to prove them. Halas' charges are like someone committing murder at the same time he is objecting to someone walking across the lawn."

Another of Halas' favorite ploys was to heap excessive praise on the Packers and make it sound as if his poor, downtrodden, talentless Bears would not have a prayer in the upcoming game. Prior to the 1940 season opener, Halas sent a telegram that described a supposedly wretched Bears team preparing to battle the great Packers.

"Given a couple of additional weeks of training, we'd be ready to give that Lambeau aggregation plenty of hell, but as it is I'm fervently hoping we can be at least sixty percent efficient," Halas' telegram read. "We are slower in developing this year than usual."

Lambeau dismissed the telegram with an "angry snort," according to an account in the *Press-Gazette*.

"We're not falling for that Bear propaganda," he said. "And we're not going to ease up no matter what Halas says. We know perfectly well the Bears are coming here with one of the greatest teams which ever played in the National League."

Lambeau was right. The Bears won, 41-10, and finished the season with their historic 73-0 victory over the Redskins in the NFL title game.

In 1958, Halas chose to sing the Packers' praises after the Bears had registered a 34-20 victory in the season opener. The Packers were coached that season by Scooter McLean, one of Halas' former players.

"We won't be better than six and six, and the Packers will do better than that," Halas said, with a straight face, after the game. "I'm not being fooled by all this. The Packers are a fearsome team."

Fearsome is the last word anyone would use to describe the 1958 Packers. They finished 1-10-1, the worst record in franchise history. The Bears, on the other hand, finished 8-4.

Halas didn't just limit his psychological ploys to telegrams and false praise. "Lombardi told me a story he had never told to anybody else," said Hall of Fame running back Paul Hornung. "I think it happened in 1965, Gale Sayers and Dick Butkus' first game against the Packers. Dad Braisher was our longtime equipment guy and, back then, the locker rooms in Lambeau Field were in the same building.

"Anyway, there was a knock on the door after both teams had come back up for last-minute instructions and it was Halas. Dad Braisher opened the door and Halas says, 'I need to talk to coach Lombardi right now.' So Dad leaves him standing there and goes and knocks on the door where the coaches are having a conference. Lombardi angrily opens the door, 'What do you need?' Dad says, 'Coach Halas needs to see you. He says it's very important.' 'Coach Halas? Where?' 'Down in the equipment room.' So Lombardi walks down there, it's like ten minutes before kickoff, and Halas says, 'Vince. I just want to tell you one thing. You better have your team ready because we're going to kick your ass.' Then, Halas turned and walked away.

"He caught Lombardi with his pants down. Lombardi was flabbergasted. We won the game. But the whole game—Lombardi later told me—he was thinking, 'Why did he do that? Why did he do that?' Halas absolutely psyched him out. And that was a great lesson for Lombardi, I think."

Max McGee, who played wide receiver for the Packers in 1954 and again from 1957 to 1967, also remembers Halas trying to play with his mind in the heat of battle. "Halas would call the snap signal," McGee said. "You'd be lined up wide near the Bears' bench and he'd go, 'Hut, hut.' He'd try to make you jump offside. That was George Halas. He didn't care if it was legal."

Canadeo, too, remembers how Halas' competitive spirit manifested itself during games. "Geez, what a con artist," Canadeo said. "He'd come out on the field before games and say, 'Hi, Tony! How are you? How do you feel?' Then I'd get knocked out of bounds during the game and he's there yelling, 'Kick that son of a bitch!'"

Halas didn't stop there, either. Tobin Rote, the Packers' quarterback from 1950 to 1956, asserted that stories about the Chicago coach putting bounties on Green Bay players were true.

"He really did that," Rote said. "One of my college teammates, Gerald Weatherly, played linebacker for the Bears. He graduated the same year I did from Rice. He told me, 'Watch your back. Halas has a $50 or $100 bounty to put you out of the game,' or something like that. He said, 'They'll take a shot at you, even after the play is over.'"

Rote said Weatherly passed on this information at a bar in Chicago the night before a game in the early 1950s. And, sure enough, the Bears knocked him out.

"Ed Sprinkle was the one who got me," Rote said. "I threw a pass about 45, 50 yards and it was intercepted. It was a desperate, last-ditch play right before the half. As it was intercepted, I was jogging over toward the sideline. Ed came and got me right behind the head with a forearm and knocked me about five yards. I was looking through two tubes for about two hours there. It was a chance for Ed to make fifty or a hundred bucks, whatever Halas was paying."

While Sprinkle denied ever getting a bonus for knocking anyone out of a game, it is safe to assume that both sides were guilty of underhanded tactics. All's fair in love and war, right? But what didn't seem fair to the Packers was Halas' seemingly substantial influence over the game officials. It is not at all far-fetched to conclude that Halas' stature as one of the league's co-founders and most powerful figures would have intimidated some officials. Other teams in the league complained about this, but none were any more vocal than the Packers.

"There was a lot of comment over the years about the fact that Bill Downes, who was one of the premier referees in the game, always seemed to work the Packer-Bear game and lived in the same building as Halas: the Edgewater Beach in Chicago," Lee Remmel said. "A lot of people were unhappy about that and paranoid about that around here. Nobody liked it, but Downes obviously was assigned by the league."

The Halas-Lambeau chapter of the Bears-Packers rivalry came to an end, in effect, after Green Bay, coming off a 3-9 record in 1948, lost its 1949 season opener to Chicago, 17-0. Lambeau resigned as coach on September 30, five days after the game. He left assistants Tom Stidham, Charley Brock, and Bob Snyder in charge, but gave them no authority. Lambeau assumed a position in the front office, although he remained an advisor to the coaching staff and the games for the remainder of that season, including the rematch with the Bears, counted toward his record.

Four months later, on February 1, 1950, Lambeau also resigned as the Packers' vice president and general manager to sign a two-year contract to coach the Chicago Cardinals. The resignation came during an attempted reorganization of the club, in which Lambeau had waged a fight for control against a faction of the board of directors which sought to oust him. Lambeau coached the Cardinals for two years, the Washington Redskins for two more, and then coached the College All-Stars from 1955 to 1957 before quietly bowing out of the game. After that, he split his time between his ranch in Thousand Oaks, California, and his summer home in Fish Creek, on the Door County peninsula in Wisconsin. By then, real estate investments had made him a wealthy man.

Lambeau kept a low profile while a new Packers era under Vince Lombardi pushed him deeper into the shadows. Eventually, he was able to put aside enough of his bitterness to attend games in Green Bay as a spectator.

Bob Harlan, the Packers' current president, will never forget his one and only encounter with the coaching legend. It occurred just after the 1963 opener, which the Packers lost, 10-3, to the Bears. At the time,

Harlan was the sports information director at Marquette University in Milwaukee.

"The only thing I remember about the game was that as I was walking out of the press box, Curly Lambeau was standing there all by himself, kind of draped over the side of the stadium wall, looking like the season was finished," Harlan said. "He seemed like such a forlorn person. He was all by himself, and it was just like it was the last game of the playoffs and we had just been eliminated. I'll never forget how terribly lonely he seemed standing there. And I'll always remember that."

On June 1, 1965, Lambeau visited a friend, Francis Van Duyse, in Sturgeon Bay, Wisconsin, and found him out mowing his lawn. Lambeau peeled off his coat for a turn at the mower. A little later, he muttered, "I feel kind of sick." Then he collapsed and died. He was sixty-seven.

Halas served as an honorary pallbearer at the funeral, and wrote a column about his relationship with Lambeau that was carried on *The Associated Press* wire. In the column, Halas reiterated Lambeau's many accomplishments—sometimes with backhanded compliments—in a businesslike tone. The column offered no insights into what Halas thought of Lambeau personally.

"Curly gave me some of my greatest battles when he had the Green Bay Packers," Halas wrote. "He did a tremendous job. I doubt if the league would exist today without the likes of Lambeau.

". . . Lambeau did the job. In fact, he did it too well. He did it so well that he kept beating the Bears. You know, that was the greatest thing that could have happened to us. He kept beating us until he started such a rivalry that I couldn't hope would end."

Halas continued to coach through the 1967 season, when he was seventy-two years old. After that, he served as the Bears' chairman of the board for sixteen more years. One of his last acts, before he died in 1983, was to hire Mike Ditka as the Bears' head coach.

While Halas viewed the Packers as bitter enemies on the field, he was an otherwise staunch supporter of the Green Bay franchise. He looked after his own interests, first and foremost, of course. In 1947, when the NFL established territorial rights extending over a seventy-five-mile radius for each city in the league, Halas opposed a special clause that gave Green Bay exclusive rights to the Milwaukee area. The Packers had started playing a portion of their home schedule in Milwaukee in 1933 and Lambeau considered it vital that they retain their hold on the city.

"When we assured Green Bay the Milwaukee territory that secured the Packer franchise," Lambeau once said. "It wasn't easy, though. Halas fought it. It was a two-day debate, but I finally got it."

At the same time, the Packers knew they could depend on Halas whenever they were faced with a serious crisis. In 1956, when they were on shaky financial ground and desperately in need of a new stadium, Halas came to Green Bay to speak at a downtown pep rally. He addressed more than one thousand fans at the Columbus Club auditorium and urged them to approve an impending referendum to build the stadium.

"I confess I have a deeper feeling of attachment for the Packers than any other club," Halas told his audience the weekend before the vote. "Sometimes I wonder if there would be a Chicago Bears today if there had not been such a terrific rivalry. . . .

"I can say to you sincerely—just as sincerely as we hope to edge out the Packers in both games next fall—that the best way for you to guarantee the current and future success of the Packers is to build a new stadium—a place where your team can grow and flourish in the future, just as it has grown and flourished here in Green Bay from the earliest days of professional football."

Three days later, the residents of Green Bay passed the referendum by an overwhelming margin.

Eighteen months later, on September 29, 1957, the Packers dedicated their new stadium—later to be named Lambeau Field—by beating the Bears, 21-17. Halas had turned over the head coaching reigns to Paddy Driscoll at the time, but attended the game and spoke at halftime.

Seven years later, Halas was honored by the Green Bay Elks at a banquet. The Bears were coming off their 1963 world championship, and the jocular Halas, feeling on top of the world, opened his address by saying, "Good evening, friends of the Chicago Bears."

"Everybody went, 'Whoa,'" Lee Remmel said, chuckling at the memory. "I can still see George. He was such a great kidder. He loved it. Everybody respected him, regardless of whether they hated him on the field."

By then, of course, Halas and Lombardi had forged a special bond, unlike anything Halas had ever experienced with Lambeau. Lombardi respected the game's traditions, and he looked up to Halas. And although

Halas' players remember the many times that Papa Bear ripped Lombardi in front of them, the feeling was mutual.

"They were very, very admiring of each other," Remmel said. "I remember Vince saying, 'Papa George, I love that man.' Halas had similar feelings about Lombardi. They were very respectful of each other."

Four decades earlier, it had been a different story entirely, when Lambeau and Halas built their respective teams into powerhouses and clashed on and off the field.

George Musso, the Bears' Hall of Fame lineman, perhaps best summarized that fascinating relationship.

"Halas and Lambeau were friends, like coaches would be friends," he said. "But when it comes to playing, hell, you're not friends. You're out to win.

"And you win any damn way you can."

Chapter 3

Sacred Fields Forever

Dan Jiggetts will never forget his annual visits to Lambeau Field, eye-opening experiences he describes much the same way an anthropologist might describe the discovery of a bizarre civilization.

Jiggetts, an offensive tackle for the Chicago Bears from 1976 to 1982 and a product of Harvard University, can still see the Packers' fans, their faces twisted in anger. He can still hear the obscenities they screamed. He can still feel their hatred, fueled by the three Bs: beer, booze, and Bears.

Before the Packers' organization mercifully built a tunnel between the visitors' locker room and the playing field in 1989, opposing teams had to pass through a concession area under the stands on the south end of the stadium as they walked to and from the field. A temporary metal fence was pulled back, allowing the players to walk through the area without being accosted by Packers fans. Well, that was the idea, anyway.

"They put up a chain-link fence, and it was like going to the zoo," said Jiggetts. "You know, you're separated by that fence, but you look at these faces and go, 'My goodness, just say no.' It was like you're walking through the zoo and the animals are on the outside looking in. They're screaming at us, looking at us. And I used to think, 'This is great.'"

The fans for both teams have been rabid and rowdy whenever—and wherever—the Bears and Packers have bumped helmets through the years. One might accurately say that while the physical environment has changed, the emotional environment has not. And so, as the venues shifted—from Bellevue Park to old City Stadium to Lambeau Field in

Green Bay, and from Wrigley Field to Soldier Field in Chicago—the rivalry took root and blossomed.

Each stadium had its own quirky character and unique atmosphere, and each added memorable chapters to the saga of Bears vs. Packers. But venerable Lambeau Field has been a special setting for professional football in general and for the rivalry in particular.

The bowl-shaped stadium on the west side of Green Bay has undergone several improvements and expansions since it opened in 1957, transforming it from a spartan, open-ended oval with 32,150 seats to a private box-bedecked jewel that seats 60,790.

Remarkably, the charm and intimacy of Lambeau Field has been more than just preserved, it has been enhanced.

"I think about that every time I go in there, how that stadium has developed," said Willie Wood, who played safety for the Packers from 1960 to 1971. "The time we were in there, it looked like a small college stadium. Now, it's probably the best in the National Football League."

In this age of high-tech stadiums, with their teflon domes, convertible roofs, exploding scoreboards, and sterile corridors, Lambeau Field stands in stark contrast as a shrine of simple elegance and a cathedral of tradition.

"That's what I love about it," said John Madden, the Fox network football analyst and former head coach of the Oakland Raiders. "If they ever build a shrine to pro football, it ought to be Lambeau Field. Every time I go there, I think, 'This is what the hell it's all about.' This is kind of how it all started, and it goes off in different directions, where you get domes and theme parks and all that stuff.

"Soldier Field is the same way. You just get the feeling that this is football. The Green Bay Packers, the Chicago Bears . . . Lambeau Field, Soldier Field. Then you get a little weather, and now you're talking."

Lambeau Field and Soldier Field are among the NFL's few remaining throwback stadiums—open-air facilities in cold-weather climates, with natural grass fields and rich histories. And no field is more revered by fans and players alike than Lambeau Field. Even ex-Bears talk about Lambeau in more sentimental tones than their own Soldier Field.

"Playing in Lambeau Field was like playing in high school," said former middle linebacker Mike Singletary, who played in ten Pro Bowls during his twelve-year career with the Bears. "It brought back so many fond memories of playing football. The field looked smaller. You looked around and it didn't seem like you were playing in a professional football game: all the business and all the hype and all the stuff that goes along with NFL football. No, when you come to Lambeau Field, we're going to take you back to what football used to be like. That's what I liked about Lambeau Field."

Revie Sorey, who played guard with the Bears from 1975 to 1982, echoed similar sentiments.

"It was a football experience," said Sorey. "It was real grass. You wore real spikes and cleats. You got dirty. If you were tough, you wore no sleeves, no gloves. To me, that was real football."

Bob Harlan, the Packers' president, recalled leaving work one day and noticing a car with out-of-state license plates pulling into the Lambeau Field parking lot. That wasn't unusual in itself, because the stadium has become a sort of drive-through mecca for Packers fans, who visit at all hours of the day and night. What happened next, however, *was* unusual. A middle-aged man got out of the car, knelt down on all fours, and kissed the ground. He was making his pilgrimmage.

Before games, the vast expanse of parking lot is turned into a menagerie of decorated RVs and costumed tailgaters, and the smoke from grilled brats hangs heavy in the air. Once the game starts, everyone gets an unobstructed view of the action. Lambeau has perhaps the cleanest sight lines of any comparable structure in the nation. And the fans who fill Lambeau to capacity for every home game are fiercely loyal and nearly unwavering in their support, even during the lean years, of which there have been many. They also happen to despise the Chicago Bears with great passion.

"The Packer fans are the best fans in the world," said Mike Ditka, Hall of Fame player and coach of the Bears, not to mention a favorite target of the Lambeau Field boo-birds. "That's a high school atmosphere. Everybody in the town is out and it's a wholesome thing. They might have called me an asshole, but that's their business. Those fans were great fans. The NFL needs a lot more Green Bays than they do New Yorks or LAs. That Green Bay feeling epitomizes what the NFL was and should be."

The Bears who played for Ditka felt much the same way as their leader and thrived on the catcalls, the insults, and the obscenities that were directed their way. They not only appreciated the setting at Lambeau Field, but they took a perverse pleasure in winning there.

"When you go there, you're in a true football atmosphere," said Kevin Butler, Chicago's kicker from 1985 to 1995. "The people who go there work all week long to make it for kickoff time. You can feel that electricity in the air. When we went there, the rivalry was great, the hatred overflowed. You were really in a hostile environment. You stepped on that field and you had the sense that you were fighting for your life.

"The great teams look forward to those challenges. When you can go into a stadium that has the character and mystique that Lambeau has, and play a team that you know wants to beat you as bad as anything, that's how you build even more character as a championship team."

Al Harris, a defensive end with the Bears from 1979 to 1984 and again in 1986 and 1987, said he would never forget the sights and sounds of Lambeau. "It was like a college atmosphere," said Harris. "Then, when you were walking up that ramp and they were yelling at you, screaming at you, throwing beer on you, you felt like you were a gladiator."

Jay Hilgenberg, who played center for the Bears from 1981 to 1991, said areas of Lambeau also had a distinct odor.

"I remember before they redesigned the stadium coming out of the locker room," said Hilgenberg, "you'd go out in between these fences and all the fans were there . . . it was great. And I'll tell you, the smell of alcohol there was incredible. Early in the morning, too. It was unbelievable."

Mark Bortz, who played guard for the Bears from 1983 to 1994, was born and raised in Pardeeville, Wisconsin, so whenever Chicago visited Green Bay, his teammates would kid him about the fans' boorish behavior. "They're standing on top of their RVs in the parking lot before the game, they're drunk, they're falling off their lawn chairs," Bortz said. "And I'd have to sit there and listen to the guys say stuff like: 'Hey, there's your family over there,' and 'Look at the cheeseheads.'"

The Green Bay fans' hatred for the Bears peaked in the mid-1980s, when Chicago fielded one of the best teams in the league and the Packers were in the midst of a string of losing seasons. For Green Bay, the frustration was evident on the field, and in the stands at Lambeau.

"In 1985, '86, and '87, when the games were as dirty as anything I've ever seen, the fans were throwing batteries, dog bones—the edible kind, milk bones, huge ones—at us." said Butler. "Those things can hurt coming from 40 or 50 yards away."

While the Bears didn't appreciate being the targets of projectiles, they did have an appreciation for the loyalty of the Packers' fans. Some Bears even recognized that not all of them were obnoxious and intoxicated; that there were pockets of civility within the stadium.

"Even when Bart Starr was coaching and they weren't playing very well, the fans were still going back and forth: 'Bart Starr! Bart Starr! Bart Starr!'" said Gary Fencik, a Bears safety from 1976 to 1987. "They used to pull those chain-link fences back, and if you were in any other stadium, the fans would be spitting on you. Here, these people are holding onto little kids, and the kids are going, 'Boo Bears.' I always enjoyed it. I still enjoy going up there. It's a wonderful environment."

Lambeau Field was built in 1957 at a cost of $960,000, which was shared equally by the Packer Corporation and the City of Green Bay. The first stadium in the country built exclusively for pro football, it was dedicated as City Stadium on September 29, 1957, during ceremonies attended by, among others, then-Vice President Richard Nixon, NFL Commissioner Bert Bell, and actor James Arness of "Gunsmoke" fame. The Packers beat the Bears that day, 21-17.

The stadium was renamed Lambeau Field in 1965, following the death of Earl "Curly" Lambeau, the team's founder and first coach.

Lambeau Field, or at least its playing surface, is known affectionately as the Frozen Tundra, a nickname that stems from the 1967 NFL championship game against the Dallas Cowboys, played in sub-zero temperatures. That classic showdown will forever be known as the Ice Bowl.

Interestingly, however, few Packers-Bears games at Lambeau have been played in arctic-like conditions.

The 1997 season opener marks the thirty-ninth Packers-Bears game at Lambeau, but only six of them have been played in December, including three straight from 1994 to 1996. The teams usually got a break in the weather because the tradition was to play the first of the two regular-season showdowns in Green Bay; it was not until 1966 that the first game was played in Chicago.

Two exceptions to the fair-weather rule occurred in 1975 and 1976. On November 30, 1975, swirling snow and winds gusting to forty miles per hour put the wind-chill index at minus-two degrees in Green Bay. The Packers won, 28-7.

The next year, on November 28, the temperature was six degrees and the wind-chill index was a bone-chilling minus-fourteen at kickoff. The turnstiles froze, and the halftime entertainment was canceled because members of the Green Bay West High School band couldn't play their ice-cold instruments. Packers guard Gale Gillingham, the only holdover from the Ice Bowl team, said conditions that day were comparable. Jiggets recalled that the plastic undersoles of his shoes melted when he tried to warm his feet on the sideline heaters.

Chicago won, 16-10, even though quarterback Bob Avellini attempted only twelve passes, completing seven for ninety-seven yards.

"That was the coldest I've ever been," Avellini said. "Guys were telling us how to keep warm: put vaseline on your face; put vaseline on your toes; wear two pairs of socks, and, in between, put a plastic bag; wear a hood; wear gloves.

"But here I'm a quarterback. I've got to be able to move a little bit. So I go out there as if it was seventy degrees out. I walked out of that locker room and my nose froze up. It was the coldest I ever felt. The first drive of the game, we had the ball for five or six minutes and we didn't throw it at all. Finally, it's third-and-ten and a pass comes in. I say, 'No way. I'm lucky I'm getting the snap.' My arm is stiff. The ball feels like glass. I go back and I get sacked. Whoever it was, I felt like thanking him for saving me the embarrassment of trying to throw the ball.

"So I go to the sideline and I put these big mittens on and I'm rubbing my hands together, and I smell something burning. I'm standing next to the heater, and my mittens had caught on fire."

The Packers have spent ten million dollars on improvements to Lambeau Field just since 1993. In 1996, they spent $3.5 million on a new scoreboard. In 1995, they spent $4.7 million to add ninety luxury boxes and an auxiliary press box. In 1993, the club spent $1.7 million on a color replay board.

The updates have modernized the stadium without destroying its aura.

Ron Kramer, who played tight end for the Packers in 1957 and again from 1959 to 1964, and returns to Green Bay for the annual alumni game, said the atmosphere at Lambeau hadn't changed over the years.

"The camaraderie and the feeling of the people in Green Bay is second to none in the National Football League," Kramer said. "This is unique. It's unique because this is the only university team in the NFL. It's wonderful to come back here, just to see the people. They have a feeling for the Packers that doesn't exist anywhere else."

Jiggetts, now a Chicago sportscaster, is one of many ex-Bears who still gets goose bumps when he returns to Lambeau.

"One of the things that will always be special is just going up there and playing in that stadium," he said. "It's football. You cut out all the B.S. and this is what it's all about. Before they put in the sky boxes, you felt like the crowd was right on top of you. Now, they've put the sky boxes in there and you feel like the whole stadium is closing in on you. You go, 'This is great. This is why you play the game.'

"I hope these young players understand that, even with the amount of money they're making. I hope they understand this will be the most special thing you'll take with you: the fact that you got to play in this type of game, in this environment. It's something you should never forget, and treasure."

Although it seems as though the Packers and Bears have played at Lambeau Field forever, they actually played at two other facilities in Green Bay before Lambeau was built.

The first two Packers-Bears games in Green Bay—a regular-season game in 1923 and an exhibition in 1924—were played at Bellevue Park, an old baseball grounds located on the north side of Main Street, just beyond Elizabeth Street. The primitive facility, located next to the old Hagermeister Brewery, was inadequate for football, but 4,451 fans filled the small bleachers and ringed the field in 1923 to boo showboat George Trafton and the Bears, who prevailed, 3-0.

"It was nothing but clay soil. Hard as a rock," said Paul Mazzoleni, a Green Bay fan who attended the first Packers-Bears game in Green Bay in 1923. "All they had was a rope. And people would drive their cars up and surround the field, pull right up to the rope."

Starting in 1925, the Packers played their home games at City Stadium, which was built behind East High School, about one mile due east of the downtown area. The Bears game that year drew a record crowd of 5,389, and the Packers won, 14-10.

City Stadium was a typical small-town park of its day. The grandstands were made of wood, and stretched roughly between the goal lines on both sides. In its early years, in particular, some fans simply stood or sat around the edge of the field. There were none of the creature comforts that today's fans take for granted. There weren't even any bathrooms.

"During halftime, you'd see guys go over, pull it out and piss on the fence," said Mazzoleni, who attended games at City Stadium over four decades. "The women would go under the stadium. If they had to use the toilet for a bowel movement, then they were allowed to go into East

High School. Of course, a lot of guys were peeking at the girls under the stadium."

The atmosphere at games was similar to that at a carnival. Fans walked to the stadium, stopping at early-opening taverns along the way to fortify themselves—a precursor to modern-day tailgating. By the opening kickoff, the crowd invariably was raucous and high-spirited.

"Remember Three Corners?" Mazzoleni asked in reference to the intersection of Main, Baird, and Cedar streets, not far from the stadium. "There was nothing but taverns over there and they'd let 'em open at seven o'clock in the morning. There were people going to the game who were getting oiled up at seven o'clock. You talk about heavy drinkers nowadays, they were pretty heavy in those days, too. A lot of these guys had to plan strategy for the game. You had a lot of football cowboys in those days."

The Bears, meanwhile, would dress at the Northland Hotel downtown, carry their cleats down to the street, and board a bus that took them down Walnut Street to the stadium. When they walked onto the field, the fans let them have it with a barrage of insults and the occasional hurled object.

"They used to throw whiskey bottles at us," said Ken Kavanaugh, who played end for the Bears in the 1940s. "We had to wear our helmets on and off the field. They threw everything at us. Maybe you'd get a pint bottle bounce off your helmet or shoulder pads. They weren't that bad during the game; the toughest part was going out on the field and coming in at halftime and after the game."

The field at City Stadium was surrounded by a six-lane, cinder track, but the stands were no more than ten to fifteen yards from the team benches. "The fans were right down on the field, right behind your bench," said Ed Sprinkle, an end with the Bears from 1944 to 1955. "They'd run up and down the sideline behind you. They had to have police there to keep them back. I never took my helmet off when I was there. I kept it on the whole game. I was afraid somebody would throw a bottle out there and whack me behind the head."

The fans were so close to the field that they were within earshot of the coaches and players. On the Bears' side of the field, the fans would carry on verbal sparring matches with George Halas.

"He'd yell right back at 'em," said Deral Teteak, a linebacker with the Packers from 1952 to 1956. "Swear? I mean that guy would swear at the officials, at his players, at us, at the fans. I can't believe the stuff he got away with. You'd see him turn his head and jaw right back at the fans. And I mean he used some bad words."

In the early years of the stadium, the biggest inconvenience for the Bears was that they could not retreat to a locker room at halftime because City Stadium had no locker room for the visiting team. The players simply gathered in the end zone or under the stands to discuss strategy for the second half. In later years, visiting teams would use the basement of East High at halftime.

Medical facilities also were nonexistent. In 1948, Bears Hall of Famer George Connor was kicked in the chin by a Green Bay player and went into a boiler room at halftime to get a nasty gash stitched. "I came out for the second half, and I was late," Connor said. "The stadium gates were locked. So I had to yell up to a couple of Bear fans in the stadium. They came down and got in a fight with the guys to get the gate open, and I walked into the stadium. The game was going on, and the Bears were on the other end of the field. So I had to wait for a timeout, and I ran across the field.

"Halas said, 'Where have you been? You're late. That'll cost you fifty dollars.' "

The Packers-Bears game in Green Bay almost always was played in September, usually the first or second week of the season, so the weather generally was good. Of the thirty-two Packers-Bears games at old City Stadium, twenty-six were played in September; the latest date the two teams ever played there was October 7, in 1956.

Rain, not snow, produced the biggest weather-related problems. On September 18, 1938, a steady rain over the weekend caused flooding throughout Wisconsin and turned the turf at City Stadium into a muddy quagmire. Chicago won, 2-0.

On October 3, 1954, torrential rains in Green Bay set records and flooded city streets. A driving rain during the game made for a slippery, sloppy mudbath, and was a contributing factor in the thirteen combined turnovers. The Bears won, 10-3.

Seating capacity at City Stadium gradually was increased to fifteen thousand by 1934 and to about twenty-five thousand before World War II. By the 1950s, however, the facility was terribly outdated. It had become an embarrassment to the league, which had expanded to the West Coast and had started to attract legions of new fans.

"The locker room was horrendous," said John Martinkovic, who played defensive end with the Packers from 1951 to 1956. "It was underneath the stands. There were concrete floors. It was from the medieval ages."

With pressure mounting on the Packers to upgrade their facilities, the citizens of Green Bay passed a referendum in April, 1956, to build a new stadium. The team moved into new City Stadium the following fall, taking a leap up in class but abandoning one of the last vestiges of a simpler era in professional football.

City Stadium still stands in Green Bay, although many of its distinguishing characteristics—its sandstone facade, the wooden bleachers, and the large band shell in the northwest corner—have been torn down. It is silent on Sunday afternoons, but is alive with football's pomp and pageantry on Friday nights. Green Bay East and Green Bay Preble high schools still use the field—the same one on which Clarke Hinkle, Bronko Nagurski, and Don Hutson ran into the history books.

In addition to their home games at old City Stadium and Lambeau Field, the Packers played at least one regular-season game in Milwaukee every year from 1933 through 1994—169 games in all.

But only once was the opponent the Chicago Bears.

On November 10, 1974, the Packers beat the Bears, 20-3, in a driving rainstorm at County Stadium—their one and only regular-season meeting in Milwaukee. It was Green Bay coach Dan Devine's decision to move the game downstate, and he was crucified for it. Devine had gone against a tradition that dated to the dawn of the NFL. Like azaleas at Augusta National, mint juleps at the Kentucky Derby, and a bottle of milk in Victory Lane at the Indianapolis Motor Speedway, the Packers-Bears game belonged at Lambeau Field.

"We caught a lot of grief up here," said Harlan, who at the time was the team's assistant general manager. "I look back on it—I wasn't making the final call at the time, but I was in on the group that sat and talked about it—as a huge public relations blunder. That game is just too important up here."

The game is equally important in Chicago, where two storied stadiums have played host to it. Wrigley Field was the Bears' home until 1971, when they moved several miles south to Soldier Field.

Wrigley Field, opened in 1914 and known by various other names until 1926, was built for baseball, and that is the sport for which it still holds sentimental value. But it also doubled as a cozy football stadium for a half-century, and the old Bears look back on its quirks and flaws with fond memories.

"There was a wonderful Americana feeling about playing in Wrigley Field," said Bob Kilcullen, a Bears defensive lineman from 1957 to 1958 and again from 1960 to 1966. "When you drove up to Wrigley Field and got out of the car, the smell that came from the hot dogs and all that stuff that was already cooking, it was just turmoil for your stomach. But it was just Chicago. The people milling around, everybody wanting to talk to you, walking through those big steel gates on Waveland; it's one of those memories that never fade."

"What a great place to play," echoed Mike Pyle, the Bears' center from 1961 to 1969. "I can't tell you how good that place was to play a football game."

Said fullback Rick Casares, who played for the Bears from 1955 to 1964: "There was a feel to Wrigley. There was a character to it. Wrigley Field was like a neighborhood. I don't think anybody had a home-field advantage like we did. Our end zone where we warmed up, the bleachers there in left field . . . those people there, you couldn't give them fifty-yard line seats. We used to carry on conversations with them, clown around. There was a closeness there. You couldn't get a ticket at Wrigley Field. I just loved it."

The intimacy was partly a byproduct of the era, when fans and athletes had a more personal bond, and partly the result of the cramped quarters at Wrigley. The stadium's dimensions really weren't big enough for a football field, but one was squeezed in anyway. Fans sitting in the end zones were literally just a few feet from the action, and the upper deck seemed to be suspended over the field. The overall effect was claustrophobic.

"You knew the north wall was about a yard past the end zone," said George Connor. "The south end zone was cut short because of the first base dugout. Then, if you were going south, you were going uphill. And Halas would place the tarpaulins in certain strategic positions along the sidelines, so if the other team ran their pass patterns down and out, they'd have to worry about the tarpaulins. And the Board of Trade Band in the northwest end zone was another thing you had to watch for. They were a nuisance. You couldn't run a pattern in that corner of the end zone. The Bears could, because the band would get out of the way. But when the other team was down there, they'd get right in the way. There were a lot of things that were very distracting."

Although most of the Packers viewed games at Wrigley Field as occupational hazards, some of the old-timers appreciated the unique atmosphere.

"I loved to play in Wrigley Field," said Hall of Fame running back Tony Canadeo, who was born and raised in Chicago. "There was such a tradition in that ballpark. Soldier Field, to me, looks like a lonesome range out west some place. But Wrigley Field, hell, if you had a relative there, you knew it. In the end zone, you'd find all your old former high school pals out there, saying, 'We're going to kill you today, Tony.' But there was a closeness out there. And tradition-wise, I just enjoyed it."

The Bears and Packers started playing at Wrigley Field—then Cubs Park—in 1921. From 1928 through 1933, the teams played two games a year there, the second often being the last game of the season. With the opening kickoff set at 2:00 P.M. in those days, the teams finished in darkness on many occasions. Lights were not intalled at Wrigley until 1988, seventeen years after the Bears moved to Soldier Field.

Weather occasionally was a factor, too; a raw wind whipping off nearby Lake Michigan was the norm, but there also were games in which the players had to deal with snow or freezing drizzle, sleet, and fog. On December 11, 1932, Chicago won, 9-0, on a field covered by more than four inches of snow.

However, no game at Wrigley, was quite like the one played December 5, 1964, following a two-day snowstorm that buried Chicago under twelve inches and forced the city's schools to close for the first time in history. At Wrigley Field, the snow was piled five feet high around the edge of the playing field. Fans pelted the Packers with snowballs throughout the game, but Green Bay prevailed, 17-3.

According to the *Green Bay Press-Gazette*, one Packers fan brazenly ran up and down the aisles waving a Green Bay pennant "despite an unremitting barrage of snowballs from Bear partisans."

Unfortunate weather was not the only discomfort with which the Packers had to cope when they played at Wrigley Field. The locker rooms were cramped and antiquated, and the showers often provided only cold water—or didn't work at all. Hank Gremminger, a defensive back with the Packers from 1956 to 1965, said he remembered wearing his uniform and taking a bus back to the hotel after a game once, so the players could shower with warm water.

"The dressing room was filthy," said Gremminger. "You'd have to put towels down to keep the dirt off your feet. We couldn't shower. There wasn't any hot water. We always blamed George Halas."

"I think our locker rooms were a little better," admitted Ronnie Bull, a running back for the Bears from 1962 to 1970. "That was the way Halas wanted it. In fact, a lot of times, Halas was accused of turning off the hot water in the visitors' dressing room. Was that true? I can't swear to it, but I heard stories it was true."

In addition, the Bears' fans could be just as rough on the Packers as the Packers' fans were on the Bears at City Stadium and Lambeau Field.

"We used to go in the dugout and we'd walk up some stairs, kind of behind a cyclone fence, up to a second floor," said Don Horn, who played quarterback for Green Bay from 1967 until 1970. "Before the game and at halftime, those irate Bear fans would throw beer at you. They'd have big old canisters of mustard and ketchup. They'd be hitting that pump, shooting mustard and ketchup at you, and throwing beer at you."

Willie Davis, the Packers' Hall of Fame defensive end, ranked Wrigley Field as one of the toughest places in which to play because of the fans.

"I think they got into the game every bit as much as the players," he said. "They started harassing you from the time you came out of the dugout until the time you left the field."

The tight quarters could be tough on visiting players, with the Bears' fans practically on top of them and the brick wall making every trip into the end zone a potentially dangerous proposition.

Gary Knafelc, who played end for the Packers from 1954 to 1962, remembers catching a touchdown pass and slamming into the wall. He was shaken up, but not seriously hurt.

"The funniest thing was, Lisle Blackbourn was our coach and he ran all the way down to the end zone," Knafelc said. "Bud Jorgensen, our trainer, thought Blackbourn was concerned whether I was hurt. But he didn't say anything about that at all; he just wanted to make sure I caught the ball."

One player who was not as fortunate was Dick Plasman, who played end for the Bears from 1937 to 1941 and again in 1944. Plasman was the last man in the NFL to play without a helmet. In a game against the

Packers on November 6, 1938, Plasman attempted to catch a pass by quarterback Ray Buivid deep in the end zone. Plasman either lost track of where he was, or momentarily forgot about the brick wall. He crashed into it head-first.

"At least one Packer player on the field at the time covered his eyes to avoid seeing what he knew was going to happen," the *Press-Gazette* reported the next day. "It was the same type of accident that Eddie Jankowski had in just about the same spot last year. But a row of spectator chairs in front of the wall broke Eddie's charge. Plasman hit the bricks with the full force of his two hundred and some pounds."

Plasman suffered a severe laceration on his scalp, a concussion, and a fractured wrist.

"He was going all out for a pass in the end zone, down where the ivy-covered walls are," said Bears teammate Dick Schweidler. "He hit it head on, full stride, and peeled his whole scalp off his head. When he hit that wall, I jumped up and thought, 'That man is dead.' I didn't see how anybody could live through something like that."

Herm Schneidman, a defensive back with the Packers, was covering Plasman on the play. "I saw the wall and yelled," Schneidman said. "I pulled up and he dove for the ball. I felt like throwing up. He was bleeding pretty bad. He peeled his head open."

Plasman continued to play without a helmet for three more seasons. He didn't don a helmet until 1944, when he returned from the service and found that the NFL had passed a rule the previous year making helmets mandatory.

As the NFL's popularity soared in the 1960s, and bigger facilities were built to seat more fans, the Bears came to the realization that they had outgrown Wrigley Field. In 1971, they switched their home games to Soldier Field, located along Lake Michigan, south of downtown. The move made sense financially, but many of the Bears loved playing in Wrigley Field and weren't crazy about moving. Soldier Field was bigger, all right, but it was stark and impersonal, lacking the aura and coziness that are important factors in a home-field advantage.

"Our advantage at home was never the same," lamented Doug Buffone, who played linebacker for the Bears from 1966 to 1979. "When opposing teams walked into Wrigley, they walked into a real hornet's nest. We lost a lot of games, but we destroyed a lot of clubs, too. In our minds, that was what football was all about. We loved it."

Soldier Field was one of the early open-air pro football stadiums to install artificial turf. In fact, the sixteen Bears-Packers games played there from 1971 to 1988—when the surface was changed back to grass—were the only times in their long history that the rivals did not play on grass.

"At that time, Soldier Field had the AstroTurf, and that was *the* thing," said Bears kicker Mac Percival. "But after we played on it a little bit, it was, like, 'Plant grass again.'"

Although Soldier Field didn't become the home of the Bears until 1971, Chicago and Green Bay played for the first time there in 1926. The eighth game of the rivalry, played on December 19 of that year, was a benefit for the P.J. Carr Memorial Christmas Fund. Carr was a well-known Chicago politician, and proceeds from the game were used to buy holiday baskets for the city's poor. The game was proposed in late November, finalized in early December, and counted in the league standings; although the Packers had played their last regularly scheduled game on November 28, and taken two weeks off before resuming practice the Monday before the game.

Soldier Field had been officially dedicated on November 27, 1926, less than a month before the Bears-Packers game. The dedication game matched Army against Navy, and drew a crowd of 110,000. One member of the Carr Fund committee, caught up in the hoopla surrounding the Army-Navy game, predicted the Bears and Packers would draw at least fifty thousand, and perhaps even one hundred thousand.

The two teams had played a thrilling game on November 21 at Cubs Park, with the Bears prevailing, 19-13. But attendance for the benefit game was just ten thousand. The game was played in mist and sleet, as lakeside temperatures hovered around the thirty-degree mark.

The Bears' permanent move to Soldier Field in 1971 coincided with a period during which both Chicago and Green Bay fielded teams that were mediocre at best and, often, downright pitiful. The Packers won the NFC Central Division title in 1972, but had only one other winning season the rest of the decade; the Bears had two.

Unlike the Bears' fondness for Lambeau Field, most of the Packers loathed the annual foray into Soldier Field. The artificial turf was hard, for one thing. And the lake-effect weather alternated between bearable and miserable. Of the twenty-five Bears-Packers games played at Soldier Field from 1971 through 1996, eight were played in November and nine in December.

Gale Gillingham, a former all-pro guard with the Packers, recalled a game in 1973, when the artificial turf iced over following a winter storm in Chicago and the grounds crew tried to melt the ice before the game.

"They had about an inch of ice and they spread that road salt, or whatever it was, on the field," Gillingham said. "People were snowballin' both teams. We played in that slop and ice. That was a tough game."

In 1994, after Soldier Field had gone back to natural grass, the teams played in a monsoon in a Halloween edition of Monday night football. The Packers won that memorable game, 33-6.

Typically, however, the weather at Soldier Field for the Bears-Packers game has been frigid and blustery. On December 11, 1977, the wind-chill index was minus-seven. The next year, on December 10, the turf was again slick with ice and the wind-chill was at minus-ten. On December 18, 1983, record low temperatures reached minus-eleven and plateaued at two above zero.

"I hated it," said Mike Douglass, who played linebacker for the Packers from 1978 to 1985. "I thought it was the worst field in the world. When we first started going there, it was before they remodeled it. It still had the AstroTurf. It was always cold or raining or snowing. The locker rooms were absolute crap. They had broken windows, showers from the 1920s that were always cold. It was like going into a dungeon."

Dave Roller, a defensive tackle for the Packers from 1975 to 1978, recalled that the showers sometimes didn't work any better at Soldier Field than they did at Wrigley Field.

"The city didn't have the water working or something one year. Shit, we put on our damn travel suits and went home, took one at home," said Roller.

One thing Soldier Field has never lacked, however, is vociferous, rowdy, overzealous fans. Cars with Wisconsin license plates occasionally are egged in the parking lot. People wearing Packers apparel are asking for trouble. Offensive tackle Ken Ruettgers, who retired midway through the 1996 season, said that his wife was pelted by hunks of cheese while she sat in the stands at Soldier Field in 1995.

The Bears fans didn't even spare Packers center Larry McCarren, who was born and raised in the Chicago area and attended the University of Illinois.

"Oh, they're vicious," McCarren said. "One year, I tore an arch, and it hurt like hell. Right before the half, they were leading me in to re-tape it so I could play in the second half. I'm walking through a tunnel where the people are leaning over, and a guy yells, 'Hey, McCarren—I hope it's broken!'"

Brian Noble, who played linebacker for the Packers from 1985 to 1993, recalled that once, fellow linebacker Tim Harris, a notorious trash talker, was standing next to him and jawing with a fan in the sixth or seventh row during the national anthem. "This big, fat guy is yelling at Timmy, and he turns around and just reads the guy the riot act," Noble said. "Well, all of a sudden, I got whacked on the shoulder. It was a ten-dollar roll of quarters. Honest to God: ten dollars worth of quarters."

After Charles Martin body-slammed Bears quarterback Jim McMahon and was ejected from a game at Soldier Field in 1986—one of the most infamous cheap shots in the history of the rivalry—he had beer dumped on him and was pelted mercilessly with flying objects when he left the field. "He got hit with everything," Noble said.

Noble's favorite Soldier Field story, however, involves a friend who came to watch him play. While Noble was waiting for the starting line-ups to be announced, his friend stood up—and stood out in his Packers jersey—and started yelling to get Noble's attention.

"He goes, 'Nobes! Nobes!' He's got my number on his jersey," Noble said. "Well, I mean, the crowd just pelted him. It looked like a rock concert. The place lit up with beer cups, soda cups, everything. They just buried him. I thought, 'Boy, you got balls standing up doing that in here.'"

Soldier Field may not be able to match Wrigley in terms of ambiance, but it does have an interesting history. Plans for the stadium, a memorial to the soldiers of World War I, took shape in 1919. It opened in 1924 as Municipal Grant Park Stadium with forty-five thousand seats. The first football game played on the field was November 22, 1924; a capacity crowd watched Notre Dame beat Northwestern, 13-6. By the time it was officially dedicated, two years later, the capacity was more than one hundred thousand.

The all-time collegiate attendance record of 123,000 was established at Soldier Field on November 26, 1927, as Notre Dame beat Southern California, 7-6. The stadium also played host to the first boxing event that drew a gate of more than $2.5 million: Jack Dempsey vs. Gene Tunney, in 1927.

When the Bears moved there in 1971, the north end of the stadium was closed off and the capacity was reduced to 55,701. Following several more renovations, capacity now stands at 66,944.

Soldier Field may not be the home of the Bears much longer. The team isn't happy with the stadium and wants a new one. Although Soldier Field does not have Lambeau Field's charm, the rivalry will lose something if the Bears move.

"We won a Super Bowl playing there," former Bears coach Mike Ditka pointed out. "If that's not tradition, I don't know what the hell tradition is."

The place even has fans among the rival organization.

"Lambeau is my number one favorite, but Soldier Field is right there," said Ruettgers. "It's the only away field I loved playing in. It just looks like you should be playing football on that field. When it was artificial turf, it was like it didn't fit. The turf didn't fit the stadium. But when they went back to grass, it was like, this is football. This is how it should be played.

"Everything is perfect for that game down there. The rivalry. The field. The fans. Football. There is not a more perfect match in the NFL than that day, that game, on that field, if you have to play away. There is something about the columns, the architecture, the name.

"Can you put a better puzzle together?"

Chapter 4
Violence, Venom, and Villains

The year was 1945. Hitler's Germany had fallen. So, too, had the atomic bomb, on Hiroshima and Nagasaki. World War II was over, and combat-weary men were returning to America's factories and farms. An uneasy peace had settled over the world.

Well, most of the world.

On the professional football fields in Chicago and Green Bay, there was no ceasefire, no truce, and definitely no peace. The Bears and Packers were still at war, in a football sense, and it was escalating.

Precipitated by a series of cheap shots, a vicious and sordid chapter in the rivalry began that fall, one that would last ten more seasons. During that span, players from both teams regularly attempted to maim each other in the name of the National Football League.

The ugliness eventually ran its course, and the teams finally cleaned up their acts in the mid-1950s.

But thirty years later, the rivalry would again turn nasty, this time sinking into a cesspool of late hits and trash talking, some of it inspired—if not encouraged—by the teams' respective head coaches.

This chapter chronicles the two most hateful and violent periods in the 77-year history of Bears vs. Packers. The stories you are about to read are true; the players' names have not been changed, because none of them were innocent.

THE ED SPRINKLE YEARS
The way the Packers looked at it, Lee Artoe had it coming.

Artoe, a tackle for the Bears and, by reputation, one of the dirtiest players in the league, had sucker-punched Packers blocking back Larry

Craig in the face during a game at Green Bay's City Stadium on September 30, 1945.

The blatant cheap shot was still fresh on the Packers' minds when the teams met again at Wrigley Field on November 4. It was time to retaliate, in accordance with the unwritten code of the NFL in the rowdy post-war era: An eye for an eye, a smashed face for a smashed face.

Every player on Green Bay's roster wanted to be the man to knock Artoe out of the game. "Everybody said they were going to get him if they got the chance," recalled Packers end Clyde Goodnight.

The honor went to halfback Ken Keuper.

"I was in on offense and had to come across and trap-block on the Bears' end, George Wilson," Keuper said. "This guy appears off our tackle, Baby Ray. I didn't realize who it was at the time, so I stepped in and hit him with a forearm.

"He went down like a cow in the stockyards getting hit with a mallet. It turned out he fractured his jaw and had quite a few teeth knocked out."

As luck would have it, the player was Artoe.

And the most brutal period in the Bears-Packers rivalry was under way. It turned into a decade-long donnybrook, a crusade of counterpunches that left a trail of broken noses, cracked ribs, and caved-in teeth. From 1945 through 1955, the Bears and Packers went at it with savage fury, trading insults, threats, and cheap shots, and, on occasion, stopping long enough to play football.

The period ran concurrently—coincidentally or not—with the career of Ed Sprinkle, a 6-foot-1, 210-pound defensive end for the Bears who was feared throughout the NFL for his raw-boned style of play. An article about Sprinkle in the September 25, 1950, issue of *Collier's* magazine was titled, "The Meanest Man in Football."

Sprinkle, a rough-and-tough Texan who played from 1944 to 1955, may not have been solely, or even largely, responsible for the brutal play during this period. But he symbolized what the era was all about.

"As far as anybody from the Bears or Green Bay trying to hurt somebody or play dirty, it wasn't in the cards as far as I'm concerned," Sprinkle said. "But if you got a chance to kill a guy, you killed 'im."

That rather neatly summed up the Bears-Packers rivalry during the post-war years. The players weren't trying to hurt each other. Oh, no. They were just trying to kill each other.

"I suppose it had a little something to do with guys coming out of the service," said Herm Rohrig, a back with the Packers in 1941 and again in 1946 and 1947. "They'd been through hell, so they were going to give a little hell to somebody else. It was pretty vicious."

Artoe, who still lives in the Chicago area, doesn't deny punching Craig in the face in the 1945 season opener. Nor, at age eighty, does he express any remorse about the incident.

"The first game coming out of the service, I kicked off and Larry followed me down the field and banged me," Artoe said. "So I turned around and punched him. As soon as you got hit by one of the other guys, your retaliation was to punch him in the face. You're not going to punch him in the headgear or the shoulder pads.

"He hit me when I didn't think he should hit me. He came from the blind side, and that's what you don't like. Oh, boy, he blind-sided me, knocked me ass over tea kettle. So I got up and punched him."

Others who witnessed the incident put a slightly different spin on it.

"I saw it with my own eyes. I did," Goodnight said. "I'll tell you what happened. They kicked off to us and Larry Craig blocked Artoe. I saw Artoe pick him up with one hand—I think Craig thought he was going to help him up—and he smacked him with that other hand. Boy, he knocked his nose all over his face."

Craig, arguably the toughest, most ornery player on the Packers' roster, finished the game. Artoe was ejected before he even worked up a sweat, much to the dismay of Ralph Brizzolara. A life-long buddy of George Halas, Brizzolara ran the Bears' front office while Halas was in the service during World War II. It was Brizzolara, the team's secretary and business manager, who had gone to considerable lengths to get Artoe a furlough so he could play against the Packers.

Brizzolara had persuaded a high-ranking naval officer to grant Artoe a leave and also had arranged for Artoe to fly from Washington, D.C., to Chicago, and then to Green Bay the weekend of the game. Artoe arrived Sunday morning, but the trip was hardly worth it.

"I got there a couple hours before the game. They started the game and I kicked off. I got kicked out of the game on the first play," Artoe remembered with a hearty laugh. "Back I go to the bench and here is Brizzolara. He looked at me and said, 'You S.O.B.'"

The Packers found little humor in the incident. They were looking for Artoe in the rematch. But the Bears had an agenda, too. They took an

0-5 record and an air of desperation into the game, which quickly deteriorated into a brutal slugfest. Chicago won, 28-24.

"It is doubtful whether there has been a more bitterly contested game in the series," the *Green Bay Press-Gazette* reported the next day. "The rough and ready Bears, keyed to a mayhem pitch through reports of dissension on the team and five straight losses, threw the rule book out the window. . . . The Bears, with tackles Lee Artoe, Al Babartsky and Al Hoptowit, and guard George Zorich leading the way, punched, elbowed, kicked and generally assaulted the Packers with what might mildly be called unorthodox football."

Packers halfback Roy McKay suffered a broken nose and had several teeth knocked lose. Halfback Irv Comp suffered a knee injury, and tackle Baby Ray sustained a one-inch cut on his upper lip. Guard Pete Tinsley was thrown out of the game for punching Bears quarterback Sid Luckman, and Goodnight also was sent to the showers for punching Hoptowit.

The Bears' casualty list included rookie halfback John Morton, who visited the Illinois Masonic Hospital to have a cut under his eye stitched, and, of course, Artoe. With one well-placed elbow, in the final two minutes of the game, Keuper broke Artoe's upper and lower jaws, along with his nose, and knocked out 11 teeth.

"Oh, boy! I can still feel it," Artoe said fifty-two years later. "I don't know whether you'd call it a cheap shot. We didn't have face masks and he hit me with his elbow, and down I went. I'll tell you, that was the roughest hit I ever got. Broke my jaw. Broke my teeth. Everything."

Even though Keuper was not penalized on the play, some of the Bears were still fuming over his handiwork after the game. End Ken Kavanaugh, Artoe's roommate, was on his way back to Chicago's dressing room when a Wrigley Field popcorn vendor yelled to him that Artoe had gotten what he deserved.

"I got so mad," Kavanaugh recalled. "I grabbed him and pushed him into a telephone booth. I had him up at the top and I started to hit him. I still had my uniform on. And I thought, 'You'd better settle down, Ken. This popcorn vendor is not worth it.' And I let him drop."

The Bears sent a film of the game to the league, and complained loudly about Green Bay's rough play, and in particular Keuper's hit on Artoe.

"Curly Lambeau says his team doesn't know how to retaliate with rough play," Chicago co-coach Luke Johnsos was quoted as saying in the *Chicago Tribune*. "These pictures will show who started all the roughness Sunday."

Keuper said his wife received telephone calls from the wives of Bears players, warning her not to let him play in the series in 1946. "They said they were going to get me and so forth," Keuper said. "But I went ahead and played, and didn't have any problems at all."

Keuper may have escaped unscathed, but the two teams were just warming up. The 1946 season opener, at City Stadium on September 29, marked one of the rivalry's lowest points. "This game turned out to be a four-round pugilistic farce," sportswriter Art Daley wrote in the *Press-Gazette*. "The gladiators didn't wear trunks, nor did they toil in a squared ring. And they didn't wear gloves, which is a shame because there wouldn't have been so much blood shed."

The *Press-Gazette* ran a "Casualty Box" that listed the Packers' injuries: end Nolan Luhn, broken nose; Rohrig, cracked rib; Comp, shredded lip; and end Carl Mulleneaux, who suffered the most frightening injury of all.

Mulleneaux was knocked out for nearly ten minutes, and had his face bloodied, on a vicious blind-side hit by Bears center John Schiechl on a kickoff. A photograph in the *Press-Gazette* showed a dazed and limp Mulleneaux being carried off the field by teammates.

"When Mulleneaux got hit, I was in the service," said Clyde "Bulldog" Turner, the Bears' Hall of Fame center of that era. "But the guy was wearing my jersey. Schiechl. Anyway, I've seen it on film. It was a dirty blow. He hit him right in the face."

Mulleneaux's injury was so gruesome, rumors circulated that night in Green Bay that he had died in the hospital. The rumors were false, but Mulleneaux never played another game. On that one play, he suffered five dislocated vertebrae, a concussion, a broken nose, facial cuts, and three broken teeth.

"Schiechl was a real mean bastard," Daley said. "He was awful. I really gave the Bears hell in the paper."

But the Bears gave the Packers hell on the field, winning, 30-7.

The rematch that year, November 3 at Wrigley Field, was tame in comparison. Turner suffered a broken nose, and Sprinkle and Packers back Walt Schlinkman were ejected for fighting. But the *Press-Gazette* termed the game "the cleanest in many a year."

Mulleneaux, who had been waived because of his injuries, showed up in civilian clothes. He exchanged words with Schiechl as he stood along the sideline during the game, then waited for him afterward outside the Bears' dressing room. What could have been another ugly scene was avoided when Schiechl offered an apology and Mulleneaux accepted it.

The Bears, it should be noted, won, 10-7, to complete the season sweep en route to a 9-2-1 record and the NFL championship.

Over the next three seasons, the tensions between the two teams boiled just beneath the surface. There were occasional fights and unsportsmanlike conduct penalties, but, for the most part, the players kept their tempers in check. The tackling and blocking, however, remained fierce and enthusiastic.

On November 9, 1947, the two teams combined to force ten fumbles as the Bears won, 20-17, at Wrigley Field. Sprinkle also caused a small scene near the end of the game when Bob Forte of the Packers lost his helmet after being tackled for a four-yard loss. Sprinkle picked up the helmet and defiantly threw it fifteen yards over the heads of the Packers' players.

The next season, three Packers were hurt in the Bears' 45-7 victory at City Stadium. Center Jay Rhodemyre suffered a concussion, Craig sustained a fractured nose, and back Bruce Smith was knocked cold from a blow to the back of the neck. In Chicago's 7-6 victory on November 14, 1948, Packers tackle Paul Lipscomb was ejected for punching Bears tackle Fred Davis.

The Bears' mascot was tackled and pummeled by several youths at City Stadium on September 25, 1949, but Chicago had the last laugh in a 17-0 victory.

Deeper hostilities resurfaced in the teams' second meeting of the 1950 season. Fullback Ed Cody of the Bears accused the Packers' Tony Canadeo of punching him in the chops on a pass play in the third quarter. Cody levied the charges on Monday morning from a Chicago hospital bed. Cody was there with a dislocated jaw and a deep cut to his chin.

Two Bears also were ejected: linemen Paul Stenn and Fred Davis. Stenn was thrown out of the game for swinging at tackle Dick Wildung of the Packers. Davis was ejected after he and guard Ray Bray of the Bears ganged up on rookie center and linebacker Clayton Tonnemaker, Green Bay's first-round draft pick, and knocked him out of the game.

"Tonnemaker snapped the ball on a punt and Ray Bray straightened him up, and Davis came in and hit Tonnemaker with a right to the mush," Wildung said. "The play was over, and I turned around and looked back, and here was a guy stretched out, forty or fifty yards back up the field. They knocked him colder than a cucumber."

The next three games were somewhat civil by comparison, but they were anything but clean. In the season opener in 1951, the Bears were penalized fifteen times for 114 yards; the Packers, nine times for 109 yards. In the rematch that year, the Packers drew twelve penalties for 130 yards; the Bears, ten for 108 yards. In the season opener in 1952, the Bears were hit with fifteen penalties for 116 yards; and the Packers, six for seventy. The total number of infractions for the two teams for those three games was sixty-seven for a numbing 647 yards.

The final crushing blow of this era of hostility occurred on November 6, 1955, at Wrigley Field. Veryl Switzer, a second-year kick returner for the Packers, was the unfortunate victim. Switzer was obliterated by Chicago's George Connor in a collision so violent, many players on the field involuntarily shuddered in horror. Even today, forty-two years later, those same players speak of Connor's hit with a mixture of awe and amazement.

"That was the worst hit I've ever seen in my life," said Gary Knafelc, an end with the Packers from 1954 to 1962 and the team's public address announcer since 1964. "To this day, it's the worst I've ever seen. I mean, the whole stadium, there wasn't a sound. They thought Switzer was dead."

Switzer, who had scored on a ninety-three-yard punt return against Chicago the year before, had just fielded the ball and was about to start up field. Connor, the Bears' 6-foot-3, 240-pound wedge buster, had his head down and was running at full speed. For some reason, none of the Packers' blockers picked up Connor, and he plowed into Switzer without breaking stride.

The impact literally knocked Switzer out of his helmet. He went flying one direction, the ball went another, and his helmet popped fifteen feet straight into the air. When the helmet was recovered, the chin strap was still fastened.

"I was right next to Switzer," said Bears defensive tackle Bill Bishop. "I picked up his headgear. I thought he had lost his head."

Actually, the injury to Switzer's chest was what bothered him most. "I bled internally, off and on, for about six weeks," Switzer said. "I could hardly walk the next day, but I continued to play and practice. If I got bumped in a game, though, for about four or five weeks, I kind of spit up blood. He tore my sternum pretty good."

Switzer still isn't sure why the wedge broke up. "I think they were pointing at folks nearest them. Or they were getting out of Connor's way," he said. "One of the two."

Bill Forester, a Packers linebacker and one of the blockers in the wedge that day, took exception to a theory voiced after the game by Bulldog Turner: the wedge had fallen apart intentionally because Switzer was black. "Turner got on television and said, 'It was two boys from Texas opening the gates on the black boy,' " Forester said. "That's terrible, isn't it? What did he know? Veryl was one of my best friends. We used to ride to practice together every day. But he really got blasted. It was about as hard a blow as I ever saw."

Connor's hit on Switzer brought a closure of sorts to the brutal postwar era. Many of the antagonists on both teams had retired, or were winding down their careers. Artoe, the man who started it all, was long gone, having left the Bears after a contract squabble with owner George Halas following the 1945 season. He then played three seasons in the All-America Football Conference before retiring. But the 6-foot-3, 235-pounder left an indelible mark as one of the great villains of the Bears-Packers rivalry. "The Packers hated him with a passion," said Sid Luckman, Chicago's quarterback. "He was really something else. He was a rough, tough, tough football player."

Running back Tony Canadeo agreed that those were the sentiments of the Green Bay players, but he said they also thought Artoe crossed the fine line between being tough and dirty. "You never could turn your back to him," Canadeo said. "He was a good football player. He was tough. But no scruples. No scruples."

The late Ted Fritsch had the teeth marks on his buttocks to prove it.

Fritsch, who played running back for the Packers from 1942 to 1950, carried around the tattoo as a permanent reminder of Artoe's aggression. He revealed the evidence one day at Paul's Standard, a Green Bay service station owned by Packers fan Paul Mazzoleni and frequented by fans, players, and coaches.

"A bunch of us are standing around and we're talking about dirty players," Mazzoleni said. "Fritsch says, 'What goes on in that pile-up, you'll never believe. They twisted your leg. They tried to gouge your eyes out. They pulled on your ears.'

"Then he pulled down his pants and said: 'If you don't believe it, look at this. That fuckin' Artoe. I've still got his teeth marks in my ass.' We got a hell of a laugh out of that."

Artoe turned his forearms into casts, or lethal weapons, by taping himself from his fingernails to his elbows. He also was nearsighted, so he had trouble seeing opposing players from a distance and drew frequent penalties for hitting after the whistle. "His excuse was that he was blind," Bulldog Turner said with a chuckle. "But I guess he couldn't hear, either."

Another Bears teammate, back Harry Clarke, once asked Artoe how he knew which player to block or tackle. "He said, 'I'll tell you what, Harry. Anything moving in front of me, I try to kill it,'" Clarke said.

Artoe, an intelligent man who earned an engineering degree from the University of California, helped organize the NFL Alumni Association and became friendly with many ex-Packers after their playing days were over.

"The Green Bay Packers are my friends," Artoe said. "I love the Packers. I've always liked them. It was the heat of the moment. When you're playing that way, you'd hit your own mother if the situation was right. In those days, you could punch because you didn't have face masks. The first thing you did was punch a guy in the face. Bang the helmet in the face, head-butt 'im. You couldn't hold, so you threw your elbows and used your headgear and your shoulders. We played to win. We fought."

Of his reputation, Artoe reluctantly admitted, "The stories they tell, they're telling the truth."

Bray was another villain in the series, at least from the Packers' perspective. A two-way lineman, Bray packed 237 chiseled pounds on his 6-foot frame and liked to show off his impressive strength by doing extended one-armed pushups. He played for the Bears from 1939 to 1942 and again after the war, from 1946 to 1951. Oddly, he finished his career with the Packers in 1952.

"He was the worst right there," said Hal Van Every, a halfback with the Packers in 1941 and 1942. "He'd slug you in the face any time. He'd make a charge and he'd start out with his fist down low to the ground and he'd come up and hit you right in the face because you didn't have face guards. He'd level you. Ray Bray. I remember him above all of them."

Paul Stenn, a tackle with the Bears from 1948 to 1951, not only was ejected for throwing a punch at Wildung in the second game in 1950, but he also was accused by the Packers of flagrantly kneeing quarterback Bobby Thomason in the season opener the next year.

"He used to tape pads on the back of his legs because he whip-kicked," said Sprinkle, revealing years later a trade secret of a former teammate. "If a guy was rushing the passer, he'd come back around with his leg. That was his forte."

Fred Davis, the Bear who went after Clayton Tonnemaker, was another player who occupied a prominent spot on Green Bay's hate list. The 6-foot-3, 244-pounder played offensive and defensive tackle for the Bears from 1946 to 1951.

"He was one of the toughest, best, meanest football players I ever played with," said Connor. "Davis had all the tricks."

If the truth be known, the Packers felt just about everyone on the Bears played dirty in those years. While the Packers were blamed for most of the mayhem that occurred in the 1980s, the Bears were considered the culprits for most of the transgressions that took place in the late 1940s and early 1950s.

"The Bears just played dirty football," said Goodnight, who practiced family medicine in Holland, Texas, after his retirement. "At least, that is what we on the Packers thought. They'd hit you on the way back to the huddle if you didn't watch it. I never played against the Bears that they didn't bloody my nose, my lips, or something with illegal punches. A man could really get hurt out there if he wasn't careful."

Of course, the Packers were not without their instigators and trouble-makers. Two-way linemen Paul Lipscomb and Ed Neal were mountainous men who had a knack for enraging the Bears with their rough style of play.

Lipscomb, 6 feet 5 inches and 246 pounds, played for Green Bay from 1945 to 1949. The Bears claimed that, among his arsenal of questionable tactics, he took a perverse pleasure in stepping on fallen opponents.

"I'll never forget Paul Lipscomb," said Stan Jones, a two-way lineman for the Bears from 1954 to 1965. "He was one of the dirtiest guys in football. He'd go out of his way to get somebody. When he was pursuing a play, he'd have a direct line and he'd take an extra step out of his way to step on somebody's back."

Pat Preston, a guard with the Bears from 1946 to 1949, remembered a particularly nasty encounter with Lipscomb.

"I was running down on the kickoff, and Lipscomb hit me in the mouth with his fist," Preston said. "He knocked my tooth out. My mouth was bleeding. The Packer ran it back to about the 50-yard line, and I grabbed my face, my teeth, bleeding all over; and, as I'm coming off the field, George Halas said, 'Damnit, Preston, you let him get by, you let him get by!' I said, 'Coach, I don't give a damn if he runs to Miami.'"

Neal, 6 feet 4 inches and as heavy as three hundred pounds, played for the Packers from 1945 to 1951. An immobile behemoth, he stood his ground in the middle and wielded his huge forearms as if they were clubs. His battles with Bears center Bulldog Turner were legendary.

"Ed Neal used to beat on Bulldog," Sprinkle said. "He outweighed Bulldog by quite a bit and he'd line up over center, and I mean he'd whack Bulldog in the nose. And they'd fight. But as far as Ed Neal breaking free and making a tackle, Bulldog was usually able to handle him pretty good."

Neal had incredibly strong arms and hands. Bears end Ken Kavanaugh remembered watching Neal roll up bottle caps "like a cigarette" with his thumb and forefinger. "That impressed the hell out of me," Kavanaugh said.

In a strange twist of events, Lipscomb and Neal both spent the final seasons of their careers with the Bears. Neal finished up in Chicago in 1951, and Lipscomb played for the Bears in 1954, arriving in a trade with the Washington Redskins.

"Just a week or two before we got Lipscomb, Halas said, 'Without a doubt, this man is the dirtiest man in football, and he should be barred from the game,'" Stan Jones said. "Then, one day, there's a knock on the clubhouse door, Halas opens it and in walks Lipscomb. We had picked him up."

As a member of the Bears, Lipscomb apparently found it just as easy to hate the Packers. "I was running with the ball and I got tackled," said Tobin Rote, the Packers' quarterback in 1954. "Lipscomb came sliding into me like I was second base and he kicked me under the nose. He broke my nose in five places."

Neal also went out of his way to inflict punishment on his ex-teammates after being cut by the Packers early in the 1951 season. "He got right over Jay Rhodemyre, who was our center and the guy who had taken his place," said Billy Grimes, a running back with the Packers from 1950 to 1952. "First play, Ed Neal jumps offsides and nearly killed Rhodemyre. I guess Jay was probably two hundred pounds or so and here Ed was 290."

Later in the first half, Neal was penalized another fifteen yards for slugging Rhodemyre.

Of all the rough and tough players during the post-war years, however, Sprinkle ranks as a unanimous selection as the roughest and toughest. He is not a member of the Pro Football Hall of Fame, but there are plenty of people who believe he belongs with that company.

Sprinkle was the epitome of the hard-nosed player. He played twelve seasons, never wore a face mask, and had an aura about him that said, "Don't mess with me." Few opponents were eager to try. Some of the Packers groused that he was a dirty player, but the evidence shows he did most of his hitting before the whistle.

"They used to talk about Ed Sprinkle being a dirty player," said Ken Kavanaugh, a Bears teammate for six seasons. "All he did was knock the hell out of people. That's all. He'd hit 'em, and, of course, they didn't like that too much. Sprinks was supposed to be the meanest man in football. But he never hit anybody dirty, no cheap shots or anything. He'd just go in and tear them to pieces."

Don Perkins concurred. He was a running back who played for both the Packers and Bears in the 1940s. "I would say Ed Sprinkle, pound for pound, was the roughest, hardest-playing football player I ever ran into," Perkins said. "He was not dirty, but he played hard. If you were going to get hit by Ed, you were going to get hit."

Sprinkle was born September 3, 1923, and joined the Bears in 1944 out of Hardin-Simmons, located in Abilene, Texas, and the same college that produced teammate Bulldog Turner. Sprinkle played both offensive and defensive end, but made his mark on the defensive side of the ball. Small by today's standards, he compensated for his lack of size with quickness and an enthusiasm for the game's legislated violence.

"Did you ever hear football being referred to as anything but a contact sport?" he asked. "The guys are taking shots at you, and I was geared that way. I loved contact. I liked to mix it up. I believed in hitting somebody."

Sprinkle had strong arms and huge hands, and he put them to good use. He perfected what he called "The Hook," which was basically a clothesline tackle, legal in those days. Any running back coming through the line or drifting wide for a short pass risked catching Sprinkle's forearm in the nose, under the chin, or in the Adam's apple. As a pass-rusher, Sprinkle often left his feet, jumping over the would-be blocker to hook the vulnerable quarterback.

"I don't know how I developed that thing," Sprinkle said. "They used to teach us, if a halfback was swinging out of the backfield, you clotheslined him if you could. That would be illegal by today's standards, but back then, it was legal. Today, that's that outlet pass these teams run, that San Francisco offense. The quarterbacks look, look, look—nobody's open—so they throw it out there.

"Well, when that guy was coming out of the backfield when I played, you clotheslined him. It was pretty effective."

The Hook definitely left a lasting impression. Tony Canadeo, the Packers' star running back in the 1940s and early 1950s, saw stars once after being hooked by Sprinkle. "You know, you get a little lackadaisical sometimes," Canadeo said. "I was supposed to swing out for a short pass. But I got too gulldarn close to the line of scrimmage. And he hit me. Not with a fist or anything, but right in the face. I had tears coming down my cheeks. I went, 'You son of a bitch. I'm not mad, because I was stupid. But don't you ever turn your back, because ol' Tone is looking for you.'

"Boy, he hit me. I had crocodile tears coming down."

When Fred Cone was a rookie fullback with the Packers in 1951, the veterans warned him about Sprinkle.

"The old-timers had pumped us, being rookies, so much about Sprinkle and the Bears that when we were getting ready to play them we were pretty nervous," Cone said. "The story they told about Sprinkle was that if you were going to run a swing—a short pass out of the backfield—don't look for the ball because Sprinkle would take your head off with a hook."

Floyd "Breezy" Reid, a back with the Packers from 1950 to 1956, was one of Sprinkle's favorite targets. "Breezy would try to cut that corner a little too tight when he came out of the backfield," said Roger Zatkoff, a Packers linebacker. "Sprinkle would put the arm out and hook him. Catch him under the throat and knock him down. John Martinkovic would say to Breezy, 'For crissakes, can't you get a little wider? You're going to get killed.' "

On offense, Sprinkle was used primarily as a blocker. There, he had linebackers looking out of the corners of their eyes and over their shoulders. "They had like a crackback block when you'd start a wide end run," Sprinkle said. "I'd split out wide to the right and come back in on the linebacker. That was my forte. I could really put those guys away."

Ever the competitor, Sprinkle didn't show much compassion for his teammates, either. Once, some of the Bears went swimming in a quarry in Rensselaer, Indiana, where the team held its summer training camp. Guard Herman Clark was a native Hawaiian and could "swim like a fish," according to fullback Rick Casares.

"Everybody was talking about Herman, and Sprinkle said, 'I'll race you,'" Casares said. "So they dove off the bank, and Sprinkle got ahold of Herman Clark by the head and hair and pulled him under. He almost drowned him to beat the guy in a race."

Hearing those stories, one imagines that Sprinkle was some kind of monster, a sadist who enjoyed hurting people. Nothing could be further from the truth. He seems genuinely surprised, even today, when he hears that some ex-Packers considered him to be a dirty player.

"One of the Green Bay coaches said once that they watched me for an entire game and I didn't do anything dirty or illegal," Sprinkle said. "I never set out to maliciously maim anybody in a football game. But I danced every step with them. I was going to hit 'em, and if they were coming to block me, I was going to be there."

No question, Sprinkle had some great games against the Packers. In fact, he may have made more big plays in the rivalry than any other lineman. He returned a fumble thirty yards for a touchdown when the Bears beat the Packers, 10-7, in 1946. In 1948, he caught two touchdown passes as the Bears won, 45-7, at Green Bay and he scored the Bears' only touchdown on a thirty-four-yard reception in a 7-6 victory at Chicago. He blocked a punt in 1950 to set up the Bears' final touchdown in a 28-14 victory. And he blocked what would have been a tying field goal in the fourth quarter of the Bears' 24-14 victory over the Packers in 1952.

"I think Ed Sprinkle was a great player," said Dave Hanner, a defensive tackle with the Packers from 1952 to 1964, as well as a longtime assistant coach and scout. "There isn't anybody who has come along who was any tougher."

Sprinkle is semi-retired and lives with Mariane, his wife of fifty years, in a tastefully decorated condominium in Palos Park, Illinois.

Occasionally, he returns to Green Bay to play in NFL Alumni golf tournaments, and he still hears boos when his name is announced on the first tee.

A Packer fan never forgets.

Still, with his white hair, quick smile, and disarming manner, it's difficult to imagine Sprinkle wreaking havoc on the football field all those years ago. But then he stands up and spreads his arms to make a point, and there it is. The Hook.

Instinctively, you duck your head.

THE DITKA-GREGG YEARS

Forrest Gregg and Mike Ditka didn't exactly get off on the right foot as rival head coaches. And, well, let's just say that things went downhill from there.

The date was August 11, 1984. It was the second of four exhibition games for each team. Gregg was in his first season as head coach of the Packers; Ditka was in his third season with the Bears, who were on the verge of becoming an NFL juggernaut.

The game was played at Milwaukee County Stadium, which, because of its baseball configuration, required that both teams' benches be placed on the same side of the field, along the outfield grass, separated by only a few yards.

The Packers took a 14-0 lead and, after a Bears field goal trimmed the margin to 14-3, they got the ball back with one minute, 44 seconds left in the first half. Gregg, obviously trying to work on his two-minute offense, called three straight pass plays. No problem there.

But after quarterback Rich Campbell scrambled for three yards to the Packers' 41, Gregg called a time out with 1:12 left.

Big problem there.

In that situation—ahead by 11 points in a pre-season game, and on your own half of the field with barely a minute left in the half—many coaches would simply call two running plays and head for the locker room.

Gregg chose to ignore protocol. Charged with turning around a team that had floundered under former coach Bart Starr, he appeared to want to make a statement—not so much to the Bears as to his own players—that things were going to be different. He was going to show the Packers how serious he was about winning.

Whatever the circumstances, Ditka thought the timeout was ridiculous. The two coaches were standing just a few yards apart, and an argument ensued that set the tone for the next four years.

"Ditka said, 'Why the hell are you calling time out? This is an exhibition game; let's just go in,'" said Mike Douglass, a linebacker for the Packers who witnessed the exchange. "Forrest said, 'I need to work on my passing game.' Ditka got really pissed and said, 'You sorry son of a bitch.' Forrest called him the same name, then he said, 'Suck my cock, Ditka.' They wanted to go at each other. They were pissed. Ditka was really mad. Players had to step between them, and they were yelling and screaming over the top. It was crazy."

Halftime passed without sanity being restored. Gregg gathered his players in the locker room and delivered a fire-and-brimstone speech. "Forrest says, 'You guys just go out and take care of the Bears, and I'll take care of Ditka,'" said center Larry McCarren.

The tension didn't ease when the second half started. Ditka was still fuming, as well. Soon thereafter, he got into a heated argument with Buddy Ryan, his defensive coordinator. Ryan called a blitz on third-and-long and the Packers beat it.

"Ditka goes up to Buddy and starts cursing at him," Bears quarterback Bob Avellini said. "He said, 'Don't you ever blitz again! Don't ever do that again!' You could see the veins popping out in his neck. He was mad at Forrest Gregg, but he was madder at Buddy Ryan.

"So maybe three more downs go by, and they have to punt. Buddy throws his headset down on the ground and goes up to Ditka and gives him an earful: 'Don't ever come by me again when I'm sending in signals. You're getting in my way.' He's as mad as Ditka is.

"Now, we've got this short, fat, chubby guy—Buddy Ryan—and Ditka, who wants to kill him. We're just looking at all this and going, 'We can't believe this is happening.' And all for an exhibition game."

Ryan remembered the exhange. "I probably told Ditka to fuck himself," he said. "It was a perfect call."

The Packers went on to win, 17-10, which was inconsequential only because the game didn't count in the standings. On another level, the game was the genesis of a series of bitter, vicious confrontations between the teams that spanned Gregg's four years as the Packers' coach.

"That was, without a doubt, the most tense time of the rivalry since I've been here," said Bob Harlan, current president of the Packers and a member of the organization since 1971. "And it wasn't good. I don't think it was good for either organization, and I don't think it was good for football. I thought during the Ditka-Gregg years, the rivalry just deteriorated. It turned into a gang fight."

The period was defined by rampant trash talking; a series of blatant cheap shots; and a string of fines and warnings, as well as one suspension, all handed down by the NFL office.

The immediate fallout from the game in Milwaukee was that the contract calling for two more pre-season games had to be scrapped. Jerry Vainisi, former vice president and general manager of the Bears, had worked with Robert Parins, then the Packers' president, to revive the annual pre-season game the teams had played from 1959 through 1975.

The agreement was essentially dead before the night was over.

"I can't say Ditka was all excited about it to begin with," said Vainisi, "but being an old Bear and as much as he hated the Packers, if he could beat them ten times a season, it was fine. But when they were nose-to-nose, I happened to spot that and said, 'Oh, shit! That's going to be a problem.' And, sure enough, on the way home, Mike says, 'We gotta get out of this game.' And about two days later, Judge Parins calls and says, 'Jerry, Forrest wants to get out of the game.'"

The teams haven't faced each other in the pre-season since. But they still had to play two regular-season games each year. And as long as Ditka was coaching the Bears and Gregg was coaching the Packers, those games were now destined to be messy affairs.

Here were two men who had been on the opposite sides of the rivalry as players. They had played the game not only skillfully, but passionately. And they were alike in many ways; among their common traits, both were strong-willed and had short fuses. They even shared the same birthday—October 18—although Gregg was six years older.

They couldn't help but clash.

"A lot of great players hate other great players," said McCarren. "Ditka was one of the Bears' top dogs when Forrest was playing, and Forrest was one of the Packers' top dogs. So there was a professional animosity between them. Let's face it: it was probably two mega-egos going after each other."

As players, Ditka and Gregg had been teammates for one season. They played together with the Dallas Cowboys in 1971, and shared in a

Super Bowl victory. "We got along perfectly," Ditka said. "There was never a problem."

However, as rival coaches, all it took was one game, one confrontation, to erect a barrier between them. Hate is a word that others throw around loosely to describe how Ditka and Gregg felt about each other, but true hate is a strong, powerful emotion. This rift seemed to be more a football thing than a personal vendetta.

There may have been some jealousy involved. Gregg played tackle in the NFL for fifteen years, fourteen of them with the Packers, and retired after the 1971 season. He was inducted into the Pro Football Hall of Fame in 1977, his first year of eligibility. Ditka retired one year after Gregg, following a distinguished twelve-year career, but had to wait eleven more years to get into the Hall of Fame. He was the first tight end ever selected, but the call didn't come until 1988, the year after Gregg resigned as the Packers' head coach.

"I can only speak for Ditka," said Mark Bortz, who played guard with the Bears from 1983 to 1994. "He hated Gregg. I don't think he ever really respected him as a player. I think that's where it started. Guys like that have big egos. Ditka made some reference one time that, 'He wasn't all that great, anyway.' It was probably jealousy. Forrest went into the Hall of Fame before Ditka. Ditka was pretty funny about stuff like that."

Ditka also remembered well his own playing days when the Packers dominated the series, other than in 1963 when the Bears won both games and the NFL championship. The year before Gregg took over as coach—in 1982, Ditka's first season as coach, both Bears-Packers game were canceled by an NFL players strike—Ditka set his own tone for the rivalry.

"I remember him saying right off the bat, 'Good things happen to the Bears, and you've got a special team when you can go up there and beat Green Bay,'" said Jay Hilgenberg, a center for the Bears from 1981 to 1991. "He challenged us. He played in all those games and he knew what it meant."

Once Gregg arrived on the scene, Ditka considered the games not only to be crucial to the Bears' success, but grudge matches, as well. In his mind, the Packers crossed the line from being merely aggressive to being dirty.

"Forrest Gregg had a bunch of guys who had no class," said Mike Pyle, who played with Ditka and then did a radio show with him in

Chicago. "The Kenny Stillses of the world. The Matt Suhey incident. That horrible Charlie Martin incident, when he injured Jim McMahon.

"Forrest Gregg had a bunch of marauders, whatever you want to call them. A bunch of streetfighters. Those guys were brutal. And Forrest Gregg wouldn't stop it. Ditka would accuse him of something and Gregg would come back with some flippant answers. I think that's what caused the problems."

The more Ditka developed a dislike for the way Gregg's teams played, the more he relished beating them. He did it regularly—seven times in eight games over four years—and he did it Chicago style; by being brash, smug, and sarcastic.

Gregg's albatross—partly because of his own making—was that he had inferior personnel. He had a ragtag cast trying to compete against a team with one of the greatest defenses ever assembled and one of the greatest running backs of all time in Walter Payton. In his four seasons as coach of the Packers, Gregg never had a winning record. The Bears made the playoffs all four years and won the Super Bowl after the 1985 season.

The more Gregg lost to Ditka, the more desperate he became. He tried to whip his players into a fever pitch every time they played the Bears, but all he did was compound the challenge of rebuilding a flagging team. On one occasion, Gregg made his players wear orange wrist bands to practice the week before a Bears game—as if they needed a reminder.

"He was wild," said Mike Douglass. "He'd get real uptight, and I think it tightened the team up, too. You'd be up to such a level, and there was so much pressure placed on that one game—it was like everything counted on it. And, sometimes, it was hard to recover, especially the week after. We had a lot of young players, and it was just too much."

The players and fans also stoked the flames of the rivalry during those four years.

Players on both teams regularly violated one of the cardinal rules of sport by directing outrageous, inflammatory remarks at each other in the days leading up to games. They didn't hesitate to say the first thing that came to their minds. There was no effort at restraint; the sound bites had bite, and the newspapers had bark.

"In this particular case, it didn't matter," said defensive back Shaun Gayle, who played with the Bears from 1984 to 1994. "Guys like Jim McMahon and Dan Hampton, they wouldn't go into a game against

Miami and say what they were going to do to Dan Marino. But versus Green Bay, it didn't matter because we knew it was going to be a battle from start to finish."

The fans, in turn, treated the games as a sort of uncivil war. The fans in Chicago were on a perpetual high for most of Ditka's years as coach; and the more the Bears beat the Packers, the more they gloated and the more condescending they became toward their neighbors to the north. In the gas stations, the bars, the restaurants, and on the radio talk shows in Green Bay, the subject of Packers vs. Bears always had been a lively topic, but now the games took on added importance. With the Packers wallowing in mediocrity, their fans viewed a Bears game as their Super Bowl. It was the only way to salvage a miserable season.

"It's the only time in the NFL where I really felt the emotional level was like when you're in college," said former Packers tackle Greg Koch, a product of the University of Arkansas. "You can't separate the business from the game in the pros. To me, in college, there was always more emotion. But that Bear game, that's as close as it came to being a college-type atmosphere."

The first regular-season meeting between the Bears and Packers during the Ditka-Gregg era took place on September 16, 1984, barely a month after the fiasco at County Stadium.

Both teams went into the game with banged-up quarterbacks. Jim McMahon took painkilling shots for a broken right hand and a sore back; Lynn Dickey played despite a back injury he had suffered in a 28-7 loss to the Los Angeles Raiders the week before.

McMahon didn't make it through the first quarter; his back stiffened after a hit by Packers nose tackle Charles Martin. He alleged that he had been the victim of a cheap shot.

"It was a hook slide. I thought it was a late hit," McMahon was quoted as saying in the *Chicago Tribune* the next day. It was a precursor of things to come, as was Ditka's sideline tirade directed at Bob Avellini, who replaced McMahon at quarterback.

"I go in and, like the first play, I take a shot at throwing the ball long to Willie Gault," Avellini said. "It's barely knocked down, just tipped away by a defensive back. So I come to the sideline, and Mike Ditka is just ranting and raving: 'I'm going to cut your fuckin' ass! I'm going to cut your fuckin' ass!' I'm thinking, 'Geez, what did I do?' Plus, he had nobody else to put in. McMahon was down. Steve Fuller was hurt. And they had just signed Rusty Lisch.

"Well, I go on and complete 11 of 17 and throw one interception. But every time I come back to the sideline, Ditka is going, 'I'm going to cut your fuckin' ass!' I'm saying, 'Geez, somebody get this madman away from me so I can just concentrate.'"

The rest of the game wasn't pretty. With Dickey hurting, the Packers could muster only 154 total yards. Avellini couldn't get the Bears into the end zone, but Bob Thomas kicked three field goals and Chicago escaped with a 9-7 victory and improved its record to 3-0.

One remarkable play turned the momentum in Chicago's favor. Years later, many of the Bears would point to the play—a spectacular interception by cornerback Leslie Frazier—as a sign of their transformation into a playoff contender.

Green Bay led, 7-6, early in the third quarter when cornerback Tim Lewis intercepted a pass by Avellini that bounced off Gault's shoulder pads. The Packers had the ball on the Bears' 24-yard line and were threatening to put the game out of reach. But Chicago got the ball right back when Frazier leaped over wide receiver John Jefferson for an interception on the seven-yard line.

"That was big time," recalled former Bears middle linebacker Mike Singletary. "We had been trying to beat the Packers and go to the next level, and we did. That was the game that signaled, 'We're moving forward.'"

The rematch that season, December 9 at Soldier Field, was memorable only because Walter Payton played quarterback and the Packers beat the Bears for the only time in Gregg's tenure as coach.

The Bears' quarterback situation was so dismal that Rusty Lisch started the game. True to his word, Ditka had cut Avellini. McMahon had suffered a lacerated kidney a month earlier, and was declared out for the season three days before the game. Chicago was down to Lisch and emergency signee Greg Landry, who had spent the previous three seasons in the United States Football League.

After Lisch had been totally ineffective for most of the first half, Ditka had Payton run the offense from a shotgun formation. The experiment lasted six plays: Payton rushed for twenty-five yards in four carries and threw two passes, one that fell incomplete and one that was intercepted.

The Packers also played their third-string quarterback, Rich Campbell, a former number one draft pick, and he connected with wide receiver Phillip Epps on a badly underthrown, but game-winning 43-yard touchdown pass in the final seconds.

"It was a crazy game, wasn't it?" an elated Gregg said. "They're the Bears; we're the Packers. Dogs and cats fight."

The defeat spoiled the Bears' chances of playing host to a first-round playoff game. Nevertheless, they won the division with a 10-6 record and made it to the second round of the playoffs before losing to San Francisco.

The Monsters of the Midway were just beginning to flex their muscles. And the rivalry was about to escalate to another level. It wouldn't be war, but it was about as close as two combatants could come to it on a football field.

The first Bears-Packers game of 1985, a Monday night showdown at Soldier Field on October 21, established the stakes. No longer was it enough to simply beat the other team. One-upmanship was now part of the equation.

The Bears' first-round draft pick that year was mammoth defensive tackle, William "The Refrigerator" Perry. He had been a disappointment in training camp, but Ditka discovered a spot role for him the previous week in a game against San Francisco. Perry lined up at fullback in goal line situations.

Perry was on the field for five offensive plays against the Packers. On the first three, the Bears scored touchdowns. Perry served as the lead blocker for Payton on two of the touchdowns and drove George Cumby, the Packers' undersized inside linebacker, five yards backward with textbook blocks. The other time, Perry scored on a one-yard run over right guard to give the Bears the lead for good, 14-7.

A 325-pound star was born, on prime-time national television, no less. Perry's touchdown catapulted him to fame and fortune, but it infuriated the Packers, and it would haunt Gregg for the rest of his tenure in Green Bay.

"I think the way Refrigerator Perry scored on us, I think Forrest thought Ditka was rubbing it in our face," said Packers defensive end Alphonso Carreker. "Forrest took a lot of that stuff personal."

He had reason to do so.

"I didn't plan Perry's touchdown for them," Ditka said several years later, "but that's where I wanted it. There was a little bit of, 'Here, take this,' involved."

Later in the season, a huge poster of Perry appeared on the Packers' bulletin board. "People would black out his teeth, draw hair on him," said Ken Stills, a safety for the Packers from 1985 to 1989. "It was hilarious. Forrest would walk past and throw stuff at the poster."

In his Tuesday news conference, however, Gregg downplayed the Bears' use of Perry with his usual dose of sarcasm.

"Once everybody gets over the idea that this is truly phenomenal and amazing, and plays defense the way defense should be played, I don't think it's really a factor," Gregg said. At that point, when it was suggested to Ditka that he had rubbed it in, he denied it. In so many words, he told the Packers and everybody else to mind their own business.

"When the opposition tells me how to coach my football team, then our record probably will be 3-4, also," Ditka snapped. "Anybody who says we were trying to rub it in . . . they're stupid. You know, maybe we ought to forfeit. All of a sudden you do something a little bit different and you're making fun of the opposition. I think the opposition has got to look at itself." The stage was set for the November 3 rematch at Lambeau Field.

It came just two weeks after the Monday night game. Chicago had crushed the Minnesota Vikings, 27-9, in the intervening week to improve to 8-0. Green Bay was reeling at 3-5 after a 37-10 loss to the Indianapolis Colts.

In the locker room, following the game in Indianapolis, assistant coach Virgil Knight had hurled a can of Coke at Mike Douglass. A scuffle ensued between Douglass and Knight that left the Packers in turmoil.

"Hell, if it it would have hit him, it would have killed him," said Dick Corrick, former director of player personnel for the Packers. "Then, it turns out, Mike didn't play that lousy of a game. Forrest never even had the class to apologize to the guy or the team."

The tension in Green Bay mounted in the days ahead as the Bears and Packers engaged in a war of words. "I have a lot of respect for Lynn Dickey," Bears defensive end Dan Hampton said, "but I wouldn't give you two cents for the whole Green Bay Packer team."

Said McMahon: "They've got a lot of good ballplayers, but they've got a lot of crybabies, too."

Ditka was as arrogant as ever. "I know the Packers don't like us, and we don't like them," he said. "Maybe they think we tried to run up the score on them. But that's the way football should be played. No buddy-buddy stuff."

Koch shot back: "I just think we see a golden opportunity to shut a lot of people up—the people that are on us—and to shut up Mike Ditka, show that everything he says isn't golden anymore."

Gregg, in an effort to both reduce the tension and prime his team for battle, passed out plastic "Bear Bats" to his players.

The game quickly deteriorated into a Pier 6 brawl, punctuated by six unnecessary roughness penalties, numerous shoving matches, several fights, and an ejection. The Bears held on to win, 16-10, and Perry scored again—this time on a four-yard pass from McMahon. More embarrassment for the Packers.

The tone of the game was set on the third play from scrimmage. Payton fumbled, and while defensive end Ezra Johnson was falling on the ball for the Packers, Stills was leveling McMahon with a forearm. The next day, when the Bears' coaching staff studied the game films, they determined that the Packers were guilty of five cheap shots on the first nine plays.

On the Bears' second possession, Packers cornerback Mark Lee was ejected after Payton gained five yards on a counter play. Lee pushed him out of bounds and both players tumbled over a bench. Television replays appeared to show Payton grabbing Lee's face mask and pulling him, but referee Bob McElwee ruled Lee was at fault.

"That's the thing nobody ever talks about," said former linebacker Brian Noble. "They called the penalty on Mark Lee and kicked him out of the game. We lost our best cornerback, but it was Payton who pulled Lee over the bench. Nobody ever talks about that."

Everybody still talks about an incident that occurred on Chicago's next possession. Stills, who had been cut by the Packers in the pre-season and re-signed just five days before the game, came up from his free safety spot and drilled Bears fullback Matt Suhey several seconds after the whistle blew. Suhey actually was starting to walk back to the Bears' huddle when Stills hit him. Stills was penalized 15 yards, but was not ejected.

"I'll tell you exactly what happened," said Stills. "The Bears were coming down the field; it was a long drive that started on about the 15. We got in the huddle and everyone is saying, 'This is getting out of control.' People were swearing. Guys were saying, 'We can't let them do this to us in our house.'

"I'm saying, 'Let's hit these guys, let's punish people.' They ran a toss to Payton; I could see the sweep developing. I remember Charles Martin knifed through and got Payton in the backfield. Most plays last about three seconds, but this play lasted only one or two seconds and it was over. But I was still running full speed. I had the mindset that I was going to hit somebody. I didn't care who it was, when it was, where it was. All I saw was this different colored jersey in front of me. Everything was flashing. I didn't even hear the whistle. And I hit somebody. I didn't know who it was."

Everybody in the stadium saw the hit coming, it seemed, but Suhey.

"Every official threw a flag. There were five flags on the ground," Stills said. "Oh, I hit him hard. I mean, I ran right through him. I hit him so hard, my head slid across the field and when I stood up, I had big hunks of turf hanging from my helmet.

"The next thing I knew, I could hear Dick Modzelewski, our defensive coordinator, yelling at me from the sideline, 'You dumb son of a bitch! What the hell are you doing?' And I could hear Forrest saying, 'Leave him alone. He's trying to do something for this team. He's trying to make a play.'

"I walked back to the huddle, and Randy Scott and John Anderson and Noble were looking at me like I was crazy. Martin and a couple of other guys were laughing at me."

The Bears didn't see the humor in the incident. Years later, Suhey went so far as to claim that the late hit not only was planned, but even was ordered by Gregg. "It was definitely a Forrest Gregg directive," Suhey said. "It was the lack of respect he had for the rules. He disregarded any sportsmanship. In my estimation, the Packer organization is one of the shining stars in the NFL. However, in that era, the Packers were a black eye. Forrest Gregg—I don't know him personally, but what I do know about how he coached, I have no respect whatsoever. That hit was per him."

Suhey wasn't hurt by the late hit. "It just knocked me silly for a while," he said. And later, he received an apology from Stills.

"I don't know if he believes my version of what happened, though," Stills said. "He probably thinks I'm a nut. From that day on, whenever there was a play where I would wind up near Suhey, he would just look at me for a second or two. He never said anything. It was weird, because he took some grief for that play, and I'm getting all the glory. And I was wrong. It was a late hit."

When Gregg looks back at the play, he almost seems to be able to justify what Stills did. "The thing about Kenny was that he had been in training camp and we had cut him," Gregg said. "All of a sudden, he wound up starting. Kenny was a very physical guy, and he was just trying to make an impression in that ballgame. He hit Suhey late and got penalized for it, which he should have been. But I don't think Kenny was a dirty football player by any stretch of the imagination."

Stills said Gregg never said a word to him about the play. "Tuesday came and went, nothing," Stills said. "On Wednesday, I got a letter from the commissioner saying I had been fined five hundred dollars, and where do you want the money to go, which charity? But Forrest never said a word. Dick Modzelewski went off on me at the meetings the next week. He kept running the play back and forth, back and forth. Everybody was laughing, and he said, 'This ain't fuckin' funny.' He just kept running it back and forth, shaking his head."

The Bears maintain to this day that Gregg's refusal to discipline Stills and other Packers who crossed the line of fair play was evidence that he condoned—if not encouraged—dirty football.

"I think Forrest Gregg coached some of those guys to be dirty," said former defensive end Al Harris. "I just think they were coached that way. I think we overmatched them physically, and I think they coached that if you can take a guy out, take him out."

Some ex-Packers claim the charges are unfair. "He did not condone that," said Noble. "It did not sit well with him, either. He barked pretty loud about it."

Ditka didn't directly blame Gregg, but said he would not have put up with some of the Packers' antics if he was their coach. "I don't care what the circumstances are," said Ditka. "Wrong is wrong and right is right. People can say what they want about the Bears. We played hard, but we played by the rules. We knocked the shit out of people. That was the way we wanted to be. And I have no apologies about that. But if something happened on the field involving one of my players that I didn't like, I got him out of there. I'd put 'em on the bench, or take the uniform off them. That's all."

The Bears chose other ways to retaliate. They flaunted their superiority in word and deed; the touchdown pass to Perry was just one example. With twenty-five seconds remaining in the first half and the Bears on the Packers' four-yard line, Perry entered the game and McMahon called a play-action pass. Cumby bit on the fake and Perry was wide open in the end zone, giving the Bears a 7-3 lead.

"We must have been at the line of scrimmage for a minute-and-a-half," said Hilgenberg. "The crowd was yelling and screaming. McMahon was eggin' the crowd on, just being irritating like he usually did. We're getting booed, but we're all laughin' about The Fridge. 'He's going to catch a touchdown pass.' And, sure enough, he caught the pass. It was great. Ditka was letting us have fun."

Once again, Ditka had added insult on top of victory. So had McMahon, the irreverent quarterback whom the Packers loathed more than any other Bear of that era. "Arrogant as shit, man," Douglass said. "He thought he controlled the field, the referees, your team, how you should line up. He was such an arrogant bastard. We just tried to kill him every chance we got."

The Bears went on to compile a 15-1 record in 1985, then crushed the New England Patriots, 45-10, in Super Bowl XX.

As a postscript to the season, Suhey ran into Gregg at a restaurant in New Orleans during Super Bowl week, and the two had words.

"I said something to him and he said, 'Stop whining about it,'" Suhey said. "Then, I made some suggestions about his character. It was just an argument. It was maybe a few beers speaking. But I don't have a whole lot of respect for Gregg professionally. He obviously was not a great coach. Great player, maybe, but not a great coach."

The 1986 season was more of the same for the Bears and Packers. The players filled the newspapers with trash talk. And Chicago swept again, winning 25-12 and 12-10.

The first game was another Monday night affair, September 22 at Lambeau Field. Again, in the days leading up to the encounter, insults and threats flew back and forth. The Packers were still woofing about Perry's touchdowns the year before. "We made the kid a millionaire," Noble said in a story in the *Chicago Tribune*. "We think he should send us a couple checks or something."

Gregg, meanwhile, was angered because Stills was quoted in a story in the *Milwaukee Sentinel* as saying the Packers were going to go after McMahon, who was listed as doubtful with a slight shoulder separation. "I think if we get the opportunity, we're going to go in there, we're going to pick him up and we're going to put him on his shoulder," Stills said in the article. "We're going to test his shoulder right out. If his shoulder's hurt, I'm going to try my best to find out if it really hurts."

Ditka issued his own warning: "If they want to play football, we'll play football. If not, we'll play on their terms."

Bob Harlan remembers visiting the Packers' locker room before the game and sensing how nervous and tense the players were.

"It seemed very uneasy to me," he said. "I thought everybody was uptight. And as I come out of the locker room, I have to walk by the Bears' locker room, too. As I walk by, McMahon is the first guy out of the locker room, and he's got all these players around him, and he says: 'Are we going to go out and kick some Packer butt?' Everybody started screaming, 'Yeah, yeah, yeah.'

"I thought, 'Oh, boy, are we in trouble. Our guys are sitting in there, almost like, 'Do we have to do it?' And they tore us up."

For all the talking that went on, the game was hard-hitting but fairly civil. "It was football, the way football should be played," Noble said. And as it turned out, McMahon didn't even play, so Stills never got a chance to test the quarterback's shoulder.

The bad blood was still coursing through the players' veins, however, and it surfaced again in the 1986 rematch, November 23 at Soldier Field. McMahon went into the game with a slight tear in the rotator cuff of his right, or throwing, shoulder. With seven minutes, fifty-five seconds left in the second quarter, he threw a pass that was intercepted by Mark Lee. Charles Martin appeared to hesitate for a moment, then charged up to an unsuspecting and vulnerable McMahon from the blind side, picked him up, and body-slammed him to the artificial turf. McMahon landed on his injured shoulder.

It was a blatant foul, and referee Jerry Markbreit immediately disqualified Martin. The Bears were incensed, and for good reason. When asked about Martin after the game, linebacker Otis Wilson said, "If I had my own way, I'd get my Magnum and blow his ass away."

Said defensive tackle Steve McMichael: "I guess he ain't in no position to win the Nobel Peace Prize for intelligence."

More than a decade later, the Chicago players who were on the field that day shake their heads at the memory.

"Charles Martin was a loose cannon long before that happened," said Mark Bortz. "He was a cheap shot guy. On film, you'd see him doing things all the time. Against the Bears, it always seemed like he had the blessing of his coaches. Like all the other knuckleheads they had up there."

To the Packers who knew Martin, the cheap shot did not exactly come as a surprise. Nor was it totally out of character. Stills said Martin had a quick fuse.

"We'd go to the clubs and Charlie would have four or five drinks, and he would want to fight," Stills said. "He'd want to fight *me*. He'd get a buzz on and start hitting me."

Some Packers also suspected Martin was on steroids.

"At that time, there were a lot of guys on steroids and doing other stuff," said Douglass, who played his last season in Green Bay in 1985. "Those guys were really aggressive. There were about five guys who ran in Martin's little clique, and they were all juicin'. Man, they were aggressive as hell on and off the field, getting in trouble. You'd get in practice, and the littlest things would turn into big things to them and they'd start fightin' in a minute. Just in passing drills, they'd start fighting, when you were going half-speed. Charlie didn't have a half-speed, so he'd piss somebody off by hitting them too hard."

Two days after the game, Pete Rozelle suspended Martin for two games without pay, the most severe penalty he had meted out for an on-the-field infraction in twenty-six years as commissioner. McMahon stayed in the game after he was dumped by Martin, but Ditka replaced him in the fourth quarter. On Tuesday, it was announced that McMahon would require shoulder surgery and was lost for the season.

Many of the Bears believe the cheap shot contributed to the arm woes that plagued McMahon for the remainder of his career, and that it also cost them the chance to win other Super Bowls. "He never had the same arm strength after that," said Harris. "That was a crucial play for us in the '80s. The way Charles Martin played, it was like he should have been in jail."

Martin's cheap shot was so ridiculously blatant, not even the Packers could defend him. Still, years later, Gregg tried.

"The thing with Martin was a tough situation because you don't ever want one of your players to injure a player on the other team with a foul," Gregg said. "What happened with Charlie was that he was rushing the passer—at least, this is how I see it, knowing Charlie as I do—and you could almost see the wheels turn. All of a sudden, McMahon throws the ball and it's an interception. One of the things that Dick Modzelewski always taught the defense was to get the quarterback on an interception. But he meant to block the quarterback; don't pick him up and throw him to the ground.

"I think Charlie got all the things in order, but he probably got confused whether he was on defense or offense; whether he was supposed to tackle the quarterback or block him. I don't think Charlie had any intentions of really hurting anybody."

Martin, Stills, and several other Packers defenders had worn white towels on their belts, on which they had scrawled the numbers of various members of the Bears' offense. Martin had number 9 on his towel—McMahon's number. Some of the Bears believed the towels were "hit lists."

"We thought there were some things that were crazy," Ditka said. "When you have guys coming in wearing towels with the opposition's numbers on them, it's like bounty hunters. That's the guy they're going to try to take out of the game. You gotta wonder, what the hell? The mentality here can't be too high. Wherever it came from, it was wrong. This was their way of being macho, having towels hanging from their ass all the way down to their ankles. It looked so stupid, anyway."

Several of the Packers denied that the towels were hit lists. "It was more that these are the players we have to slow down to win the game," Stills said.

As the game wore on, Ditka offered his players one hundred dollars for every towel they brought to him on the sideline. "I had a guy bring me about three towels," he said. "We just ripped them off those guys."

When the game was over, Noble was so embarrassed about Martin's hit, the towels, the cheap shots, and the acrimony, he said he went to the Bears' locker room to apologize personally to Ditka.

"This was my second year in the league," Noble said. "I'm twenty-three. But I knew this was bad. So I went to the Bears' locker room. The guards knew who I was, but they weren't going to let me in. But Mike

Ditka's wife was there, and she hollered, 'Get out of his way and let him in.' She opened the door for me and pushed me in the locker room.

"So I walked right by Bortz and all those guys, and I went to Ditka's office. I said, 'Coach, can I talk to you for a minute?' He said, 'Sure, Brian, come on in.' I said, 'I just want to apologize to you for what's going on right now: the Kenny Stills deal, now the Charlie Martin deal, all that's transpiring on the football field right now.' He looked at me and said, 'Brian, you just keep doing what you're doing. You're a hell of a football player, and you play the game the right way.' Here was a Super Bowl coach telling a twenty-three-year-old man that. That meant a lot to me.

"Those two incidents right there really tainted a wonderful thing for me. I can say I played against all those guys. The Jimmy Macs, the Walter Paytons. It was a tremendous rivalry. But, inevitably, those two incidents always come up."

Players from both teams were guilty of making disparaging remarks during the Gregg-Ditka years, and the Bears weren't totally innocent on the field, either. But it seemed that the Packers more often showed a lack of class, not to mention common sense.

"After one of those games, Matt Suhey saw me coming out of the locker room and he stopped me," Harlan said. "We shook hands, and he said, 'You guys have got to clean this up. You're really becoming a dirty team.' And I knew what he was saying. It embarrassed me."

One year, when the Bears arrived at Lambeau Field, they found a bag of manure had been delivered to their locker room.

"To this day, I can't figure it out," Bortz said. "I watch TV, and they talk about the great legacy of the Packers and how wonderful the small-town atmosphere is. To me, growing up in Wisconsin, I have a hard time dealing with it. To be professional, they wouldn't have let that happen. Somebody in the clubhouse let that bag of manure in. I just thought it was classless."

Bortz also never trusted anyone again in the visitors' locker room: not the cops, not the clubhouse attendants, not anyone.

A sister of one of his high school coaches had someone deliver a pie to him in the locker room after the manure incident, but he never ate it.

"I didn't trust it," said Bortz. "To this day, I've lied to her when she asks, 'How was the pie?' I threw it away. I wouldn't eat it. You know, they're bringing manure in the locker room."

Even when the two teams met in off-season charity basketball games in the mid-1980s, they couldn't drop their mutual hatred. Those basketball games were supposed to be fun, light-hearted, and entertaining. More often than not, they became physical.

"It was just as violent as the football games," Gayle said. "I can remember one year, we played after the Bulls had played at Chicago Stadium. It was just unbelievable. Pushing and shoving—that was mild. That was in warm-ups. When you went in for a layup, you took your life in your hands."

There were behind-the-scenes developments, as well, that also illustrated the disdain the teams and coaches had for each other. One such incident occurred in 1987, Payton's final year in the league—and, as it would turn out, Gregg's last season as Green Bay's coach.

Payton had announced that he would retire following the season, and Harlan thought it would be appropriate to honor the great running back before the game at Lambeau Field on November 8. "I heard that all the teams were paying tribute to him, so I went to our public relations staff and said, 'Hell, we've got to honor him when he comes to town,'" Harlan said. "So one of the things we were going to do was give him a Packer helmet. We had a lot of different things: a plaque, a picture. I didn't want to tell Forrest about it. We were going to do it before the game. He'd be in the locker room. I didn't think it was any big deal."

Gregg found out about the plan and stormed into Harlan's office.

"Oh, he was livid," said Harlan, who was assistant to the president at the time. "He said his wife, Barbara, was livid. I said, 'All we're going to do is honor him. I know every other team in our division is going to honor him and we're really going to look second-class if we don't. I said, 'Forrest, who he plays for doesn't make a bit of difference.' If he had played for Tampa Bay, I'd say, 'Let's honor him. This is a great name. A great player.'"

Gregg wouldn't back down. He hated the idea, and he absolutely insisted that Payton not get a Packer helmet. "The helmet was what really set him off, so we withdrew the helmet from the list of gifts," Harlan said. "He didn't get that. But we had the ceremony. We were honoring a person who was a Hall of Famer. He just meant a lot to the game of pro football. And I really believe my relationship with Forrest deteriorated from that point on. I really do."

The game that day was marred by a combined twenty-three penalties for 193 yards and epitomized the entire four-year era. Later that season, the Bears beat the Packers, 23-10, on a miserable, rainy day at Soldier Field in the final chapter to the Ditka-Gregg era. But the game was anticlimatic. By then, Gregg's fate had been sealed in Green Bay.

The Packers never finished better than 8-8 in any of his four seasons. They had played the Bears tough, but beat them only once in eight tries.

The loss in Green Bay in 1987 was the most painful of all.

With exactly one minute left, Al Del Greco kicked a 47-yard field goal that gave the Packers a 24-23 lead. Lambeau Field was rocking.

The Bears got the ball on their own 24 with fifty-six seconds remaining. McMahon hit Ron Morris for twenty-one yards and Dennis McKinnon for twenty more, and suddenly, Chicago was in field goal position.

With four seconds left, Kevin Butler lined up to attempt a fifty-two-yarder. Gregg called a time out to make him think about it.

"Forrest wanted to ice me, but it really gave me an opportunity to make the surface where I had to plant my foot and get the ball down usable, because it was kind of a muddy game," Butler said. "Inside the 45-yard line, it was chewed up. So he helped me by calling time out."

The noise was deafening as Butler's foot met the ball and, a moment later . . . dead silence. The kick was good.

The Packers had lost again.

Butler turned directly toward Gregg and punched the air defiantly.

"Forrest had a hatred for me that surpassed football," Butler said. "And I shared that feeling right back for him. He was a mouthy coach and I was a mouthy player. That was the most exciting kick I had as a Chicago Bear, strictly because of where we were at, the intensity, and the rivalry. I made my scar in every Packer that day."

McMahon was so overcome with joy, he flipped the finger at the Packers' bench. "I saw it," Noble said. "There was a big smile on his face. There was a grin from ear to ear. I think there were two messages there. One, he was letting us know we had lost the game. And two, he was letting us know how he felt about us. That was a crushing blow. Both of them. Not only the field goal, but the bird."

Chapter 5

Hard-Edged Names in Hard-Nosed Games

The Bears and Packers have contributed their share of stylish and gifted athletes to the National Football League over the years. Players such as Don Hutson, Gale Sayers, Walter Payton, and Paul Hornung moved with a balletic grace that transcended their sport.

This chapter is not about them.

This chapter is about another group of Hall of Famers, a group every bit as remarkable but not nearly as glamorous. The point is the Bears-Packers rivalry would not have been the same without them.

The seven men to which this chapter is devoted had two things in common. One was that their names didn't roll off the tongue, but rattled around in the mouth and forced their way through the teeth. Hard-edged names, full of consonants and resonance. The other was that their rugged style of play not only perfectly suited their names, but personified the sometimes brutal nature of Bears vs. Packers. These men wielded vicious forearms and nasty attitudes. They played in pain, and inflicted it on others. They lived for the big hit, the crunching block, the head-snapping tackle. They intimidated opponents and, sometimes, even their own team-mates.

Other players in NFL history may have been as tough.

But nobody has ever been tougher.

BRUTE TRAFTON

As a product of the Roaring '20s—when America cultivated a fascination with both flamboyant heroes like Babe Ruth and outrageous villains like Al Capone—George "Brute" Trafton recognized the value of showmanship.

A calculating 6-foot-2, 235-pound braggart and bully, Trafton was the first great anti-hero of the Bears-Packers rivalry. He also was the first great center in professional football and was inducted into the Pro Football Hall of Fame in 1964. But during his 13-year career, from 1920 to 1932, his talents were sometimes overshadowed by his antics on the field or his exploits off it.

Known for baiting opponents and egging on the opposing team's fans, Trafton was universally disliked in NFL towns across the Midwest. In Green Bay, his rough play and his blustery act made him the most hated player on the most hated team.

"Oh, he was a dirty player," said Paul Mazzoleni, a Packers fan who attended nearly every game that Trafton played in Green Bay. "The fans booed him terrible. If you had to make an analogy, he was a guy like this Dennis Rodman. He knew how to get people excited. He was always ready to scrap."

A wire service story in 1944 conveyed, in no uncertain terms, how Packers fans felt about the Brute during his playing days, comparing him with the three hated H's of the time: Hitler, Hirohito, and Bears coach George Halas.

Born in Chicago on December 6, 1896, Trafton joined the Decatur Staleys in their inaugural season in 1920. When Halas moved the franchise to Chicago the next year, Trafton went with him and played the remainder of his career there.

He was credited with introducing the one-handed center snap to professional football and also with being the first roving center on defense.

He wore jersey number 13 out of defiance, billed himself as "Trafton the Great" and acquired the reputation, mostly deserved, as a cheap-shot artist, rogue, and rebel in the loosely governed, anything-goes infancy of the pro game.

"At the time, he was a pretty big guy," said Norm Pigeon, another longtime Packers fan who attended the first Bears-Packers game in Green Bay in 1923. "He'd try to harass the other team. He'd get down on the ball and say, 'You can't make this many yards,' or, 'You can't make an inch.' He'd mark it in the sand."

The *Green Bay Press-Gazette* prominently mentioned a bit of gamesmanship by Trafton in its coverage of the sixth game of the series, a 6-6 tie on September 26, 1926. "Even before the opening whistle blew," it was noted, "Brute Trafton started wolfing about the tee that Moose Gardner was using for the kickoff."

Mazzoleni said he recalled a similar incident at old City Stadium in Green Bay in 1932 involving Trafton and the Packers' Clarke Hinkle.

"Hinkle was getting ready to kick off," Mazzoleni said. "So the fans are all standing up, waiting for the kickoff, and here comes Trafton. He kicks the ball. Holy cripes! Curly Lambeau came out on the field. George Halas came out on the field. I happened to be selling programs that day. Halas and Lambeau were shaking fists at each other. The fans wanted to get on the field. It was a good thing we had police protection. The fans were really aroused."

Stories about Trafton and his escapades against the Packers abound, but most of them don't meet the burden of proof.

There are tales, but little, if any, supporting evidence, that Trafton was chased off the field by irate Packers fans after a game in Green Bay; that he and longtime Packers center Francis "Jug" Earpe used to chew tobacco and spit on each other during games; and that he blocked a punt for a touchdown one time with the Bears trailing, 10-0, told punter Verne Lewellen that teammate Bill Hewitt had blocked it, and then blocked a second punt for the winning touchdown when Lewellen instructed his teammates to overshift toward Hewitt's side.

Yet, as crude and as uneventful as pro football games often were in the 1920s, Trafton had his moments in the spotlight in the Bears-Packers rivalry. He recovered a key fumble when the Bears beat the Packers in Chicago in 1926 and blocked a kick in another narrow victory in Chicago in 1927.

No doubt, he was a whale of player. He also was a whale of a story-teller. Here is one of Trafton's apocryphal tales that the *New York Times* printed in 1964 when he was nominated for enshrinement to the Pro Football Hall of Fame.

On October 2, 1927, the Bears were leading, 7-0, at City Stadium when Lewellen scored on a one-yard run late in the game. Everett "Pid" Purdy, a drop-kick specialist, came in to attempt the game-tying extra point. Trafton grabbed the referee by the arm and walked over to meet Purdy. As the Bears captain, Trafton was exercising a prerogative, checking to see that Purdy did not speak in accordance with the rules of the era. But Trafton, because he was captain, could talk. He didn't waste the opportunity.

"Boy, what a hero you'll be tonight, my lad," Trafton said to Purdy. "There will be free champagne at every bar in Green Bay and they'll probably nominate you for mayor. But brother, if you miss! What a bum you'll be. They'll run you out of town."

Purdy, forced to seethe in silence while Trafton delivered his soliliquy, put everything he had into the kick.

"The attempted drop kick didn't go within a mile of the uprights," the *Press-Gazette* reported the next day, "and the gloom at the stadium was so thick that it could be cut with a knife."

The next day a still furious Purdy supposedly went out and drop-kicked ninety-two consecutive extra points before he missed.

Aside from his football fame, Trafton also dabbled in professional wrestling and boxing. In 1929, he took a five-round decision from Chicago White Sox first baseman Art Shires in a ballyhooed grudge match. Trafton then signed to fight Primo Carnera, the Italian heavyweight contender who later became world champion. Just fifty-four seconds into the fight, Trafton tumbled comically to the canvas after Carnera flicked a pawing jab in the general direction of his chin.

In 1944, coach Curly Lambeau shocked Packers fans by signing Trafton as line coach. This occurred after a chance encounter between the two during which Trafton supposedly said: "What's wrong with that club of yours? They don't scrap back like those old Green Bay teams. Why, right now, in this dinner jacket, I could chase those mugs out of the park."

The story goes that Lambeau replied: "You've got a job."

Trafton spent just one season in Green Bay, but the Packers won the NFL championship that year; it would be their last until Vince Lombardi's Glory Years. Trafton later served as an assistant coach with the Los Angeles Rams from 1946 to 1949, and as head coach of the Winnipeg Blue Bombers of the Canadian Football League from 1951 to 1953.

He died on September 5, 1971, at the age of seventy-four.

BRONKO NAGURSKI

The name is almost unbelievably apropos, the sort of corny tag a screen writer would dream up for a movie about a larger-than-life fullback from the leather-helmet era of the National Football League.

But no writer invented Bronislav "Bronko" Nagurski.

He was the real deal, and nearly every football player who banged heads with the Bears' tank-like fullback in the 1930s came away with the bruises—or broken bones—to prove it.

Nagurski carried 235 pounds of muscle, bone, and sinew on his 6-foot-2 frame. With a natural strength that bordered on the freakish and a battering-ram running style that made tough defenders go weak at the knees, he was one of the NFL's first great fullbacks—and, some would argue, one of its best ever, including the players of the modern era.

Although Nagurski never rushed for one thousand yards in any of his nine seasons with the Bears, he was a dominating physical presence, a plowhorse who was bigger and stronger than many of the linemen of the time. He not only was a bruising north-south runner, but he also was a tenacious blocker, and, on defense, a punishing tackler whose style was simply to slam ball-carriers to the ground with a well-aimed shoulder. When he was being tackled himself, he had the habit of catching the opponent under the chin with his shoulder, resulting in what the *New York Times* once described as "a jolt like an uppercut."

"He struck the fear of God into people," said Sam Francis, a Bears fullback who backed up Nagurski in 1937 and 1938.

As fate would have it, Nagurski came along at a time when the Bears and Packers were becoming bitter rivals and, not coincidentally, battling for the NFL championship on an almost annual basis. His clashes with Packers fullback Clarke Hinkle were sights to behold; his memorable collisions with other Green Bay players, such as Cal Hubbard and Ted Fritsch, became an important part of the rivalry's rich lore.

Nagurski was born in Rainy River, Ontario, but lived most of his life in International Falls, Minnesota. Legend has it that he was recruited to play football for the University of Minnesota when coach Clarence "Doc" Spears saw him plowing in a field—without a horse. When Spears asked directions, the story goes, Nagurski picked up the plow with one hand and pointed the way.

Other similar stories about the "Human Bulldozer" or the "One-Man Thundering Herd," as the press called him, were embellished over the years and became part of the legend. And while those stories may have been exaggerated, they painted an accurate picture of Nagurski's prowess. There is little doubt that he was the roughest, toughest player in an era that produced more than its share.

"We said he ran his own interference," said Charles "Ookie" Miller, who played center for the Bears from 1932 to 1936 and played for the Packers in 1938. "Bronk was all man."

Nagurski signed with the Bears in 1930 for five thousand dollars and played his first game against the Packers on September 28 of that year. The Packers won, 7-0, at City Stadium, but Nagurski led the Bears in rushing, based on what were then unofficial statistics, with thirty-six yards in eleven carries.

The Packers were on their way to their second of three consecutive NFL titles that season. But in the rematch at Wrigley Field on November 9, Nagurski almost single-handedly kept the Bears in the game. He was credited with gaining 104 of Chicago's 196 total yards in a 13-12 loss, and although Green Bay kept him out of the end zone, he had runs of thirty-two and twenty-eight yards.

"The 'Big Nag,' Bronko Nagurski, led the Bear attack—and what a whale of a game he played," the *Chicago Tribune* reported. "Smashing, driving and ever fighting his way forward, the former Gopher star loomed up like a man mountain in Green Bay's path to another pennant."

In that rookie season, Nagurski showed his brute strength by knocking out the Packers' Hurdis McCrary with a knee to the chin. And he more than held his own in a collision with Cal Hubbard, Green Bay's 250-pound tackle and future Hall of Famer.

The encounter with Hubbard occurred on a punt. Nagurski and Red Grange were assigned as deep blockers to protect the Bears' punter. Hubbard wanted to test Nagurski's strength and toughness, so he asked Grange to step aside on a punt in the fourth quarter, promising not to block the kick. Grange agreed. He let Hubbard through, then turned around just in time to see the big tackle go down in a heap. "Hubbard caught up with me as we left the field," Grange would say years later. "He said he'd seen enough. He said, 'The kid is as hard as they said he was.'"

Two years later, the Packers were marching toward a fourth consecutive world championship—that is, until they ran into Nagurski. On December 11, 1932, on the snow-covered turf at Wrigley Field, Nagurski scored on a 56-yard run and recovered a Packers fumble that led to a field goal in Chicago's 9-0 victory.

"He smashed inside of the Packer right tackle," was how the *Tribune* described the run, "bowled over the supporting secondary and ran fifty-six yards down the sideline for a touchdown. Once in high speed,

Nagurski outran all but one of the Packers, and he disposed of this opponent with a stiff arm which flung him aside as if struck by a two-ton truck."

Chicago's victory in that game not only ended Green Bay's chances for another title, but it put the Bears on the inside track for the championship with a 6-1-6 record. One week later, Nagurski threw a jump-pass to Grange for the only touchdown as Chicago beat Portsmouth, 9-0, in a playoff game that settled the league championship.

In 1934, the Bears scored two victories over the Packers, winning the Western Division title, and Nagurski was the dominant player on the field. He gained a combined 173 yards in twenty-seven carries and scored two touchdowns. One was on a 34-yard run in the Bears' 24-10 victory in Green Bay. In the second game, won by the Bears, 27-14, his punishing lead blocks enabled rookie halfback Beattie Feathers to rush for 155 yards in fifteen attempts.

Most of Nagurski's carries were simple plunges into the middle of the line. They were easy to diagnose, but stopping the plundering fullback was another matter.

"He had excellent, excellent speed," said Bob Snyder, who played with and against Nagurski during his six-year pro career. "He had a 21½-inch neck. The guy was just a strong power runner. And when you think about it, all the yards he made—and he was the fear of the league—was inside the tackles. They didn't have splits in the lines. In those days, they had a tight line. You were the center and your left foot was next to the left guard, your right foot next to the right guard. Now, they have splits a yard-and-a-half, two yards and they pitch out. If you had pitchouts to Bronk, he'd turn that corner and you would have never had to block those cornerbacks.

"If they would have had the offenses they have today, I swear to God, he would have killed somebody."

Like most players in the 1930s, Nagurski had his salary cut during the Great Depression. He turned to professional wrestling to supplement his income, apparently with Halas' blessing.

"He was heavyweight wrestling champ," Francis said. "He'd go out and wrestle for two weeks, and I'd get to play. Then, he'd come back, play a week or two, and go again."

After the 1937 season, Nagurski asked for a raise to six thousand dollars, but the penny-wise Halas turned him down, so he retired. However,

Halas came calling in 1943, when World War II depleted the Bears' roster, and Nagurski agreed to return.

After reporting to camp a week before the game, he played nearly the full sixty minutes as the Bears and Packers battled to a 21-21 tie in the season opener.

"He played offensive tackle, defensive tackle, and sometimes backed up the line," said Snyder, who also came out of retirement to play with the Bears that year. "He was one pound lighter than he was in his last year in 1937. He didn't limp, nothin'. The only thing he got was a blister on his foot."

Nagurski also got in his licks. On one particular play, Ted Fritsch, Green Bay's second-year fullback and a tough customer himself, hit the Bronk with everything he had. The story goes that when Fritsch regained his senses, he saw a hulking Chicago player staring down at him.

"I knew it was you, Bronk," Fritsch supposedly said. "You didn't even budge."

Although Nagurski was thirty-five years old and had been out of football for five years, he helped the Bears to an 8-1-1 record. He played tackle for most of the season, but moved to fullback and played a prominent role when Chicago beat Washington, 41-21, in the NFL championship game.

Nagurski then retired for good, opening a gas station in International Falls. He also farmed, raised cattle and poultry, and continued to wrestle professionally until 1960, when arthritis finally caught up with him. After that, he granted few interviews and made even fewer public appearances. He died on January 7, 1990.

Nagurski was officially credited with 633 carries for 2,778 yards, a 4.4 average, during his professional career. Against Green Bay, in the nine games that he played fullback and official statistics were compiled, he gained 330 yards in seventy-five carries, a 4.4 average. While those aren't exactly staggering numbers, Nagurski played nine games against the Packers before the NFL kept track of stats, missed two others in 1935, and never carried more than fourteen times in the games for which there were official stats.

Nagurski was a charter member of the Pro Football Hall of Fame in 1963, and his size 19½ ring, one of the biggest ever made by the L.G. Balfour Co., is still on display in Canton, Ohio.

More than fifty years after he played his last game, his name remains one of the most magical in the history of the game.

"You get in a conversation today—I go out and give talks—and they never ask about the glamour guys," said Snyder, also a former NFL coach now in his eighties and living in Toledo, Ohio. "They want to know what the hell Nagurski was like."

CLARKE HINKLE

The fleeting image on the archival game film—a Depression-era Packers player with an obvious zest for contact—so thoroughly intrigued Paul Zimmerman that the senior pro football writer for *Sports Illustrated* rewound the film and watched it, again and again.

Zimmerman was researching the exploits of Nagurski and Don Hutson, the Packers' great end, for a story that was published in SI in 1989. But the tough-as-nails Green Bay player wearing jersey No. 30 left an indelible impression on Zimmerman.

He watched the grainy film in awe as Hinkle repeatedly trampled defenders as a fullback and flattened ball-carriers as a linebacker. Not only was Hinkle a load, Zimmerman noted, but he was a gifted athlete who punted, kicked, caught the ball, and even threw it.

Hinkle and Nagurski were contemporaries, and while Nagurski enjoyed more notoriety and lasting fame, Zimmerman concluded that Hinkle was every bit the Bronk's equal.

"My impression was that Hinkle was a lot better than people gave him credit for," Zimmerman said. "He was a well-kept secret in Green Bay. He made the all-pro teams because he was a dominating back, but he never got the publicity or notoriety that Nagurski got. Bronko was a great name, and Nagurski was bigger.

"But Hinkle, shit, he was an iron man. He played like a fucking maniac. So, yeah, I think he was every bit as good. I saw him make a tackle and he went flying. You saw a blur coming into the screen, like he was possessed. And he smashed some guy out of bounds and into the seats. Jesus!"

Hinkle and Nagurski are forever linked because of their literal head-to-head clashes in the 1930s, when the Bears and Packers were the pre-eminent teams in the young NFL. The Bears won two NFL titles and the Packers one during the six-year span, from 1932 to 1937, when these hard-charging Hall of Famers played against each other.

Hinkle stood six feet and played at 205 to 210 pounds, giving away about thirty pounds to Nagurski. But, possessing both an iron will and a steel body, Hinkle not only didn't back down from the Bronk, he relished his encounters with the raw-boned Minnesotan and dished out his share of punishment.

"They talk about the duels between Hinkle and Nagurski; I don't know who came out better, but Clarke was really tough," said Harry Jacunski, who played end for the Packers from 1939 to 1944. "Helluva guy. I just admired the hell out of the guy as a person and as an indestructible football player."

Hinkle joined the Packers out of tiny Bucknell College in 1932 and played for ten years. During that time, he established himself as perhaps the most complete player in the NFL. He ran hard, blocked savagely, passed effectively, had outstanding range and a mean streak as a linebacker, and was an accomplished punter and place-kicker. In 1994, he was named to the league's all-time two-way team.

"Meaner than a rattlesnake," said Bob Adkins, who played with the Packers during Hinkle's final two years in the league. "Hink was great. He did everything. He was an all-around man."

A four-time all-NFL selection, Hinkle's name peppered the league record book in the pre-World War II era.

He carried 1,171 times for 3,860 yards, a 3.3 average, and also completed twenty-five of fifty-three passes for 293 yards. He scored forty-three touchdowns, kicked twenty-eight field goals, and finished his career with 372 points. He led the league in scoring with fifty-eight points in 1938, and was the NFL's field goal leader in both 1940 and 1941. Hinkle also punted eighty-seven times for a 40.8-yard average.

In twenty-two games against the Bears, Hinkle gained 665 yards in 223 carries, a 3.0 average. Again, the numbers aren't spectacular by today's standards, but the game back then revolved around plunges into the line out of tight formations. Moreover, until his final game against the Bears in 1941, Hinkle never carried more than fifteen times against them. He also never looked to sidestep a would-be tackler.

"He'd just run over people," said Tom Greenfield, a center with the Packers from 1939 to 1941. "He never tried to dodge anybody. He just knocked them over."

With Hinkle at fullback, Arnie Herber and later Cecil Isbell at quarterback, and Hutson at end, the Packers had one of the most dangerous run-throw-catch combinations in league history. Green Bay compiled an 80-35-4 record during Hinkle's ten seasons.

His greatest legacy, however, was his incredible toughness. The evidence bears out that, pound for pound, he has had few peers in NFL history. And he saved some of his best efforts for the hated Bears.

"I think he was the hardest runner I ever played against," said Clyde "Bulldog" Turner, who played center and linebacker for the Bears from 1940 to 1952. "When you tackled him, you could feel it."

And when Hinkle tackled people, they felt it.

"I would fake into the line and he'd hit me every time I came through there—whether I had the ball or not," said Dick Schweidler, a back for the Bears in 1938 and 1939, as well as 1946. "He just about murdered me."

Hinkle and Nagurski were destined to clash many times on the football field, but three particularly violent collisions—in 1932, 1933, and 1936—were the stuff of which legends are made.

In 1932, Hinkle's rookie year, he squared up on defense and tried to tackle Nagurski, who ran him over and in the process opened a seven-stitch cut in his chin.

"As I sat there, I said, 'Clarke, you better learn how to play this game, or they'll kill you,'" Hinkle said in the book *The Game That Was*. "From then on, I tried to get to Bronk before he got to me."

The next season, Hinkle was ready for Nagurski. And on September 24, 1933, in a 14-7 Packers victory at City Stadium, Hinkle returned the favor with a hit so violent that it "shook the stands," according to Hutson.

On third down, Hinkle went into punt formation, a fairly routine practice in those days. He had the option to run, pass, or kick, and on this occasion, he chose to run. He broke through a hole on the right side and veered toward the sideline.

Nagurski, in typical all-out pursuit, had the angle and was about to smash into Hinkle when, at the last instant, the Packers' fullback pivoted and drove his shoulder into Nagurski, delivering the blow instead of taking it. Both players were shaken up on the play, but the Nag suffered the worst of it. He was knocked out, and his nose was badly broken and pushed sickeningly to one side of his face. Hinkle got up and finished the game; Nagurski was carried off the field. Old-timers who witnessed the play still refer to it with reverence as the most brutal collision they have seen.

"It was like two engines hitting head-on," said Paul Mazzoleni, who has been a diehard Packers fan since the team's first year in the NFL.

"Nagurski was completely flattened out. His nose was broken. There was blood all over his face. Hinkle was lying on the ground. . . . It was the talk of the town for years."

In a story three days before the rematch on October 22, 1933, the *Press-Gazette* reported: "Clarke Hinkle, Packer fullback, will enter the game with a wary eye cast on the Bear backfield, as Bronko Nagurski, injured in a collision with Hinkle at Green Bay several weeks ago, will be back in the regular lineup. Nagurski's face was disarranged and the lines of his nose rerouted, necessitating several weeks' rest."

Old-timers remember one particularly nasty collision in the game, but newspaper accounts do not reveal anything extraordinary. Three years later, however, Nagurski and Hinkle had the sort of bone-jarring hit that solidified their reputations for posterity.

It occurred during a 21-10 Packers victory at Wrigley Field on a rainy November 1, 1936. In the second quarter, Hinkle took a handoff and ran through a hole created by teammates Charles "Buckets" Goldenberg and George Svendsen, who double-teamed George Musso, the Bears' Hall of Fame lineman. Just as Hinkle burst into the open field, however, he was met head-on by the bull-rushing Nagurski.

The impact knocked Hinkle into the air and several feet backward. But he somehow made a two-point landing, and, legs churning, again ran past a surprised Musso—and Nagurski—for a career-long 59-yard touchdown. Musso later would say it was the only time in his career that a back passed him three times on the same play.

Although Hinkle and Nagurski were mortal enemies on the football field, it was nothing personal. In fact, they had a mutual respect and admiration for one another. Nagurski, who was inducted into the Pro Football Hall of Fame with the charter class of 1963, lobbied for Hinkle's inclusion. Not that the voters needed much persuasion; Hinkle was inducted the next year.

Incredibly, Hinkle never suffered a serious injury on the football field. Up until the day he died in 1988, at age seventy-nine, he remained relatively free of the arthritic pain that crippled so many ex-pros, and especially the two-way players.

"In the five years I played with Clarke, he was never hurt," said the late Eddie Jankowski, a back with the Packers from 1937 to 1941. "That was amazing."

In fact, Hinkle rarely missed a play, let alone a game, because of injury. One of the times it happened was in 1941, when Bears fullback Bill Osmanski caught Hinkle with his cleats, opening a gash on his shin that exposed the bone. Hinkle stayed on the field for two or three plays, but then called a time out and jogged to the sideline to get the wound dressed. He was greeted by Curly Lambeau, who berated him for wasting a timeout.

"I said to Lambeau, 'Listen, my shinbone's showing,'" Hinkle said in *The Game That Was*. "I came over here to get a bandage on it, because, you know, it kind of makes me sick to look at my shinbone."

Hinkle not only went back into the game, but he kicked a 38-yard field goal that proved to be the winning points in a 16-14 Packers victory. After the game, there were no taxis to be found on the deserted streets around Wrigley Field, so Hinkle walked the fifteen blocks to the team hotel.

"He was a great ballplayer," said Greenfield. "You know, he wasn't a big man, but, God, he was powerful. He was just a hard-nosed player. And the madder he got, those eyes would just pop out like nobody's business. You could tell when he was ready to play football. You could see the intensity in his eyes."

That intensity, along with his versatility and explosiveness, is why old-timers nearly always talk about him in the same breath as Nagurski.

"Hinkle was a great fullback," said Bob Snyder, who played with the Cleveland Rams and Bears in the years before World War II and then served as an assistant coach with the Packers in 1949. "I played with Nagurski and I played against Bronk my first year. I played against Hinkle. It's hard to explain, but when Nagurski hit you, it was 240 pounds of power and then there was a big surge forward. Bronk never really hurt you, if you got him on the line of scrimmage. But, ol' Hink, he'd sting you. He had extreme take-off speed and leverage. He was always square to the line.

"And, boy, when he hit you, you knew you had been hit."

BULLDOG TURNER

Clyde "Bulldog" Turner earned everything he ever got, from the pennies he made for picking cotton in Texas as a youth to the contracts he fought over with Bears owner George Halas in the 1940s.

But Turner, now in his late seventies and living on a ranch near Gatesville, Texas, isn't so sure he earned his nickname, despite playing center and linebacker for thirteen seasons, from 1940 to 1952.

"Not really. I wasn't no real tough guy," he said modestly. "I thought I was tough enough. I played against a lot of guys I didn't fear at all on the football field, but I wouldn't get caught in an alley with 'em."

Talk to Turner's teammates, however, or players on the Packers who engaged the Bears in a series of brutal slugfests after World War II, and the truth emerges. "Bulldog was one of the roughest, toughest men who ever walked on the football field," said Dick Schweidler, a Bears teammate in 1946. "Man, he'd run down and hit somebody on the sideline and it sounded like a horse hitting the wall. He was one tough cookie, I'll tell you."

Don Perkins, who played in the backfield for the Packers from 1943 to 1945 and then played two more seasons with the Bears, vouched for Turner's ability to dish out punishment as a linebacker.

"I think I got hit the hardest in my life by Bulldog up in Green Bay," Perkins said. "It was just a dive play. We ran the single-wing. He hit me from the blind side; I did not see him. He put me in the nickel seats, I'll tell you. He was just a regular old, hard-nosed football player. He played ball for keeps."

If nothing else, Turner, who stood 6 feet 2 inches and weighed 232 pounds, earned his nickname just by blocking Ed Neal, a massive, 300-pound middle guard for Green Bay at a time when 250-pounders were rare. Neal had limited mobility, but he had a blacksmith's arms and unbelievable strength.

"Ed's forearms were like big hamhocks," said Tobin Rote, the Packers' quarterback from 1950 to 1956. "I saw him break a beer bottle over his forearm. He'd just flex his muscle and wing a bottle right into it, and it would shatter."

Neal put shinpads on those forearms, and wielded them like clubs on the football field. Turner was on the receiving end more times than he cares to remember; by his own count, Neal broke his nose five times.

"His forearm was like an anvil," Turner said. "We didn't have face masks and he'd just throw his arm into my face. It was perfectly legal, but it hurt."

It was true trench warfare, conducted on dirt fields and in relative obscurity. Elbows, fists, knees, and forearms were the weapons of choice, and not even the advent of plastic helmets helped soften the blows.

"You know when they first came out with a hard, plastic helmet?" Turner said. "It was just some kind of fiber board. It wasn't leather, and it wasn't that strong plastic they've got now. And when I'd duck my head, Neal would hit me on the top of the head and crack those helmets. I used to take two or three helmets with me when I was going to play against Green Bay. I knew Neal would break a few of them."

But Turner won more battles than he lost. And the Bears usually won the war: they had a 19-6-1 regular-season record against Green Bay during his career, and won four championships to the Packers' one.

Turner anchored the offensive line and had outstanding range and instincts as a linebacker, intercepting four passes in five NFL championship games. He led the league with eight interceptions in 1942, and returned an interception 96 yards for a touchdown in 1947. He also played guard, tackle, and even running back in a pinch. The only time he ever carried the ball, he scored on a 48-yard run.

"Bulldog Turner is one of the greatest athletes who ever played in the National Football League," said Sid Luckman, the Bears' Hall of Fame quarterback. "In my honest to God opinion, I don't think there ever was a greater football player, a smarter football player. He was unbelievable. He could run like a deer and he weighed 245 pounds.

"Whenever we were in trouble and needed one yard, I'd give the ball to George McAfee or Hugh Gallarneau and they'd hit right off his position, and I don't ever remember him failing."

Turner was one of the first great students of the game. He soaked up information from other players and coaches, experimented with blocking techniques, and mastered the art of holding.

"He was highly intelligent, which, in those days, you didn't expect from a big, husky center," said Gallarneau, a halfback who ran behind Turner's blocks for five seasons. "Plus, he was extremely mobile for a big man. He was a great linebacker. And he was tough in the sense that he could give it and take it."

After the 1952 season, Turner hung up his cleats and spent four more seasons with the Bears as an assistant coach. In 1962, he served as head coach of the New York Titans, who became the Jets the following year. In 1966, he was inducted into the Pro Football Hall of Fame. By then, he had retired to his ranch in central Texas, where he bred racehorses and raised cattle, sheep, and goats.

And to this day, nobody calls him Clyde.

RAY NITSCHKE

As Bears running back Brian Piccolo lay on his deathbed in June, 1970, his body ravaged by cancer, he asked to see Ed McCaskey, the son-in-law of George Halas and a close family friend.

McCaskey had been assigned by Halas to take care of Piccolo's every need. He had been there to support the player and his wife, Joy, many times in those terrible final months. So McCaskey caught the first train from Chicago to New York and went straight to the Sloan-Kettering Cancer Center. He had steeled himself for the inevitable, but the sight of Piccolo, in horrific pain and gasping for breath, was more than he could bear.

"I looked at him and tears burst from my eyes, involuntarily," McCaskey said. "Brian saw that and said, 'Don't worry, Big Ed, I'm not afraid of anything—only Nitschke.'

"He died that day."

The story is testament both to Piccolo's wonderful sense of humor and to Ray Nitschke's stature as one of pro football's legendary toughmen.

Never was a football player more perfectly suited to play a position than was Nitschke to play middle linebacker. At 6 feet 3 inches and 235 pounds, he had ideal size, speed, and strength. He also had the ideal disposition: ornery, intense, fearless, tough, and emotional. He had the perfect look, too. Prematurely bald, he appeared to be older and harder than his years. In college, he had taken a helmet to the mouth, and he was missing most of his upper teeth. When he was in uniform, padded and taped, with eye black on his cheeks and, occasionally, speckles of blood on his jersey—his own or an opponent's, it didn't matter—the effect was chilling.

He was the monster Frankenstein, come to life and wearing No. 66 for the Green Bay Packers.

"He was scary looking," said Willie Davis, who played defensive end for the Packers from 1960 to 1969. "He just gave you the sense that he would destroy anything that came within range."

Nitschke was born in Bears country—Elmwood Park, Illinois, a working-class suburb of Chicago. As a prep star at Proviso East High School and a standout fullback and linebacker at the University of Illinois, Nitschke dreamed of playing for the Monsters of the Midway. But in 1958, the Packers drafted him in the third round.

"I didn't know too much about Green Bay," Nitschke said. "I grew up a Bears fan. I grew up going to Wrigley Field as a kid. I was disappointed I wasn't drafted by them."

It didn't take long, however, for Nitschke to become a Bear-hater, like the rest of the Packers.

As a member of the College All-Star team—before he even began his professional career—Nitschke traveled to Rensselaer, Indiana, to take part in a scrimmage against the Bears.

"I'll never forget it," he said. "I'm playing against the team I grew up watching. I knew all about the Luckmans, the Osmanskis, the Nagurskis. So we're warming up, and I'm really scared and nervous. And I think one of the first players I saw was Doug Atkins, who was just huge and built like a Greek god. Big and strong. I said, 'Oh, my God.'

"Then, we get into the scrimmage, and I get comfortable after the first few plays. I remember knocking Rick Casares, the Bears' big fullback, out of bounds near their bench. And George Halas starts calling me all these names. I couldn't believe it. Here was my boyhood idol, cussing me out.

"So I found out very early I didn't like the Bears."

The dislike grew stronger when he played his first game at Wrigley Field on November 9, 1958. "I thought, being from Chicago, I'd get a few cheers from the fans," Nitschke said. "But wearing that Packer uniform, they cussed me out. So right there, at that moment, I said, 'The Chicago Bears are my enemies now.'

"We played the Bears three times a year, counting exhibition games, and I always said I didn't need Vince Lombardi to get me ready to play the Bears. No matter how I felt, I'd be out there giving it my best."

As a young professional, Nitschke was cocky, undisciplined, and, by his own admission, immature. His father had died when he was three years old, and his mother when he was thirteen; he had been raised by two older brothers. "I felt I was somebody who didn't have anything," he said. "And I took it out on everybody else."

Nitschke was obnoxious. He was stubborn. He drank too much and stayed out too late at night. And he languished on the bench behind Tom Bettis.

Two things happened to change his life. He got married, to Jackie, and settled down; and coach Vince Lombardi began to see in him the qualities that would someday earn him induction into the Pro Football Hall of Fame.

Once Nitschke moved into the starting lineup fulltime in 1962, he quickly became an emotional leader who set an example with his ferocious style of play. The Packers' defense was built to take advantage of his strengths; the linemen occupied the blockers, freeing Nitschke to roam and make tackles.

But he didn't shy away from going helmet-to-helmet with a guard when the opportunity presented itself. "The way he played middle linebacker was different," said Ted Karras, who played guard for the Bears from 1960 to 1964. "He'd play the blocks head-on, especially the guards. He always wanted to play real tough, hit, and hold his ground. He tried to play with power. Guys like Sam Huff and even Dick Butkus, they were quick and shed the blocker quickly. Butkus didn't waste his energy on the block. Nitschke's style made him more hated by the offensive linemen. He tried to punish them."

It was nothing personal. Nitschke simply rose to the occasion against the Bears. He never forgot the disappointments at Rensselaer and Wrigley his rookie year. He embraced the rivalry, and his personal feud with Chicago tight end Mike Ditka only served to fan the flames.

"I think Ray got excited about every game," Willie Davis said. "But he would go to another level when it was the Bears."

Nitschke had interceptions in Green Bay victories on November 4, 1962, and October 16, 1966.

On December 15, 1968, he did it again, intercepting a pass by Jack Concannon in the final minute to preserve a 28-27 victory over the Bears. Ronnie Bull, the fullback, and Piccolo, who was playing halfback, had both run patterns over the middle, but Nitschke correctly diagnosed the play.

"He not only was a tough football player, he was a smart football player," said Bull. "I was open, but the quarterback made the choice and Nitschke anticipated right and made the interception. The quarterback was supposed to key the middle linebacker; if he comes to me, the quarterback goes the other way. But Nitschke anticipated which way it was going to go."

That loss, in the season finale, was especially painful to the Bears. Had they won, they would have clinched the Central Division title. "That was probably the toughest loss I ever experienced," Bull said.

Like other great middle linebackers, Nitschke mastered the art of intimidation. Gale Sayers, Chicago's Hall of Fame running back, remembers Nitschke trying to rattle him with verbal abuse in 1965, his rookie year. Nitschke also was fond of barking "hut-hut" to try to draw opposing linemen offside.

Those he couldn't pysche out, he simply tried to wipe out. "The hardest I ever got hit was by Nitschke," said Bull. "My rookie year, running around end, I cut back and he lowered the boom on me. It was like getting hit by an eighteen-wheeler."

While Nitschke loved contact, he played by the rules. He went all-out until the whistle blew, but he didn't believe in late hits or cheap shots.

Bull shared a story that spoke volumes about Nitschke.

"One time, we were playing in Green Bay and Willie Wood intercepted a pass," Bull said. "He was running across the field, and I'm chasing him to make the tackle. Before I got there, the whistle blows. Somebody grabs me by the shoulder from the blind side. I didn't even see him, didn't even feel him coming. I turned around, and there was Nitschke, smiling, no teeth and all. He said, 'Saved by the whistle.' I was so shocked, I just said, 'Yes, sir.' If I had been a rookie, he would have killed me. Luckily, I guess, he had enough respect for me that he didn't do it."

In 1971, Packers coach Dan Devine replaced Nitschke in the starting lineup with twenty-three-year-old Jim Carter, a second-year player. "He wasn't a coach," Nitschke said of Devine. "There were a lot of frustrations when you're not playing. I thought I should be playing. But they wanted me just to run out the clock."

On December 12, 1971, the Packers honored him with "Ray Nitschke Day" before the final home game of the season. Nitschke was moved to tears during the festivities at Lambeau Field.

Devine started him against the Bears. Nitschke played well, and the Packers won, 31-10. "I couldn't have chosen a better opponent," he said. "If Dan Devine ever did anything for me, the best thing he did for Ray Nitschke was let me have an opportunity to play in that game."

Nitschke hung on for one more year, then retired after his fifteenth season. It was the second-longest tenure in Packers' history behind quarterback Bart Starr. He was named to the NFL's All-50 Year and 75th Anniversary teams, and was inducted into the Pro Football Hall of Fame in 1978.

On December 4, 1983, Nitschke had his number 66 retired in a pregame ceremony, again on the day of a Packers-Bears game at Lambeau Field. Nitschke still lives in Green Bay, and is a visible and popular figure in Wisconsin, where he does television commercials and makes appearances at store openings, charity golf tournaments, and card shows.

To this day, the debate continues about whether Nitschke or Butkus was the greatest middle linebacker of all time. Nitschke, who owns a Siberian Husky named "Butkus," refuses to get dragged into the debate.

"What I liked about Dick Butkus was his tenacity as a player," he said. "He played every down with everything he had. That's the way you're supposed to play the game."

Certainly, that's the way Nitschke played it.

MIKE DITKA

It didn't take long for Mike Ditka to make an impression on the Packers.

In the 1961 Midwest Shrine Game, an exhibition played in Milwaukee, the rookie tight end out of Pittsburgh angered Ray Nitschke with his roughhouse tactics, then nearly came to blows with the Packers' middle linebacker in a bar afterward. It was the beginning of an eye-for-an-eye feud that lasted several years.

"Actually, I pulled up on him," Ditka said, remembering the incident. "I was coming across the field and the play was over, and when I pulled up, I kind of put my hands out and I kind of pushed him from behind. If I had wanted to block him, believe me, I could have done anything I wanted to because he never saw me coming.

"But when I put my hands up—and believe me, I did a lot of things that weren't innocent, but this was totally innocent—he took that the wrong way."

In those days, Bears coach George Halas allowed his players to take their cars up to Milwaukee for the Shrine Game, so after the game, Ditka joined a few teammates, including Rick Casares and Bill George, for a beer. Some Packers players—Nitschke among them—were in the same bar.

It wasn't long before Nitschke was in Ditka's face. Nitschke was an imposing figure and a four-year veteran, but Ditka didn't back down. The two had to be separated by their respective teammates.

"He told me I was a dirty player," Ditka said. "I said, 'Fine.'"

After that, Nitschke and Ditka made it a point to seek each other out and renew old acquaintances during Bears-Packers games.

"I think it was the next year when I peeled back on him in a game up there and I'll tell you what, I put a helluva block on him," Ditka said, relishing the memory. "It was clean. It was legitimate. And I'll tell you this, if it had been somebody else, I probably would have hit him high, but I hit him low. And what happened was, he went out of the game. Then, I couldn't believe he came back in the game. He taped his knee and played a helluva game."

But Nitschke scored his share of knockdowns, too, and even registered a knockout on December 5, 1964.

"I had been thinking about number 89, that I owed this guy somethin'," Nitschke said. "He caught the ball right in front of me and I hit him pretty good. I thought I killed him. It was some experience. You got this 'I'm going to get this guy attitude,' and then all of a sudden, you say, 'Man, I saw the whites of this guy's eyes and I thought I killed him.' I knocked him out and they had to carry him off the field."

Ditka returned, but the rest of the game was a blur.

"He knocked me out in the first quarter," said Ditka. "I continued to play, but I had no recollection of anything until I saw the films."

The Ditka-Nitschke collisions certainly added spice to a rivalry that didn't need extra seasoning. But there was much, much more to Ditka as a player. Many put him on a pedestal, along with Baltimore's John Mackey, as one of the greatest tight ends in NFL history.

At 6 feet 3 inches and 230 pounds, Ditka had ideal size. He also had great hands, better-than-average speed, and an innate feel for the game. "He was the best football player I've ever seen play," said Bob Wetoska, a tackle for the Bears from 1960 to 1969. "He could have played, give or take some poundage, just about every position on the field except for defensive back. He was that good. An incredible football player."

Perhaps Ditka's biggest strength was his blocking ability. He is generally regarded as the finest blocking tight end in history. "Nobody blocked middle linebackers like Mike Ditka," said Casares, who played fullback for the Bears from 1955 to 1964. "He relished it. He used to wipe them out. You could see the middle linebackers' heads spinning, looking for where Mike was. He used to clean their clock. Sweeps and cutbacks. He was a fierce blocker."

Ditka also didn't shy away from defensive linemen. "No question in my mind, he was one of the most aggressive and stay-after-you football players that I have ever seen," said Willie Davis, Green Bay's Hall of Fame defensive end. "He would be absolutely dogged in his attempt to get you. When he was lining up there, he was my first concern. I always said, 'Shit, don't get caved by Ditka.'"

Dave Robinson, a linebacker who played behind Davis in Green Bay's defense, said Davis was almost obsessed with Ditka, whom he always feared would take out his knees with cut blocks.

"The first time I played against the Bears, Willie told me, 'No matter what you do, don't let Ditka block back on me,'" Robinson said. "That was my one job against the Bears: keep Ditka off Willie Davis' legs. He said, 'If you keep Ditka off me, I'll take care of all the running plays.'"

Once, Davis remembers, he and Ditka "going after each other big time." Near the end of the game, Davis issued a challenge. "I said, 'Hey, Ditka, let me tell you something. Goddamnit, if you're so tough, maybe we ought to settle this after the game,'" Davis said. "He said, 'Just name the place, buddy.'"

The Bears selected Ditka with the fifth pick in the first round of the 1961 draft. He had been an All-American end at Pitt, but rarely caught the ball there. Over the next few seasons, however, Ditka's prowess as a receiver would forever change the way teams used their tight ends. In his rookie season, he finished fifth in the NFL with fifty-six receptions for 1,076 yards and twelve touchdowns, second-most in the league. He was named all-pro and selected to the Pro Bowl, as well as being named rookie of the year.

Once he caught the ball, Ditka turned into a fullback-type runner. Tackling him in the open field was not a fun proposition, particularly if you were a safety or cornerback and giving away thirty to forty pounds.

"When you tackled him, you had a handful," said Hank Gremminger, a defensive back with the Packers from 1956 to 1965. "He was fast for a tight end, particularly when he got an inside release. He wasn't a John Mackey. He was a bull on the loose. He just didn't want to be brought down."

Ditka saved some of his best efforts for the Packers, of course. When Green Bay took a 31-7 lead in the third quarter on November 12, 1961, the game appeared to be over. But Ditka led a comeback that almost resulted in victory. He caught nine passes for 190 yards, a 21.1 average, and scored three touchdowns on receptions of forty-seven, fifteen, and twenty-nine yards. The Packers held on to win, 31-28. "He's a real fine rookie, no doubt about it," Packers coach Vince Lombardi said after the game.

Lombardi issued the praise with typical reticence. What was perhaps a more revealing response on his part came to light the next year. The Packers revamped their secondary. Herb Adderley, who was starting his second year, took over permanently for Gremminger at left cornerback. Gremminger, in turn, replaced six-year veteran John Symank, a gritty, tough-tackling, but short, slow strong safety who had been largely responsible for the coverage on Ditka the previous season.

In 1963, when the Bears beat the Packers twice to win the NFL championship, Ditka caught just three passes for forty-four yards in the two games. But he had another big game on September 13, 1964, catching seven for seventy-four yards, including a 13-yard touchdown, in a 23-12 loss.

"Ditka . . . blasted three Packers out of his way in scoring the Bears' only touchdown." the *Chicago Tribune* reported the next day. "(He) left Hank Gremminger, Willie Wood and Ray Nitschke prostrate as he churned into the end zone with the pass."

In twelve games against the Packers when he was playing with the Bears, Ditka caught forty passes for 554 yards, a 13.9 average, and four touchdowns. Unfortunately for him, his career overlapped the Glory Years in Green Bay. He was on the winning team just three times.

The losses to the Packers certainly tore at Ditka's guts, and they undoubtedly influenced the way he approached Bears-Packers games in the 1980s, when he was Chicago's head coach. Above all else, Ditka was a fiery competitor who hated to lose at anything.

"All I can say is he was the greatest competitor who ever walked on the fooball field," said Sid Luckman, an assistant coach with the Bears during Ditka's playing career. "There was none any greater."

That competitiveness surfaced even during a friendly card game with Packers guard Jerry Kramer at a golf outing in Phoenix.

"We got in the lounge and started playing gin rummy," Kramer said. "I'm beating him pretty bad. I beat him several games in a row. And he got so frustrated, so angry, he stood up and tore the deck of cards in half, threw 'em at the wall, and walked around the table two or three times. He wanted to kill me, I suppose, but I'm gigglin' and probably too big to kill. So he screams, 'Give me another deck of cards!' We sit down and start playing some more. I loved his intensity, his emotions, the way he played. That kind of personified the Bears."

After six seasons in Chicago, Ditka signed with the Houston Oilers of the American Football League. However, shortly after that, the AFL-NFL merger voided his contract. The Bears retained Ditka's rights, but a disgruntled Halas traded him to Philadelphia. Ditka played two seasons for the Eagles before being traded again to Dallas.

In Ditka's four years with the Cowboys, they won three divisional titles and two National Football Conference championships. In his next-to-last season as a player, Dallas won Super Bowl VI, beating Miami, 24-3.

He finished his career with 427 receptions, a record for tight ends at the time. In 1988, Ditka became the first tight end to be inducted into the Pro Football Hall of Fame.

In Green Bay, he is remembered for his many encounters with Packers defenders, most notably Nitschke.

"It wasn't a matter of getting anybody back," Ditka said. "It was how we both played the game. You know, football isn't for the faint of heart. You don't ask any quarter, you don't give any quarter. That's just the way it was. Listen, I have no regrets at all. I don't have any regrets about the guys who knocked me on my ass, and I have no regrets at all about the guys I knocked on their ass. Life is too short. If people don't like the way I played the game, I couldn't care less. I played the game as well as I knew how, as hard as I knew how. And I will never apologize for that."

DICK BUTKUS

Dick Butkus was a broken-down gladiator in 1973, his ninth and final season in the NFL. He had had four knee operations. He couldn't run, he couldn't cut, and his lateral movement—that trademark sideline-to-sideline pursuit—was now an exercise in agony.

Larry McCarren, a rookie center with Green Bay that year, remembers feeling sympathy for Butkus as he watched the Bears' great middle linebacker warm up before a game against the Packers.

McCarren, like Butkus a native of the Chicago area and a University of Illinois graduate, had long admired number 51. Now, however, he found himself feeling sorry for him.

"I was on the taxi squad," McCarren recalled. "And, you know, I grew up watching Butkus, so I watched him the whole warm-up. And he's dragging that leg through warm-ups, and I'm thinking, 'How can this son of a bitch play?'

"On the first series, (Packers guard Gale) Gillingham—you might disagree, but he should be in the Hall of Fame, because he could play— comes smokin' right into Butkus one-on-one—this poor guy I saw dragging his leg around. Boom! Butkus just drops his ass like it was nothing and stuffs the ball-carrier.

"I thought, 'This guy is really something special.'"

The Nitschke camp would beg to differ, but many believe that Butkus was the most intimidating man who ever put on a pair of shoulder pads. Whenever his name comes up, former teammates and opponents lower their voices and speak in solemn, hushed tones about his talent, his drive, his indomitable spirit, and his love for the game.

"Butkus, hell, we used to put three people on him and we still couldn't block him," said Dave "Hawg" Hanner, who played for the Packers but was an assistant coach by the time Butkus entered the league. "I've never seen a better defensive player than him."

At 6 feet 4 inches and 245 pounds, and with the temperament of a pit bull, Butkus was born to be a middle linebacker. In his prime, he struck fear into the hearts of offensive linemen, quarterbacks, running backs, and even wide receivers. He could shed blocks with his cat-like quickness and balance, or use his strength to bull the would-be blocker backward into the ball carrier, sometimes tackling both.

"He was just hard to hit," said Forrest Gregg, the Packers' Hall of Fame tackle who tangled with Butkus many times. "It seemed like you never got a solid blow on him. You'd try to cut him, he'd jump over you. If you went too far upfield, he'd slip inside of you. If you waited too long to negate that move, then he'd go over the top of you."

But what truly separated Butkus from the rest was his all-out effort, from snap to whistle, on every play of every game. While Pete Rose was earning a reputation as "Charlie Hustle" in baseball and John Havlicek was diving after loose balls for the Boston Celtics, Butkus was their equivalent on the football field. He pursued from one sideline to the other. He hustled to make tackles forty yards downfield. He didn't know how to let up. No one can remember him quitting on a play, no matter how hopeless his chances of making the tackle seemed to be.

"I remember the first time we ever watched him play," said Jerry Kramer, the Packers' right guard under Vince Lombardi. "We were getting ready to play the Bears and coach Lombardi had said something about him in the scouting report, that he was a pretty good football player. So we were curious about him.

"And I remember watching him in the films. I don't remember who the Bears were playing, but Butkus blitzed and the fullback caught him under the chin. Put just an absolutely beautiful block on him. Knocked him flat on his ass. And the quarterback threw like a square-out to the wide receiver. The guy jigged a couple of times and came back into the middle, and Butkus tackled him. Everybody is going, 'Run that back! Run that back! How the hell did he get out there?'

"I think that was his great strength, his great hustle. Dick absolutely never quit. He had incredible hustle. He just never gave up."

Packer receivers Carroll Dale and Boyd Dowler said they tried to keep track of Butkus' whereabouts while they ran pass routes and even after they caught the ball down field. "I remember him getting into the passing game areas," Dowler said. "I remember seeing his eyes as he was coming toward you, twelve, fifteen yards deep. Some guys have a look to them that can be a little intimidating. Butkus sure did. He was always yelling and frothing at the mouth."

MacArthur Lane, a hard runner and all-out blocker who played halfback for the Packers from 1972 to 1974, once said about Butkus: "If I had a choice, I would sooner have gone one-on-one with a grizzly bear."

The Bears selected Butkus with the third pick in the 1965 draft; they also had the fourth pick, and used it to take running back Gale Sayers out of Kansas. Butkus and Sayers may have been the finest rookies ever to break in with the same team at the same time.

After the Bears beat the Packers, 31-10, on October 31, 1965, coach George Halas gushed about his rookie middle linebacker, who had beaten out incumbent Bill George for the starting job. "Butkus is a lot farther along than I ever felt he would be at this point," Halas said. "I started playing him from the very first day. I said, 'Mistakes or no mistakes, he's going to play,' and it's paid off."

Like many players on both teams over the years, Butkus got fired up for the Bears-Packers rivalry. Although Green Bay won the NFL title his first three years in the league, Butkus always made his presence felt.

He recovered two fumbles in a 13-10 Bears loss at Lambeau Field on September 24, 1967. The next season, he forced a key fumble by running back Donny Anderson in the Bears' last-second, 13-10 victory at Lambeau.

"Butkus always had a great game against the Packers," said Mac Percival, Chicago's kicker from 1967 to 1973. "Of course, Nitschke was there. And whenever Butkus played against Nitschke or Tommy Nobis—those were the two premier linebackers at the time—he always had phenomenal games. He'd gas up for those."

Not that his tank was ever empty. Butkus got so wound up during games that he cast an almost maniacal profile and always seemed to be sputtering guttural noises. "He was extremely intense," said Gillingham. "He'd be swearin', cussin', hollerin', bitchin', chewin' people out. His own players, and us. Hell, they'd have a fight in their own defensive huddle half the time."

Butkus had some epic battles with Packers center Ken Bowman, one of the few players in the league who kept his cool when Butkus did his animal act. Bowman studied Butkus carefully and concluded that the pyrotechnics were mostly calculated.

"His tactic was to try to intimidate the quarterback and intimidate anybody who was going to block him," Bowman said. "And if he could get you mad at him, he'd have a field day. So what he'd do in the first quarter of the game was get you angry. He'd cuss at you. He'd come up in the hole and pound on your head. He might give you a couple dirty licks. He'd try to get you mad to the point where you were coming out of control trying to stick it to him. That's when he started grabbing you and winging you on by.

"Ray Nitschke would stick in the middle and cover his hole first, then try to slide out. Ray would give you the bone almost all day. With Butkus, it was like the first quarter, trying to get the center's goat, trying to get him out of control. And it was amazing to me how successful he was at it. I'd watch those films and watch those films and watch those films, and those centers, almost to a man, would start flying out, and he had 'em right where he wanted 'em."

On punts, Butkus would start about five yards off the line of scrimmage and time his rush so that he walloped the center an instant after the ball was snapped. Sometimes, the carnage he left was a pathetic sight. Larry Krause, a running back with the Packers from 1970 to 1974, remembers reporting to the training room after the Packers had played the Bears his rookie year.

"We had a center named Malcolm Walker, and Butkus about killed him," Krause said. "We went in on Monday, and Malcolm had two ice bags on each shoulder, his knees, his ankles. He was like engulfed in ice. He was totally beat to hell."

Butkus had such an impact on the game that Lombardi was even forced to alter the blocking schemes for his famed bread-and-butter sweeps when the Packers played the Bears, according to Don Horn, a quarterback for Green Bay from 1967 to 1970.

"Dick was so quick and so good—before he had the knee injuries— that he could chase it down from behind," Horn said. "Our traps, too. We had to change our whole blocking schemes, because he was that good."

Horn was thrown into the fire against Butkus on December 15, 1968. Bart Starr, the Packers' starting quarterback, sat out the game with a rib injury, and his backup, Zeke Bratkowski, was hurt in the first quarter. Enter Horn, ten days out of the Army and activated the morning of the game.

"I go in there and I proceed to lose like seventeen yards in three plays," Horn said, chuckling at the memory. "Butkus intimidated me. My last name is Horn, but I don't think it was even in the program. Butkus was calling me 'Tin Horn' and 'Green Horn.' He'd lean over Kenny Bowman and say, 'Hey, what's your first name? Tin? Is it Tin Horn? Green Horn? Here I come, Tin Horn.'"

Horn said he suffered a broken nose in the game, but he collected himself to complete ten of sixteen passes for 187 yards and two touchdowns, leading Green Bay to a 28-27 victory.

Later, when Butkus was on the decline physically but still up to his old tricks, he still tried to intimidate Horn. "I actually felt sorry for him," Horn said. "We had a running back, Travis Williams, who was very quick. I isolated him on Dick, and Dick couldn't change directions fast enough. I beat him a couple times on one-on-one stuff. Dick would yell at me, 'Quit pickin' on a cripple.' He yelled some four-letter words. He said, 'You should be ashamed of yourself. If you really want to come after me, come after me head-on.' He was intimidating."

By 1969, in just his fifth season in the league, Butkus was living— and playing—with tremendous pain in his knees. Although he had lost mobility, he continued to spit venom, brow-beat, and generally harass the opponent. And he continued to make plays.

"We were watching him play against the Browns two weeks ago on film," Starr said in a *Green Bay Press-Gazette* story in December, 1969.

"He was limping around on one leg and making tackles all over the field. He's unreal."

On December 13, 1970, Butkus knocked Starr out of the game with a concussion in the first quarter, and the Bears went on to win, 35-17. However, Green Bay's running backs were, on occasion, starting to run wild on Butkus and the Bears.

On December 14, 1969, in the game Horn referred to, Williams scored on a 39-yard run and caught a 60-yard touchdown pass when Butkus bit on a play-action fake. The Packers won, 21-3. On November 7, 1971, Packers rookie John Brockington rushed for 142 yards in thirty carries, and, according to the *Press-Gazette*, "repeatedly bowled over would-be tacklers, including, on occasion, the redoubtable Dick Butkus."

The end was not a pretty sight.

"It was terrible what happened to him," Gillingham said. "People were knocking him down and stuff. He was still trying to play, but he couldn't get out of anybody's way at the end. It was tragic he was still out there."

Despite his abbreviated career, Butkus is the Bears' all-time leader with twenty-five fumble recoveries and is second with forty-seven take-aways, including twenty-two interceptions. He was a seven-time all-NFL selection and was inducted into the Pro Football Hall of Fame in 1979.

"He was a super football player," said Stan Jones, a lineman who was winding down his career in Chicago when Butkus broke in. "I'll tell you, if I was a coach, I'd show the highlights of his career to every guy who comes into the team. He was something else. He was an animal back there."

Chapter 6

Twenty Memorable Games

Over eight decades and more than 150 games, Bears vs. Packers has produced plenty of showdowns, storybook finishes, and heroic performances. But one of the charms of the rivalry is that even games that were artistically flawed, lacked suspense, and had no bearing on the division race had compelling appeal.

Here are twenty memorable games and the stories behind them.

1. Marcol's Miracle
Packers 12, Bears 6 (overtime)
September 7, 1980; Lambeau Field

When Packers kicker Chester Marcol caught his own blocked field goal in overtime and scurried untouched into the end zone in the 1980 season opener, he brought new meaning to the words "sudden death"— Bears fans everywhere felt like dying.

It was the most illogical, improbable ending to a game in the history of the series. By far. The sight of Marcol, holding the ball awkwardly and running for his life past the stunned Bears, was almost comical.

"The guy looked like a rugby player, carrying the ball like a sack of potatoes," said former Bears fullback Robin Earl, smiling ruefully at the memory.

Until the dramatic finish, the game was unremarkable, even boring. Marcol had kicked field goals of forty-one and forty-six yards in regulation, and Bob Thomas matched him with kicks of forty-two and thirty-four yards for Chicago.

In the sudden-death overtime period, a 32-yard pass from Lynn Dickey to James Lofton set up Marcol's 34-yard attempt with nine minutes left. Before the teams lined up, Bears defensive end Alan Page told teammate Jim Osborne that he thought he could block the kick.

"Alan had it down to a science, where he'd take so many steps and just put his hand up at the right time," said Osborne, a defensive tackle who lined up next to Page on the play. "He just had a knack for blocking field goals. I got a good jump on the ball and drove the center back and, sure enough, Alan took his couple of steps, the hand went up and I heard this thud. I knew the field goal was blocked, but I was buried under the pile.

"Then, I hear the fans going crazy, and I go, 'We're in Green Bay. This is not good.' When I looked up, I saw Chester Marcol crossing the goal line with the ball in his hands. I'm saying, 'How did he do this?' And then, when I saw it on the replay, I couldn't believe it."

The ball ricocheted off Page straight back into Marcol's chest. The kicker had no choice but to catch it and run. After Jim Gueno, the Packers' left upback, took out the only Bear who had a chance to make the tackle, Marcol had a clear path into the left corner of the end zone. "The Red Sea parted," said Dickey, "and he walked right in."

"I was just thankful I played other positions in high school and had some experience," Marcol said. "I knew what to do. It was a heads-up play."

The Bears had a few other descriptions for the play, none of which related to Marcol's alertness or his prowess as a runner. "I gotta tell you, you could've knocked me down with a straw," said defensive end Dan Hampton. "We bat the ball back, and that little weasel runs it in. It was like bursting a balloon."

Even Packers coach Bart Starr had a hard time believing his own eyes.

"Oh, God, what a happening!" Starr said. "A power runner. I was speechless at the time. I was cheering, and chuckling underneath. You're rooting for him, yet you are almost exploding with laughter at what's happening."

It wasn't the first time Marcol had beaten Chicago. In fact, given the long list of great athletes who have played for Green Bay over the years, it is incredibly ironic that one of the biggest Bear-killers of them all was a bespectacled, frizzy-haired, soccer-style kicker from Poland.

The first time Marcol faced Chicago, as a rookie out of tiny Hillsdale College in 1972, he kicked a 40-yard field goal with seventeen seconds left to give Green Bay a 10-7 victory in the pre-season Shrine Game at Milwaukee County Stadium.

Six weeks later, he did it again, this time in a game that counted. Marcol booted a 37-yard field goal into the teeth of a crosswind with thirty seconds left to give the Packers a 20-17 victory at Lambeau Field on October 8.

By now, Bears coach Abe Gibron, a rotund, animated man with a strong and genuine disdain for the Packers, had seen enough. He sarcastically dubbed Marcol the "Polish Prince," and made reserve running back Gary Kosins a designated hit man for the rematch at Soldier Field on November 12.

Kosins' lone mission on Packers kickoffs was to seek and destroy Marcol. "My job was to go after Marcol, try to intimidate him and try to get him to think about it—that every time he kicked that ball, he was going to have someone come and try to knock his block off," Kosins said. "Abe used to really get me going. He'd say, 'Get going, he's no Polish Prince. Go knock his ass off.'"

Marcol made a beeline for the Packers' bench after every kickoff that day. But he also kicked field goals of fifty-one, twenty-one and twenty-one yards, and Green Bay won again, 23-17.

"Gibron decided he could shake me up sending people after me," Marcol said. "I never took anything personal, because that's the way he was. That's how he coached."

Kosins again went after Marcol on August 4, 1973, in the pre-season Shrine Game in Milwaukee. This time, Marcol missed a 39-yarder with three seconds left, and the Packers had to settle for a 13-13 tie.

Packers fans were mad enough to lynch Kosins, who happened to be Polish and whose family was from Milwaukee. "There was nothing ever dirty or foul in what we were doing," Kosins said. "I was just trying to knock him down. It was a blocking assignment."

Chuck Johnson, sports editor of *The Milwaukee Journal*, wrote a column calling Gibron's tactics "bush" and imploring then-Commissioner Pete Rozelle to order the practice stopped. "If you want to play two-handed tag or touch or something, we'll just let Marcol go out there and give an exhibition," Gibron responded in a story in the *Chicago Tribune*.

Unfortunately, after Marcol's rookie season, in which he led the NFL in scoring, was named rookie of the year, and helped the Packers to a 10-4 record and the National Football Conference Central Division title, things went downhill for both the kicker and his team. Green Bay had only one other winning season in Marcol's nine years with the team—8-7-1 in 1978—and the Polish Prince developed serious problems with alcohol and drugs.

By the 1980 season, he was a full-fledged alcoholic who had dabbled with just about every type of recreational drug. In fact, just a few weeks after scoring his unforgettable touchdown, Marcol was released.

But going into the 1980 season opener, Marcol wasn't the only one with problems. The victory over the Bears was as much a team miracle as it was Marcol's. In five exhibition games that year, the Packers were outscored, 86-17. They lost four of the five games and the other ended in a 0-0 tie. Then, four days before the opener, Green Bay's defensive line coach, Fred vonAppen, resigned, plunging the team into deeper turmoil.

The previous weekend, during the second half of the Packers' 38-0 loss to Denver in the final exhibition game, defensive end Ezra Johnson was observed eating a hot dog on the bench. Starr's reversal of his original decision to suspend Johnson apparently triggered vonAppen's resignation.

"That thing got blown out of proportion, and Fred was so adamant about it," Johnson said. "When I ate the hot dog, I was really hungry. I had an ankle injury, and they let me play about one quarter. Toward the end of the game, I was absolutely starving. The thing about it, nobody on the team knew I even ate it. It was like three bites and it was gone. I guess somebody in the media saw it, and they were using me to whip Bart because we lost the game. They were saying, like, 'We got players who don't care.'"

First-year defensive coordinator John Meyer took over vonAppen's coaching duties, literally days before the season opener. "I spent half the week trying to talk Fred into coming back," Meyer said. "I sure found it to be disruptive. I don't know if the players did. It was my first year as coordinator, and I needed all the help I could get."

Meyer said he cried "tears of joy" when Marcol crossed the goal line. "I remember I was just spent emotionally," he said.

One player who was spent physically was Packers center Larry McCarren. On August 14, McCarren, the team's offensive captain, had undergone hernia surgery. He had missed the last three exhibition games, and was listed as questionable for the season opener. But he extended his string of consecutive starts to sixty-four and wound up play-ing the entire game.

"Bart said at the team meeting the night before, 'To keep your streak alive, we're going to have you go out for a play and then sit down,'" McCarren said. "They sent me out there for the first play and I didn't come back. So I stayed there for the first series. I stayed out for the next series, and pretty soon, the fucking game is in overtime. I hadn't prac-ticed. I was hurtin' for certain.

"I was glad when that fucker got over the goal line. Matter of fact, I think it was my fault Page blocked the kick. He came right on the inside and I heard the double thud. I thought, 'Oh, fuck! This thing is going to go on forever.' All of a sudden, I heard the crowd roar, and Chester took it in.

"I was so happy it was over, regardless of the result. I was just happy the son of a bitch was done."

Today, Marcol is clean and sober and living in Michigan's Upper Peninsula, where he is an avid hunter and fisherman. Far removed from those heady days in Green Bay, but finally content with his life, he regrets the self-destructive path he chose. At his nadir, he tried to commit sui-cide by drinking battery acid; to this day, he must make periodic visits to a doctor to have his damaged esophagus stretched.

"The only thing that hurts, that I kind of ponder, is that I had to leave my job the way I did," he said. "It's not that it was anybody's fault. I made some poor choices, and I made some decisions that almost destroyed me."

Fifteen years after his career ended, Marcol took a kicking tee to the high school football field near his house. In his mid-forties and wearing street clothes, he said he easily kicked 40-yard field goals.

"I deeply believe that if I had dedicated myself and not just lived off my talents," he said, "I would have played in the league into my forties."

2. Prelude to a Title
Bears 26, Packers 7
November 17, 1963; Wrigley Field

No professional football game in Chicago, before or since, has been more eagerly awaited than was the dramatic 1963 showdown between the two-time defending NFL champion Packers and the grimly determined Bears. Both teams entered the game with 8-1 records, and

the winner clearly would have the inside track to the Western Conference championship. Green Bay had won eight straight games since its
season-opening, 10-3 defeat to the Bears. Chicago had lost only to
San Francisco.

The Monday before the game, the Bears placed fifteen hundred standing-room tickets on sale. The tickets, priced at $2.50, sold out in forty
minutes. As game day drew nearer, scalpers' prices shot up to a hundred
dollars, an unheard-of sum in those days.

Because of the television contract then in effect, the game was
blacked out for a seventy-five-mile radius around Chicago, so Bears fans
fled the city Sunday morning by the thousands. A Chicago bowling estab-
lishment even constructed a special antenna to try to pull in the telecast
from Channel 13 in Rockford, Illinois, but the device failed.

At 2:45 A.M. on game day, lines began forming in front of the bleacher
box offices at Waveland and Sheffield avenues for nine hundred
additional standing-room tickets. As game time approached, the 350
ushers on duty kept busy trying to stop non-ticket holders from vaulting
the turnstiles.

"Tickets to the Russian circus and baseball rainchecks were
among the most common items shuffled through the pass window, to no
avail," the *Chicago Tribune* reported. "A few agile youths tried scaling
the cyclone fence to crawl into the upper deck."

The importance of the game was lost on neither Packers coach Vince
Lombardi nor Bears coach George Halas, then sixty-eight years old. Lombardi closed practices the week before, locking the stadium gates. "We're
not going to put in anything fancy," Lombardi said. "If the Bears beat
us, they will beat us doing what we do best."

Meanwhile, in Chicago, the Bears' practice on Wednesday was halted
for a time when a cameraman was spotted in the window of a third-story
apartment overlooking Wrigley Field. The man turned out to be a press
photographer, hoping for an exclusive shot of a secret drill.

Halas took pains to talk about the Packers' mental edge, a ploy he
often used in an attempt to soften the opponent. "It isn't even necessary
to mention their overall strength," he said. "But in addition to manpower,
they will have the psychological advantage. In view of our 10 to 3 victory over them in the opener, the Packers will be primed emotionally."

Lombardi simply laughed when informed of Halas' statements, and
said, "I always agree with the master."

There was no denying, though, that the Packers were supremely confident going into the game, even though quarterback Bart Starr was out with a broken hand and running back Paul Hornung was serving his NFL suspension that season for gambling. Green Bay, after all, almost never lost must-win games under Lombardi.

"In all the years I was there, I don't ever recall going into a game thinking, 'If Bart's not here, we don't have much of a chance,' or, 'If Paul's not here, we don't have a chance,'" said wide receiver Boyd Dowler. "I think that's a tribute to Lombardi. He impressed that you had to step it up a little bit, and it didn't make much difference who played."

Plus, the Packers, despite their season-opening defeat, still weren't sold on the fact that the Bears were a championship-caliber team.

"I think we kept expecting that somebody was going to knock them off," said defensive end Willie Davis. "When it didn't happen, it was almost like it was hard to believe. There were a lot of folks that felt Bill Wade was not a quarterback who could take them to a championship."

The night before the game, Bears defensive lineman Bob Killcullen had dinner at the Drake Hotel with Robert Riger, an artist and photographer for *Sports Illustrated*. After dinner, Riger excused himself to talk to Green Bay players Jerry Kramer and Fuzzy Thurston; the Packers stayed at the Drake when they were in Chicago in those days.

"Riger came back down and said, 'Bob, I've got to tell you, those guys are loose. They don't think there is any way they're going to lose this game,'" Kilcullen recalled. "Brother, that was all I had to hear.

"Then, on top of that, a little while later, Vince Lombardi came into the dining room. When I turned around and looked, he was standing on a step and his pearly whites were showing. He was smiling and waving at people. There was nothing wrong with what Lombardi was doing. Just, to me, he was saying, 'There is no way we can lose this ballgame.'

"So the next morning, I got to Wrigley Field early and I told everybody I could about the night before. They just listened. I think that had some effect. I'll tell you, we were ready that day."

The tone was set on the opening kickoff, when Bears defensive back J.C. Caroline streaked down the field and made a vicious tackle on Packers kick returner Herb Adderly, upending him inside the 20-yard line.

The Bears went on to a dominating performance, captured eloquently by sportswriter George Strickler in Monday's edition of the *Tribune*: "Under the overcast in Wrigley Field yesterday, the Team of Destiny rose up in all its muscular might to hammer the regal Green Bay Packers into ignominious defeat. . . ."

Chicago's ball-hawking defense forced seven turnovers, intercepting Starr's replacements, John Roach and Zeke Bratkowski, five times. The Bears also shut down the Packers' vaunted running game, holding fullback Jim Taylor to twenty-three yards. Green Bay managed just seventy-one yards on the ground and 232 total.

"On their sweep, whenever they tried to come around left end, somebody picked up that Forrest Gregg would cheat out about six inches," Kilcullen said of the Packers' all-pro left tackle. "So one of our linebackers, Joe Fortunato, and I talked about it. If I moved outside, that let him know that I was thinking they were coming around the outside. Each time Forrest cheated out there, sure enough, here they came."

The late Willie Galimore rushed for seventy-nine yards in fourteen attempts, leading the Bears' 248-yard assault on the ground. Galimore scored on a 27-yard run in the first half, and the Bears built a 26-0 lead. Green Bay averted the shutout when Tom Moore scored on an 11-yard run in the fourth quarter.

After the game, Bears assistant coach Chuck Mather told Chicago sportswriter Bill Gleason that Lombardi's decision to trade veteran defensive end Bill Quinlan after the 1962 season and replace him with rookie Lionel Aldridge had come back to haunt him.

"Mather told me, 'We won this game when Lombardi got pissed off with Bill Quinlan. We ran the left end all day long because Bill Quinlan wasn't there anymore,'" Gleason said. "He said, 'That was one time when the Italian outsmarted himself.'"

Caroline made several other crunching tackles on special teams that day, earning the praise of his teammates. "When we came back on Monday, before we broke down on offense and defense, we watched the special team film together," said Johnny Morris, who played wide receiver for the Bears from 1958 to 1967. "Everybody knew J.C. had made a great tackle to start the game, but he had made so many great tackles in that game.

"Football players are hard-nosed, but they were watching it and watching it, and everybody kept saying, 'Good play, good play.' Then, when the film was over, the guys gave him an ovation. I never saw football players do that before. It was just a spontaneous thing."

In hindsight, the Packers admitted that the absence of Starr and Hornung was too much to overcome against a keyed-up Bears defense. "Bart was such a steady, dependable guy," cornerback Jesse Whittenton said. "John Roach was a pretty nervous-type guy. He was pretty high strung. He wasn't near the quarterback that Bart was."

Tight end Ron Kramer said the Packers could compensate for Hornung's physical contributions, but not the intangibles he brought to the team. "Hornung had a great *esprit de corps*," Kramer said. "He had more of an influence spiritually, psychologically, than he ever did physically. Don't get me wrong. He was as good as anybody around. All he could do was beat your ass. But everybody had these great feelings for him. We still do."

The Bears went on to compile an 11-1-2 record, then beat the New York Giants, 14-10, to win the NFL title. The Packers finished 11-2-1.

Willie Davis still contends that the Packers had just as good a team in 1963 as they did in 1961 and 1962, when they won championships. Other Packers believe the Bears were lucky that season. "I remember watching games where they'd fumble the ball and it would jump right back up in their hands," said guard Jerry Kramer. "They'd kick it and slop around, step on it, and it would jump right back in their hands. They had two or three things like that happen to them, and I just went, 'Oh, bullshit. It's just their year.'"

But linebacker Tom Bettis, who relinquished his middle linebacker job to Ray Nitschke and wound up playing for the Bears in 1963, said luck had nothing to do with it. "I think they came into Chicago thinking there was no way in the world they were going to get beat by us," Bettis said. "I don't think they really respected us, or felt we were that good a football team. And we ended up beating them pretty convincingly. I don't think they realized we were a better football team than they were, at that point in time.

"Maybe not on paper. But we were a better team."

3. Offshoot of Instant Replay: An Asterisk
Packers 14, Bears 13
November 5, 1989; Lambeau Field

If you open the Bears' media guide to "All-Time Results" and scan the 1989 season, you will find an asterisk next to their loss to the Packers on November 5.

The notation at the bottom reads: "Instant Replay Game."

"It still irritates people around here that in their media guide, they've got that asterisk in the 1989 season," said Packers President Bob Harlan, whose son, Bryan, is the Bears' director of public relations. "After we beat the Bears, 40-3, in 1994, I went over to Bryan after the game and said, 'I don't want to see any asterisk after this score.'"

Actually, the asterisk was the idea of Mike McCaskey, the Bears' president and CEO. "It's the only game in NFL history," said McCaskey, "that has been decisively determined by instant replay that was wrong."

That's open to debate. The Bears swear to this day that Packers quarterback Don Majkowski was over the line of scrimmage when he released his game-winning, 14-yard touchdown pass to Sterling Sharpe with thirty-two seconds left. Line judge Jim Quirk saw it that way, too, throwing his flag from his position fifty yards across the field on the line of scrimmage.

For nearly five minutes, a surrealistic atmosphere enveloped Lambeau Field while replay official Bill Parkinson rewound the tape and watched the play over and over on his Sony videocassette equipment on level three of the press box. Finally, Parkinson overruled Quirk. The touchdown stood.

Green Bay had ended an eight-game losing streak to Chicago—the longest streak in the history of the rivalry—winning for the first time since 1984.

"We had fought 'em tooth and nail a lot of times, but I had never beaten them," Packers linebacker Brian Noble said. "Then, there was that long pause, where we didn't know. It's one of those situations where you're going, 'Not again. They can't do this to us again.' Then, to have the after-further-review deal . . . I can say that was the first time in a long time that I cried."

The Packers faced fourth-and-fourteen and trailed by six points when they lined up in their four-receiver flush formation. The play called in the huddle was a slant-in to Jeff Query, who lined up as the inside receiver on the left side. The Bears were in a zone defense, but the play was designed for man coverage.

With nobody open, Majkowski improvised. He ran to his right, with Bears defensive end Trace Armstrong in pursuit. As he got closer and closer to the sideline—and to the line of scrimmage—Majkowski could feel Armstrong coming. He saw wide receiver Perry Kemp running along the back of the end zone and was ready to wing a pass when Sharpe entered his peripheral vision. Majkowski planted his foot at the 15-yard line, jumped in the air, and hit Sharpe with a perfect spiral.

Then came the penalty flag, followed by Parkinson's review behind the tinted windows of the press box. The question was not where Majkowski's foot was when he released the ball, but whether his arm and hand were beyond the line of scrimmage.

"We knew it was real close," said Packers tackle Ken Ruettgers. "We kept asking Don, 'What do you think? What do you think?' He said, 'I don't know. It's going to be close.' And it was. They could have called it either way. It was that close. We looked at film later; we looked and looked and looked. Man!"

To the players milling about on the field, the delay that followed seemed to last an eternity. "How long it took the referees was the biggest joke about it," said Bears kicker Kevin Butler. "I remember turning to players on the sideline and going, 'They're not going to give it to us, because if they do, these poor referees might get killed.' They had let it go that long, and the crowd anticipation was building up. I remember the stadium just shaking when they called the touchdown."

Bears guard Mark Bortz, who was born and raised in Pardeeville, Wisconsin, recalls being disgusted not only by Parkinson's decision to overrule Quirk, but by the pandemonium that followed. "The visiting clubhouse guy was out there going absolutely berserk after the game," Bortz said. "He was on his knees, like Willem Dafoe in 'Platoon.' He was just happy as hell. I had to walk off the field next to the guy. I'm not going to tell you what I said to him, but I thought what he did was really unprofessional."

Nearly an hour later, when the Bears' bus started to pull out of Lambeau Field, the still-celebrating fans swarmed around it. "They were literally rocking our bus, just beating on it," Butler said. "They were letting out many, many years of frustration. They had gone berserk. We were inching out of the stadium and they just had us surrounded, screaming and yelling. I thought they were going to tip our bus over; they were rocking it that hard."

In 1992, McCaskey helped lead the drive to get rid of instant replay. It failed to get a three-fourths vote by the NFL owners, and was scrapped. In March, 1997, the owners voted on a new form of instant replay, and again, it did not pass. McCaskey, still bitter about the 1989 defeat, has said he would never again vote for instant replay.

"The team that deserved to win didn't win," he said. "No right-thinking person could ever doubt that. It was absolutely clear. Majkowski was over the line of scrimmage, and the officials on the field ruled correctly that the touchdown did not count. The game was over. The rulebook said it had to be indisputable, visual evidence. If it takes six or seven minutes to stare at it, it is not indisputable, visual evidence."

To Packer fans, this sounds like nothing but a bunch of sour grapes.

Even former Bears linebacker Mike Singletary figures Chicago simply didn't deserve to win that day. "Our feeling was that we didn't play a very good game," Singletary said. "I thought Green Bay kicked our tails."

4. The Fridge Becomes a Celebrity
Bears 23, Packers 7
October 21, 1985; Soldier Field

To say William Perry was in the right place at the right time on the night of October 21, 1985, would be a 325-pound understatement.

In five plays that resulted in three touchdowns, Perry went from curiosity to national celebrity. And those plays helped him become financially secure for the rest of his life.

The stars were aligned favorably for Perry as Chicago played host to Green Bay in a Monday night game in an electric atmosphere at Soldier Field. The Bears were 6-0, and eager to show the world they were for real. Furthermore, there was bad blood between the two head coaches: Mike Ditka and Forrest Gregg.

Perry, a mammoth defensive tackle, had been selected by the Bears in the first round of the draft that year. A gregarious rookie with a gap-toothed grin, he was nicknamed the "Refrigerator," for obvious reasons.

"When I think back to the time we drafted the Fridge, there was a lot of hype and hoopla," said Shaun Gayle, who played defensive back for the Bears from 1984 to 1994. "It was, 'Wow, look at this big guy.' He was probably one of the first three-hundred-pounders. Now, every team has one. He just liked to play the game. He didn't care for the notoriety, the limelight. The Fridge just enjoyed playing football. And he had the ability to run and jump and do all the things most people that big can't do, so he wanted to do it."

The Packers, and a nation of football fans, were about to be bowled over—literally in the former case, figuratively in the latter.

In the second quarter, the Bears drove to the Packers' two-yard line, and Ditka inserted Perry at fullback. He knocked 225-pound linebacker George Cumby five yards backward, paving a wide path for Walter Payton to score an easy touchdown.

Less than five minutes later, the Bears drove to the Packers' one-yard line, and again, Perry waddled onto the field. With Soldier Field rocking, and millions of viewers laughing and pointing at their TVs in disbelief, quarterback Jim McMahon called a dive play, handed the ball to Perry, and got out of the way.

Touchdown.

"That," said Packers offensive tackle Ken Ruettgers, "was just another notch in Ditka's belt."

Before the quarter ended, Payton had added a third touchdown, on a one-yard run, again following Perry's lead block on the undersized Cumby.

The Packers had an idea Ditka would use Perry on offense, because he had done so the week before, in a victory over San Francisco. But knowing Perry was coming and stopping him were entirely different matters.

"Nobody on our team was big enough to take that fat guy on," said Dick Modzelewski, then Green Bay's defensive coordinator.

In the second half, Perry was in for two offensive plays near the goal line. He blocked on a run that was stopped for no gain, then McMahon threw an incomplete pass.

Perry's agent, Jim Steiner, was inundated when he arrived at his office the next day.

"It was a huge response," Steiner said. "Over the next couple of days, as I recall, we must have had eighty to one hundred inquiries about William, from large companies to small companies, from licensing arrangements to charities and personal appearances. You name it, we had it."

How much was the game worth to Perry financially?

"Millions," Steiner said. "Millions of dollars. I'm going to say two million to four million."

Steiner could not think of another athlete who has been a bigger overnight sensation.

"We've never been involved with anything quite like that," he said. "He became a world renowned figure and, in some respects, still is today. He transcended sports. Our mothers and grandmothers knew who the Refrigerator was. Although his marketing power obviously has dried up, he still is a very well-known, world-wide figure."

While Perry became rich and famous, the joke was on Cumby. The hard-working, soft-spoken linebacker unfortunately is best remembered as the Fridge's personal blocking dummy.

"I think our entire team was unfair to him," said Packers offensive tackle Greg Koch. "Here's a guy 350 pounds in the backfield, and on Monday night football, George gets run over by the guy.

"Whatever the media said, his teammates were twice as vicious. It's good-natured. It's not like they're riding you derisively. But you get ribbed so much, it has to get to you. You'd hate for that to be the defining moment of your career."

A few years later, Bears offensive guard Mark Bortz attended a devotional service before a game in Houston, and was surprised to see Cumby leading the prayer session. This guy gets up there and says, 'You probably don't know who I am, but I have a lot of history with the Bears. My name is George Cumby,'" Bortz said.

Perry lasted nine years with the Bears, but he did not have a spectacular career. A one-dimensional run-stuffer who couldn't control his weight—he ballooned to 350 pounds or more on more than one occasion—Perry never endeared himself to some people in the Bears' organization.

Modzelewski didn't think much of Perry, either. "He was not a good football player," he said. "He couldn't rush the passer. To this day, I could rush the passer better than he could."

But Perry's coming-out party on Monday night football was symbolic of what the Bears were, and what they were about to become. Chicago went on to compile a 15-1 record, and crushed the New England Patriots, 45-10, in Super Bowl XX.

"When that happened, the Fridge was huge, he became a folk hero," said Mike Singletary, the Bears' middle linebacker from 1981 to 1992. "But that was just the start of it. I think that season the Bears took football to another level. But that was the start. That night. Monday night football. Everybody had a chance to see the Bears were coming. The media, the whole country. It was like, 'Wow, look at the Bears. They're a force to be reckoned with.' And that's what we wanted to show.

"The magic started, and it started with Green Bay that night."

5. The Monsters of the Midway Fall
Packers 16, Bears 14
November 2, 1941, Wrigley Field

A 73-0 demolition of the Washington Redskins in the NFL championship game the year before. An explosive, T-formation offense led by Hall of Fame quarterback Sid Luckman. Five consecutive victories to start the season, and fourteen straight overall, including exhibitions and the 1940 title game.

The 1941 Chicago Bears had acquired the nickname "Monsters of the Midway," and for good reason.

The Bears already had beaten the Packers, 25-17, in the season opener. Green Bay had won its other six games, however, and had pointed to the rematch for weeks.

"Our players kept reading, day after day, about the Bears being the wonder team, the unbeatable team," Packers coach Curly Lambeau said later. "We knew the Bears were reading the same stuff. We hoped they believed it. We didn't."

A crowd of 46,484 jammed into Wrigley Field—at the time, the biggest turnout for a professional football game in the Midwest. An estimated three thousand Packers fans were in attendance that day, many of them having arrived on four special trains: two from Green Bay, one from Appleton, Wisconsin, and the fourth from Iron Mountain, Michigan.

They were treated to one of the greatest Packers' victories in franchise history.

Green Bay unveiled a seven-man defensive front that completely befuddled the Bears. Chicago's ballyhooed T-formation accounted for only 156 total yards, including a mere eighty-three on the ground.

"We'd be damned if we knew what to do," Luckman recalled. "They had one linebacker, two halfbacks, and a safety. The seven men were really coming at us, and we didn't know how to block them. They just controlled us. They were fabulous."

Behind Clarke Hinkle, who rushed for sixty-nine yards in twenty attempts and also kicked a field goal, the Packers built a 16-0 lead. Then they held on as the Bears scored two touchdowns in the fourth quarter.

Chicago drove into Green Bay territory late in the game, but coach George Halas bypassed a field goal attempt. Luckman faded back to pass and was tackled by bull-rushing defensive end Harry Jacunski. He fumbled, and Pete Tinsley fell on the ball to complete the underdog Packers' victory.

"I was looking left, and Jacunski came around on the blind side," Luckman said. "As I went to throw the ball, he knocked it out of my hands. I was just devastated. It just broke my heart that we'd lost to Green Bay that way."

Jacunski smiled at the memory. "That probably got me a couple dollars' raise from Lambeau," he said.

The game was so intense, nine people at Wrigley Field reportedly suffered heart attacks. Two of them—Halas' sister-in-law, and a forty-eight-year-old bar owner from Racine, Wisconsin—died.

Chicago and Green Bay both finished the season with 10-1 records, forcing the first-ever Western Division playoff game.

6. An Unbelievable Comeback
Packers 17, Bears 14
October 27, 1935; Wrigley Field

When halfback Johnny Sisk rumbled fifty-five yards down the sideline to give the Bears a 14-3 lead with less than three minutes left in the game, the fans began a steady stream toward the exits at Wrigley Field.

As many as 5,000 of the 29,389 paid admissions were Packers fans from points north, and most of them shuffled glumly out of the stadium to catch the early train back to Green Bay.

They missed one of the most thrilling comebacks in Packers history.

Green Bay stunned Chicago—and what was left of the crowd—with a remarkable rally, as Arnie Herber threw two touchdown passes to Don Hutson in the final two and one-half minutes to pull out the victory.

Lee Remmel, the longtime *Green Bay Press-Gazette* sportswriter who became the Packers' director of public relations, cherishes the frantic finish as one of his favorite boyhood memories. "I was eleven years old, living in Shawano, Wisconsin, and I listened to the game on the radio," Remmel said. "Many people had left Wrigley Field to go to the railroad station to catch the milk train back to Green Bay. They didn't even know until they got back that the Packers had won the game."

A report in the *Press-Gazette* on Monday typified what happened to many of those fans: "Councilman Joseph Donckers left the game three minutes early and caught an early train for Milwaukee in very low spirits. He laid over in Milwaukee and joined the other Packer fans on their way to Green Bay. He was unable to understand the jubilant spirits of the returning fans. He inquired but when he was told the score, he refused to believe it from his friends. Then he slipped back into the next car, and made some inquiries among strangers. It was so. Councilman Donckers joined the celebration."

The Packers rally started on second-and-eight from their own 32-yard line. With the Bears playing far off the line in an early version of the pre-vent defense, Herber flipped a pass to Hutson in the flat. The fleet receiver zig-zagged across the field, squirming away from defenders Gene Ronzani and Keith Molesworth and sprinting into the end zone.

"Hutson was so darn fast," said George Musso, the Bears' Hall of Fame lineman. "He'd lull you to sleep. You'd think he was coming full speed, and he'd be coming about three-quarters speed. Then, when he got to you, he'd leave you. He was that kind of ballplayer—he could fake you out of your jockstrap. Oh, hell, he was the best."

The Packers' spirits were lifted, but the outlook was still grim. Coach Curly Lambeau marched up and down the sideline, exhorting his players.

"Curly said, 'We're going to win this,'" said back Herm Schneidman, who played for the Packers from 1935 to 1939. "We were going to kick off, and Lambeau went up and down the bench, and whoever had a tough look in their eye, he put 'em in. He said, 'I want the ball! Get that ball!'"

Bears quarterback Bernie Masterson obliged on first down, the ball squirting out of his hands like a cake of wet soap. "The oval went bouncing and dribbling along the ground toward the Bears' goal," the *Press-Gazette* reported. "A wild scramble ensued, but it was Packer tackle Ernie Smith, blood covering his face from a nasty cut on the forehead, who slumped over it on the 13-yard line."

The Packers quickly drove to the Bears' three. In the huddle, Herber was thinking about sending fullback Clarke Hinkle crashing into the line, when Hutson spoke up. "I can outrun Molesworth," he volunteered, "in case you want to try fifteen to the left."

"Fifteen it is," Herber said, and the team hurried to the line.

Hutson hesitated at the goal line for an instant, then cut hard to the left; Molesworth tried to stay with him, but the receiver had him by a step. Herber delivered the ball, and the Packers had a most improbable victory.

7. Rubbing it in and Relishing it

Bears 61, Packers 7
December 7, 1980; Soldier Field

The weekend started out the wrong way for the Packers. Their plane was fogged in when an unseasonably mild weather front stalled in the area, and they had to bus to Chicago the afternoon before the game.

"The temperature was like sixty degrees," recalled quarterback Lynn Dickey. "We waited forever for the fog to lift and found out it wasn't going to happen, so we bused down. I remember walking through the streets of Chicago to get something to eat with our kicker, Jan Stenerud. It was so weird; it was sixty degrees at night. Then, Jan ran up for the opening kickoff and slipped on his butt.

"He said, 'Boy, this is going to be an awful day.'"

Boy, was it ever—for the Packers. For Chicago, still smarting from its fluky, 12-6 overtime loss in Green Bay in the season opener, it was the most beautiful day of the year. "There was a lot of ill will in that game," recalled Bears tackle Dan Jiggetts.

In the mist and drizzle at Soldier Field, everything went right for the Bears, and everything went horribly, horribly wrong for the Packers. "It was Pearl Harbor Day," recalled Packers center Larry McCarren, shaking his head at the memory. "Boy, wasn't that appropriate. We just went out there and got smacked. I mean, big time."

The loss was the second-worst in Packers history, superceded only by a 56-0 defeat to the Baltimore Colts in 1958. It was the Bears' biggest margin of victory in the 152 meetings between the teams. The sixty-one points also were the most given up by Green Bay in its seventy-eight-year history.

The 6-8 Bears looked like an invincible juggernaut. Unproven fourth-year pro Vince Evans, making just his eleventh career start, became the first Chicago quarterback in ten years to throw for three hundred yards. Evans completed eighteen of twenty-two passes for 316 yards and three touchdowns.

Behind crushing blocks by guards Revie Sorey and Noah Jackson, Walter Payton rushed for 130 yards in twenty-two carries. The Bears finished with 267 rushing yards and a staggering 594 total yards.

"All I could hear on the PA was, 'Another Chicago Bear rushing record for Walter Payton,'" McCarren said.

Bill Tobin, then Chicago's player personnel director, said the Bears had decoded Green Bay assistant coach Zeke Bratkowski's system of hand signals to send in the offensive plays. The idea of stealing the signals, Tobin said, came directly from team owner George Halas, who was then eighty-five years old.

"Halas thought if they were going to stand there and signal their plays in from the sideline, why can't we figure out what they're doing?" Tobin said. "So we figured it out. I spent the off-season working on it. I still have the films. We taped Zeke, then the play. That particular game, they started out with two signal-callers, so you didn't know which one was live and which one was the dummy. So it was hard to decode. But they got caught with the forty-five-second clock early and there was a delay of game. All of a sudden, they only used Zeke. He'd call a play, I'd relay it to Buddy Ryan, and he would call the defense."

There is considerable debate among the players and coaches that day whether the stolen signals played a big role in the rout. "There is no way," said Dickey. "The information sent to me was so minimal. There was no way they could do that. You know what the real problem was? We were really bad."

Said Bears safety Gary Fencik: "We knew it, and it absolutely screwed us up. We thought we had an idea when they were going to run draw plays, and everybody completely blew their assignments. Sometimes, you're better off not knowing and just reacting to a play."

Even Ryan, the Bears' defensive coordinator, said the signals weren't of much use. "We couldn't get it to the players on the field fast enough," he said. "That never worked out."

But Tobin said the advance knowledge of Green Bay's plays definitely was a factor in the victory. "Buddy is full of shit," Tobin said. "Whether it was going to be run or pass, which way, whether it was going to be a draw or screen—we had the whole bit."

Things got out of hand when Bears reserve quarterback Mike Phipps threw two passes late in the game—completing both for twenty yards—long after the result had been determined.

"We're in the huddle and the play comes in from the sideline to run the ball," Jiggetts said. "We're up by fifty points, but Phipps hadn't had a lot of opportunity to play. They're telling him to run the ball, and he goes, 'I don't think so.' So he starts putting it back up in the air. It was a beautiful thing. Were we trying to rub it in? Absolutely. We wanted seventy points."

Meanwhile, Bart Starr, the Packers' head coach at the time, had inserted his backup quarterback, David Whitehurst, when the score was 48-7. It was Whitehurst's first appearance of the regular season.

Ryan kept calling blitzes until the bitter end.

"Buddy was one of these guys, when you get 'em down, kick 'em and stomp on 'em, and kick 'em and stomp on 'em," Tobin said. "Buddy was different."

After the game, Starr charged across the field and angrily confronted Bears coach Neill Armstrong. Starr was more upset about the blitzes than he was the passes by Phipps or the fact that Payton came back in the game with the score 55-7 to pad his rushing total. Starr refused to shake Armstrong's hand, then stormed off the field.

"I felt there was an excessive effort on the part of Ryan to take advantage of an inexperienced quarterback and continue to literally rub it in," Starr said. "I harbor no feelings about it now, but at the time, I was really ticked off."

Ryan remains unrepentent. "Starr told Neill that I was blitzing his young quarterback," Ryan said. "But the guy had played the year before. He was a regular. But it didn't make any difference. That was the way we played. They were trying to run a two-minute drill, and they didn't think we would blitz. So they were running their backs out of there in a hurry. So we blitzed 'em. If you didn't have it picked up, we came and got you."

Fencik could understand Starr's anger, but he thought it was misdirected. "If anything, his anger should have been vented to his own players, rather than us," Fencik said. "I think when you walk on the field, you don't expect any favors from anyone."

After the shellacking, Starr told reporters, with a straight face, that he was proud of his team's effort.

His pride, however, was nothing compared with what the Bears felt. "We wanted one hundred points," said defensive end Dan Hampton. "It couldn't have happened to a nicer bunch of pricks."

8. Lombardi Gets a Ride
Packers 9, Bears 6
September 27, 1959; Lambeau Field

On the first day of training camp in 1959, new head coach Vince Lombardi let the Packers know that things were going to be different in Green Bay.

Shortly after he gathered the team to introduce himself, Lombardi announced that he was fining wide receiver Max McGee, running backs Paul Hornung and Howie Ferguson, and cornerback Jesse Whittenton. "He introduced himself as head coach and general manager," recalled Whittenton. "Then he said, 'Mr. McGee, Mr. Hornung, Mr. Whittenton, and Mr. Ferguson, it'll cost you $250.'

"What happened was, we came to training camp early and went out and played golf and all that stuff. Howie said, 'What's the fine for?' Lombardi said, 'You missed curfew.' Ferguson said, 'Camp don't start 'til now.' And Lombardi said, 'It started the day you brought your luggage into this dormitory. You were out after eleven o'clock. If you don't like it, let me know what club you want to go to.'

"That was how he introduced himself. He fined four of us."

Lombardi's no-nonsense approach and stern demeanor was in sharp contrast with that of his predecessor, Ray "Scooter" McLean, whose players admitted he let them get away with murder in 1958, his only season as head coach. The Packers, perhaps not coincidentally, had a 1-10-1 record that year, worst in franchise history.

Lombardi's stated goal was a winning season, and he knew he had to whip the players into shape, mentally and physically, from Day One. He put them through a grueling camp to get them ready for the opener against the Bears, picked by many as favorites to win the Western Conference title.

"Vince was so hell-bent on getting off to a good start that year," said Red Cochran, one of Lombardi's assistant coaches. "He had made the statement when he came in that he had never been part of a losing season, and he didn't want to start with a loss."

Defensive back Bobby Dillon, who had been talked out of retirement by Lombardi, arrived in training camp late and noticed an immediate difference in the Packers. "The players were in much better condition,"

Dillon said. "Everything was much better organized. We had a plan. Lombardi got guys to have confidence in themselves. Coaches would always say, the guy you're playing across from, you've got to play your best game to beat him. Lombardi would go the other way. He'd tell you, 'The other guy couldn't make our team, and if you can't beat him, you don't belong on my team.' It put a lot more pressure on the guys."

The Wednesday before the game, Lombardi closed training camp at the Oakton Manor resort in Pewaukee. By then, the Packers were in magnificent shape and champing at the bit. "He had us ready to play the first week of camp," defensive tackle Dave Hanner said with a hearty laugh.

Lombardi decided to start Lamar McHan at quarterback over Bart Starr, and the underdog Packers fell behind, 6-0, on two field goals by John Aveni. Then, the momentum—and Green Bay's fortunes—shifted in the fourth quarter.

First, rookie Richie Petitbon fumbled a punt, and Green Bay's Jim Ringo recovered on Chicago's 26-yard line. A few plays later, fullback Jim Taylor crashed over from the five and Hornung converted the extra point to give the Packers a 7-6 lead.

Minutes later, McGee got off a 61-yard punt, with the ball rolling out of bounds on the Bears' two-yard line. On first down, Ed Brown dropped back to pass, but Hanner and three other Packers dumped him for a safety.

As the fans counted down the final seconds, several jubilant Packers hoisted Lombardi on their shoulders and trotted off the field. Only once before, with Gene Ronzani, had a Green Bay coach been given such treatment. The legendary Curly Lambeau, who won six NFL titles, was never carried off the field on his players' shoulders.

"When we got ready to play the Bears that first time, our preparation was so fundamentally sound and strong and intense—without being overly psyched—that we were ready," Starr said. "And because of that, we were able to win. It was such an exhilirating feeling, we grabbed Lombardi and carried him off. It was a very spontaneous thing."

The Packers went on to compile a 7-5 record, and a dynasty was born.

"That was just the start of what he was preaching through training camp coming true," said defensive back Hank Gremminger. "He told us if we listened to him and did what we were told to do, that we'd win. I think that was just the start. We didn't know how good we were. It gave us confidence."

Fred Williams, who played defensive tackle for the Bears from 1952 to 1963, vividly recalls watching the Packers carry their new coach off on their shoulders.

"Yeah," Williams quipped, "they should have kept carrying him."

9. The Monsoon Bowl
Packers 33, Bears 6
October 31, 1994; Soldier Field

The Bears had grand plans for the special Halloween edition of Monday night football. They planned to retire the numbers of Hall of Famers Gale Sayers and Dick Butkus in a halftime ceremony. And, before a national TV audience, they planned to beat the arch-rival Packers.

But Mother Nature rained on the Bears' plans.

Then, it was the Packers' turn to reign.

Things went awry when an all-day rainstorm, driven by an incessant, howling wind, pelted the Chicago area with 2.26 inches. Earlier in the day, an American Eagle turboprop bound from Indianapolis to O'Hare International Airport had plunged into a farm field near Roselawn, Indiana, killing all sixty-eight people aboard.

The Soldier Field grounds crew began removing the tarp two hours before game time, in accordance with NFL rules that allow teams that much pre-game practice time. However, neither team came out of its locker room until 7:00 P.M., by which time the field—which had been resodded four times in the previous five months—was a muddy swamp.

Only 47,381 fans attended the game; another 19,563 ticket-holders stayed home. At kickoff, the temperature was forty-seven degrees, but the wind-chill index was in the teens. The peak wind gust, six minutes before kickoff, was measured at forty-three miles per hour. The rain was being driven horizontally into the players' face masks. There was absolutely no escaping it.

"That was the worst weather, at any level, I had ever participated in as a player or coach," said Packers coach Mike Holmgren. "I can remember playing in high school where it rained so much in old Kezar Stadium in San Francisco that the mud would be so thick, it would literally suck the shoes right off you. You'd go into a pile, and you couldn't breathe because of the mud. But this had it all. This had the wind. The rain was coming right at you. It was just awful."

The players were almost in awe of the elements.

"I thought one goal post was going to come down, the wind was blowing so hard on one end," said Bears kicker Kevin Butler. "The rain was just sideways, literally sideways."

"A California boy like me, man, I didn't understand that one," said Bears safety Mark Carrier. "I was waiting for them to call the game off."

Said Packers running back Edgar Bennett: "That was ridiculous. I don't think I've ever played in anything that bad. You couldn't even dream something like that up."

Both teams wore throwback jerseys, in honor of the NFL's 75th anniversary. They proceeded to play a throwback game in the hog-wallow slop that passed for a football field.

The Bears won the toss, and coach Dave Wannstedt elected to kick off. It didn't take a genius to figure out that this game would boil down to field position. Wannstedt figured that by taking the wind in the first quarter, the Bears would have a huge advantage. Holmgren said that if the Packers had won the toss, he would have done the same thing.

The Packers punted on their first five possessions, but Craig Hentrich turned out to be an unsung hero with four consecutive punts of twenty-seven yards into the gale. "That game could have been decided in the first quarter," Holmgren said, "but Craig kicked three or four of the most beautiful twenty-seven-yard punts I've ever seen."

Hentrich said catching the snap from center was actually more difficult than kicking the ball into the wind. "The rain was coming in my face mask and the ball was slippery," Hentrich said. "The ball was so slimy and muddy, and the wind was blowing so hard, you didn't know where it was going to go."

The Bears failed to score in the first quarter, which proved to be their undoing, because their punter, Chris Gardocki, was not nearly as effective as Hentrich. "We punt one, and the ball goes eight yards," Wannstedt said, shaking his head. "Straight up in the air, caught the wind and came straight down. Once they turned the field position around on us, we were in trouble."

The Packers scored two touchdowns in the pivotal second quarter, one of them on a 36-yard run by quarterback Brett Favre. The rout was on.

Bennett rushed for 105 yards as Green Bay totaled 223 on the ground. Amazingly, Green Bay did not turn the ball over once, while Chicago had five turnovers. Favre completed only six of fifteen pass attempts for eighty-two yards, but he did not throw an interception.

"Favre is one of those rare types," said Bears defensive back Shaun Gayle. "A lot of players tend to lose their way when the obstacles mount. Only a few players are able to play better when the times are tough. In fact, they look forward to it. It's a real test of mental strength. Not many guys can block that out, especially at the skill positions. Favre has shown he can."

The halftime ceremony honoring Sayers and Butkus went on as planned, but it lacked the intended dramatic impact. Whipped by the wind and rain, the two all-time greats wore plastic rainsuits and gave short speeches that few in the stands even heard.

"It could have been thirty below, and I wouldn't have felt it," Sayers said. "Yeah, it was a tough night. But I think Dick felt the same way. When something like that happens, you just get caught up in the event. You don't worry about the weather. It's too bad, because it could have been a better night for the ceremony and the Bears, because they got blown out, too, but it was something I'll never forget."

There were a few other interesting sidelights in the game. Defensive tackle Steve McMichael, who had played thirteen distinguished seasons with the Bears, made his one and only appearance in Soldier Field as an opponent. McMichael finished his career with the Packers in 1994.

"The thing that stands out was McMichael," said Bears guard Mark Bortz. "He almost had tears in his eyes out there before we played. I kind of chuckle. He was one of those guys who gave me a lot of grief about being a cheesehead, and there he was, in the green and gold."

Mostly, though, the game will be remembered as one of the sloppiest, slipperiest mudbaths in the history of the rivalry. "I remember at the end of the game, I was so cold and we had the game won, but I was upset with an official's call," Holmgren said. "He had his hands in his pocket, so I asked him—just to be a jerk—'How many timeouts do we have left?' He had to reach in his pocket and pull his card out. I wanted his hands to be as cold as mine."

Packers equipment manager Gordon "Red" Batty figured the game cost the team fifteen thousand dollars in ruined equipment. Every player went through two complete uniforms, and Batty said at least eight hundred towels were used.

"Everything was ruined—shoes, coaches' clothing, uniforms," he said. "We came in at halftime and every single player changed."

When the game was over, nearly every player dumped his shoes into a garbage can. Batty and his crew pulled them out and let them dry out; the team then sold them at various auctions for charities.

The Bears had the same problems. But they also had to deal with a lopsided defeat. "Most guys, when you get wet, you change your shoes, you change your socks," Bortz said. "But it was so bad, when you stepped out on the field, you stepped halfway up to your shinbone in mud and water. It was just a joke. What do you do?

"Then, when you get your ass kicked, it makes it ten times worse."

10. Hutson Breaks in With a Bang
Packers 7, Bears 0
September 22, 1935; City Stadium

As the Bears prepared for their 1935 season opener, coach George Halas made sure his defense was ready for Packers rookie end Don Hutson, a lanky lightning bolt from the University of Alabama. He reminded defensive back Beattie Feathers on several occasions that the kid could run. Feathers, no slouch himself in the speed department, assured the old man that he'd have no trouble handling Hutson.

"I remember Halas telling Beattie, 'Now, you're going to have to allow him some more space, because he's going to lull you to sleep back there,'" recalled Bears Hall of Fame lineman George Musso. "Beattie would tell Halas, 'Don't worry, coach, I'll have him covered like a blanket.' That went on all during practice.

"Then, before the game, Halas called Beattie off to the side and reminded him again about Hutson. Beattie said, 'Don't worry coach, I'll have him covered like a blanket.'"

Chicago kicked off, and Green Bay started on its own 17-yard line. On their first play from scrimmage, the Packers came out in what was then an unusual formation, similar to the pro set that is used today. Hutson was split to the left, and Johnny Blood McNally was flanked to the right.

Arnie Herber dropped back to pass, and the Bears' defense converged on the veteran Blood. Hutson, running what today is known as a fly pattern, drew even with Feathers, then put on a burst of speed and simply ran past him.

Hutson hauled in Herber's bomb at midfield and never broke stride, leaving Feathers lunging at air. The electrifying 83-yard touchdown provided Green Bay with the only points it would need that day.

"We practiced that play all week," said Chester "Swede" Johnston, who played fullback for the Packers from 1934 to 1939. "If we received, the first play would be to Hutson. He would run as fast as he could down the field, and in those days, nobody was as fast as he was. Herber threw it as far as he could, and Hutson caught it on the dead run."

In those few seconds, the game of professional football was forever changed. Hutson redefined his position, teaming with the rifle-armed Herber, and later with Cecil Isbell, to form one of the most prolific pass-catch combinations in NFL history. In 1963, Hutson was one of the initial inductees into the Pro Football Hall of Fame.

"I'll tell you, you put him right out there today, and he'd be one of the top receivers," said Tony Canadeo, who had a Hall of Fame career himself as a running back for the Packers in the 1940s and 1950s. "I don't give a damn what name you throw at me. Jerry Rice, or anybody."

Fifty-two years after he retired in 1945, the "Alabama Antelope" is still the Packers' all-time leading scorer with 823 points. He had 105 career touchdowns—in 117 games—and added 172 extra points and seven field goals. He finished his eleven-year career with 488 receptions for 7,991 yards, a 16.4 average. He also played defensive back, and when he left the game, he ranked second in the NFL in career interceptions.

"In 1942, he led the league with seventy-four receptions; the second guy had twenty-seven," said Lee Remmel, the Packers' director of public relations. "That just shows you what a man apart he was."

It wasn't just the gaudy numbers Hutson put up that made him great. He invented many of today's standard pass patterns, and he ran like the wind, moving with such a fluid style and grace that he often left defensive backs hopelessly corkscrewed as they broke the wrong way on his fakes.

"Oh, gosh! That guy would tear your nerves all to pieces," said George McAfee, a standout halfback and defensive back for the Bears. "We had two or three special defenses for him. He was great. He really was."

Halas had tried to sign Hutson himself in 1935, offering him seventy-five dollars per game. The football Brooklyn Dodgers also joined the bidding war. But Hutson wound up with the Packers when Lambeau got reckless with his bankroll and also convinced Hutson that Green Bay's offense was tailor-made for the receiver's skills.

At first, Lambeau's enthusiasm about Hutson was not universal in Green Bay. Many people thought that the end, a stripling at 178 pounds, wasn't big enough for the professional game.

On the day of the Bears game, Emmet Platten, a rabid Packers fan, bought fifteen minutes of air time on a Green Bay radio station—as was his weekly practice—and criticized Lambeau for shelling out so much money for Hutson, who had made his pro debut the week before. "What's Lambeau thinking of to sign a little guy like that?" Platten said, according to a story written years later by Oliver Kuechle of *The Milwaukee Journal.* "What's he thinking of, starting him today? Those Bears will kill him. Let's get some size in there."

Hutson was aware that he had his skeptics.

"That was a very, very important game for me, because there were some people around Green Bay that thought Lambeau made a mistake by paying me," Hutson said before his death in June, 1997. "So that took care of that."

Hutson went on to terrorize every defense he faced, but he especially tormented Halas and the Bears. In twenty-two games against Chicago, he caught eighty-four passes for 1,465 yards—a 17.4 average—and scored fifteen touchdowns.

"Don had such an impact, the story was that for three years after he retired in '45, Halas dusted off his special Hutson defenses," Remmel said. "Halas always expected Don to come out of retirement. He had threatened to retire four or five years before he ever did, but every year he came back and played. Halas didn't trust him to stay retired.

"He was that good. He required special defenses."

11. Kicking Off a Memorable Season
Bears 10, Packers 3
September 15, 1963; Lambeau Field

As the 1963 season dawned, the mighty Packers were poised for a run at a third consecutive NFL championship.

They were coming off a 13-1 season in which they had outscored their opponents, 415-148. Their roster was peppered with thirteen players who had been named to the Pro Bowl in 1962, or would be that season. Ten of those players were future Hall of Famers.

The Bears probably didn't match up on paper, but they were anxious to avenge embarrassing 49-0 and 38-7 losses to the Packers the year before.

"That was the game we pointed to from the first day of training camp," said Ronnie Bull, then a second-year running back with the Bears. "From the time we went into training camp, that was all Halas talked about—our opening game against the Green Bay Packers. "He said, 'If we win that game, we have a chance to go all the way.'"

Chicago had the makings of a stalwart defense, but there were question marks on the left side of the line. Stan Jones had been moved from offense to defense, and had replaced Fred Williams at left tackle. Bob Kilcullen had replaced an injured Ed O'Bradovich at left end.

They would have to fight off the blocks of Packers guard Jerry Kramer and tackle Forrest Gregg, the best in the business. And there was little doubt that the Packers would pound Hall of Fame fullback Jim Taylor off the right side of their line, directly at Jones and Kilcullen.

"I remember Bill Gleason, who was with the *Chicago American* at the time, wrote a column saying the Bears' defense looked pretty solid, except for the school teacher and the artist on the left side," said Jones. "I was a school teacher in the off-season and Kilcullen was the artist. And we were lining up against the best in the world."

The night before the showdown, Kilcullen and Jones were eating dinner at The Spot Supper Club in downtown Green Bay. Kilcullen happened to spot Gleason and had some words for him.

"He said, 'Hey! Bill! I just want you to know Jones and I are going to show up no matter what you think,'" said Jones. "I said, 'Thanks a lot, Bob. Jesus, we have enough problems without causing more attention to ourselves.' I think they ran most of the plays at us the next day and I think they had minus yardage in the first half. But the main thing is we won the game. It was a big thrill, probably the biggest thrill of my football career."

The duo helped the Bears shut down the Packers' powerful running game, holding Taylor to fifty-three yards. Green Bay had just nine first downs and 150 net yards, and never advanced deeper than the Bears' 33-yard line. Kramer's 41-yard field goal accounted for their only points.

Former linebacker Joe Fortunato said there was a reason for the Bears' success against the Packers that year. In two games against them, the Bears allowed a total of ten points. "George Allen became the defensive coordinator and that was when we started with tendency charts," said Fortunato. "We found that the Packers had tremendous tendencies."

As it turns out, the Bears' coaching staff didn't pick up all those tendencies on film. Halas also had some inside information. He had acquired former Green Bay linebacker Tom Bettis from the Pittsburgh Steelers in February, and brought him to Chicago to go over the Packers' scheme. Bettis had been traded to Pittsburgh after he had words with Vince Lombardi in 1962, and he was more than eager to cooperate with Halas. He also was someone with a keen football mind; he would spend more than twenty-five years as an assistant coach in the NFL after he retired as a player following the 1963 season.

"Halas picked my brain, no question about it," Bettis recalled. "I knew the Packers like a book, having played there. So I gave him a pretty good rundown on their personnel and the things they would go to: different plays, their system. It helped, no question about it. Halas even told me that later."

Did Halas actually have the Packers' playbook?

"He may have," Bettis said. "I had certain things I accumulated over the years. I don't know if I had a playbook."

Still, Jones and Kilcullen had to stop the Packers' running game, and they rose to the occasion magnificently.

On Monday, Gleason wrote a column gushing about the two players he had questioned just a few days earlier.

"I started it with a poem," Gleason recalled, then recited the verse off the top of his head: "'Stanley Jones has no bones, and Bill Kilcullen is rarely sullen.' Those were the two lines I led off with in italic. Then, I went into the column and how brilliantly they had played."

12. The Dedication of Lambeau Field
Packers 21, Bears 17
September 29, 1957; Lambeau Field

On a beautiful autumn weekend, tiny Green Bay was the center of the football universe. The city dedicated its new football stadium on the west side of town with a two-day celebration unlike anything that had ever been seen in northeastern Wisconsin.

The citizens of Green Bay had passed a referendum in April, 1956, to build the stadium, solidifying the city's future in the rapidly expanding National Football League. As the 1957 season approached, the excitement built to a crescendo as the city proudly braced for a phalanx of arriving dignitaries, not to mention the hated Bears, the opponent in the season opener.

But this was a rare occasion on which the rivalry took a back seat. The huge, double-decked headline in the *Green Bay Press-Gazette* the day before the game conveyed the city's fervor: "Miss America, Matt Dillon Arrive To Start Off Dedication Weekend." Miss Marilyn Van Derbur— Miss America—and James Arness—Marshal Matt Dillon of the popular "Gunsmoke" television series—were joined in Green Bay for the game by then-Vice President Richard Nixon and NFL Commissioner Bert Bell.

On Saturday, more than seventy thousand people choked a two and one-half mile route for the kickoff parade, which the *Press-Gazette* described as "the greatest and most colorful in the city's history, and thoroughly enjoyed by the greatest crowd ever to cram the long route." Another eighteen thousand attended a farewell program at old City Stadium, and fifteen thousand watched a Venetian Nights boat parade on the Fox River.

The Packers capped a perfect weekend by upsetting the favored Bears before 32,132 ecstatic fans. Green Bay overcame a 17-14 deficit when backup quarterback Vito "Babe" Parilli threw a six-yard touchdown pass to end Gary Knafelc in the fourth quarter. "I remember spotting Gary Knafelc under the goal post," said Parilli, who had replaced Bart Starr in the second quarter. "I was scrambling around and saw him waving in the end zone. He kind of used the goal post to screen himself from the defense."

Speaking at halftime, Nixon praised the citizens of Green Bay for building their stadium without looking for financial help from the federal government. He said the stadium made Green Bay "the best-known little city in the United States today."

Bears owner George Halas, who had visited Green Bay to support the referendum drive, also waxed eloquent. "I've been coming up here since the beginning, and never have I been more impressed than I was today," he said after the game. "It's a real tribute to the fine Green Bay fans and the Packer spirit."

Looking back, many of the Packers and Bears who played that day remember more about the hoopla surrounding the event than they do the details of the game itself. "I stood next to Miss America before the game," Parilli said. "She was quite a beauty. It was pretty exciting—here I was, a twenty-some-year-old kid."

Some of the Bears saw Arness, who stood 6-foot-6, walking through the Northland Hotel the day before the game and thought he was a new member of the Packers.

"Some of the Green Bay rookies used to stay at the hotel," said Bears lineman Stan Jones. "So I waved at him and said, 'Hey, how you doin'?' Then I got on the elevator and on the way up, I said, 'My God! That's James Arness!'"

After the game, Nixon toured both locker rooms and shook hands. Safety Stan Wallace of the Bears and tackle Ollie Spencer of the Packers had been ejected for fighting in the first half, and when Wallace stood up to shake Nixon's hand, the vice president had some advice for him. "He said, 'Number 40, I've got two suggestions for you,'" Wallace recalled. "He said, 'One, I wouldn't pick on the biggest guy on the field. And, two, your left hook needs a little work.'"

As he waited to shake Nixon's hand, Bears defensive tackle Fred Williams thought of his high school, Little Rock Senior High. In 1957, President Eisenhower had dispatched U.S. Army troops to Little Rock to desegregate the school, after Governor Orval E. Faubus sent the Arkansas National Guard to block integration.

To Halas' great horror, Williams gave Nixon some unsolicited advice. "Halas was a big Republican, of course, and he had given us all instructions," Williams said. "He said, 'When Nixon comes by you, all you say is, 'I'm Joe Blow from Kokomo.' So I'm waiting, and Nixon comes by and says, 'Hi, son.' I says, 'Fred Williams from Little Rock, Arkansas; and how about getting those troops out of there?'

"Well, Halas just about had a heart attack. Of course, Nixon was a politician; all they do is smile. They don't listen to what you say. But Halas got hot about that. It could have been the king, I wouldn't have cared what I said. Bill George, my runnin' buddy, was standing right beside me, and he just died laughin'.

"But Nixon, he just ignored it."

13. Sayers Runs Wild; Percival Wins It

Bears 13, Packers 10
November 3, 1968; Lambeau Field

As Donny Anderson got ready to punt from the Packers' 15-yard line with forty-two seconds left in the game, Bears assistant coach Abe Gibron informed his punt returners, Cecil Turner and Gale Sayers, to call for a fair catch.

Turner fielded Anderson's 28-yard punt on the Packers' 43.

"Gibron said, 'Kicking team!'" recalled Bears kicker Mac Percival. "We looked at each other. 'Kicking team?' He said, 'Yeah, free kick.' I had never heard of a free kick."

Ahh, but the Bears coaches had. They remembered that four years earlier, then-Green Bay coach Vince Lombardi had taken advantage of a little-used rule that allows a team to try a field goal without a rush by the opponent, following a fair catch. Paul Hornung had kicked a 52-yarder just before halftime in a 23-12 Packers victory. At the time, it was believed to be the first successful free kick in NFL history.

After that game, a smug Lombardi had said, "The chance of your seeing it in your lifetime or me seeing it in mine again are nil." Lombardi may have been a prophet about many things, but this time he was dead wrong.

Percival trotted onto the field, but he didn't have the faintest idea what to do. "Richie Petitbon was my holder, and I'll never forget, we took a kicking tee out," Percival said. "But you can't kick a free kick off a tee; your holder has to hold the ball for you. Then Petitbon stuck out his leg, like you always do when you're holding. The official came running over and said, 'You're offsides.' You had to be behind the ball.

"So we lined up behind the ball, and it was kind of easy with nobody rushing you. It was like practice."

Percival's 43-yard field goal split the uprights, giving the Bears the victory.

"Green Bay had done it to us; that's where we got it from," recalled Bears running back Ronnie Bull. "That was just a payback."

The weird finish overshadowed a career performance by Bull's backfield mate, Sayers, who ran over, around, and through the Packers to the tune of 205 yards in twenty-four carries.

"It was one of those games that it probably could have been three hundred yards," Sayers said. "On several plays, I broke some runs for fifteen, twenty-five yards that got called back for penalties. It was just one of those games, we ran up and down the field, but couldn't score."

After the game, Lombardi, who had stepped down as coach but was still the Packers' general manager, saw Ed McCaskey, George Halas' son-in-law, outside the stadium.

"He came over to me and said, 'That was the greatest exhibition I've ever seen by any football player,'" McCaskey recalled.

To this day, nobody has ever rushed for more yards at Lambeau Field, although in 1977, Walter Payton—another Bears Hall of Famer—tied Sayers' mark.

Sayers, at least when he was healthy, haunted the Packers throughout his career. In nine games against them, he rushed for 754 yards in 160 carries, a 4.7 average, and scored five touchdowns. "He was a magician," said Packers defensive back Bob Jeter. "The best thing you could do as a defensive back was try to turn him in and hope for your help coming from the inside. If you thought you were going to get him one-on-one, forget it. It was impossible."

Said Packers tackle Forrest Gregg, who played against Sayers and later coached against Payton: "I think Gale Sayers was one of the most beautiful runners I've ever seen. His career was shortened by a knee injury, but, man, this guy was just awesome. He was so smooth, so agile; just a glider and a slider. He had subtle moves to make people miss, and he had great speed along with it."

Packers defensive end Willie Davis put Sayers on a level with Jim Brown, generally considered to be the best running back in NFL history. "I always said Jim Brown was the greatest running back, and I haven't backed away from that," Davis said. "But if you were looking for somebody who was the most elusive and difficult to tackle, I thought Gale Sayers wore that crown."

14. Helmet-less Bill Hewitt is a Hero
Bears 14, Packers 7
September 24, 1933; City Stadium

With just three minutes left in the game, the Packers looked like sure winners. They had a 7-0 lead and had outplayed the Bears at every turn, "knocking them down, whipping them and rubbing it in," as the *Press-Gazette* reported.

Packers fullback Clarke Hinkle had even knocked Bears bruiser Bronko Nagurski out of the game with a shattered nose on a vicious sideline collision. Everything was going Green Bay's way.

Then Bill Hewitt, Chicago's rugged two-way end, took matters into his own hands.

First, Hewitt blocked a field-goal attempt by Green Bay's Roger Grove, and the Bears recovered on their own 35-yard line. Three plays later, Hewitt took the ball from Carl Brumbaugh on an end around. As he ran wide across the field, he saw Luke Johnsos running free downfield. Hewitt pulled up and threw the ball, and, with "no defensive player within hailing distance," according to the *Press-Gazette*, Johnsos easily scored the tying touchdown.

On their ensuing possession, the Packers were forced to punt from their own 20-yard line, with barely one minute left in the game. Hewitt flashed in from the left end and blocked Arnie Herber's punt with his chest. The ball bounded toward the Packers' goal line and Hewitt chased it down, picked it up in stride, and scored the winning touchdown.

Later in the season, Hewitt again played a great game—although he did not score—as the Bears rallied to beat the Packers, 10-7.

"Hewitt was a team by himself on the left side of the Bear line," the *Press-Gazette* reported. "The Packers would send two men and often three at him, trying to clear the way for a ball carrier. But Hewitt would smash through all of them to break up the play. When the Packers got into scoring territory the demon end would turn on even more steam and stop plays on the opposite side of the field. It was the most brilliant individual performance ever turned in by a player in a Packer-Bear game."

The 1933 season was generally considered to be the finest of Hewitt's nine-year career. Sophisticated statistics were not kept by the league then, but Hewitt is unofficially credited with throwing opposing ball-carriers for at least three hundred yards in total losses during the season.

He was known as "The Offside Kid" because his quickness made it appear as if he was jumping offside on every play.

"He was fast; he was quick," said Charles "Ookie" Miller, who played center for the Bears from 1932 to 1936, and finished his career with the Packers in 1938. "He'd get in the backfield before the blockers knew he was coming. And he didn't wear no hat, and hardly any pads."

Hewitt died in an automobile accident in Pennsylvania in 1947. In 1971, he was enshrined posthumously into the Pro Football Hall of Fame.

15. Frolics of the First Game
Staleys (Bears) 20, Packers 0
November 27, 1921; Wrigley Field

Chicago had honky tonks and gangsters, vaudeville acts and theatres, skyscrapers and upscale stores. The bustling city boasted not one, but two professional baseball teams. There was plenty to do, plenty to see, in a city that already was the social and business hub of the Midwest.

In contrast, Green Bay had a three-year-old football team, sponsored by the local Acme Packing Corporation, and comprised mostly of Midwest-bred players, and not much else to brag about.

No wonder, then, that Chicagoans were amused and bemused when more than three hundred fans from the tiny northern outpost invaded their city on November 21, 1921, for a professional football game. It's safe to assume that many people in Chicago hadn't even heard of George Halas' Staleys.

The Green Bay fans arrived on a special excursion train in the early morning hours. What a curiosity they must have been, parading in and out of downtown hotels, led by their strangely dressed, twenty-two-piece Lumberjack Band.

While the Packers lost the game, their hard-partying fans didn't allow the outcome to dampen their fun.

The *Green Bay Press-Gazette* report on Monday reflected the excitement in breathless fashion: "Staid old Chicago got a new thrill on Sunday and the college authorities who claim that 'There ain't no such thing as spirit in professional football' stood back and gasped as the rooters from Green Bay, Wisconsin, took the town by storm Sunday morning and held full sway until the last car of the special excursion pulled out from the North Western about three bells Monday morning."

History shows that Chicago's Pete Stinchcomb, a back from Ohio State, scored the first touchdown in the most frequently played rivalry in pro football. George Calhoun, a *Press-Gazette* sportswriter, described Stinchcomb's run in his long-winded game report:

"His dash for a touchdown early in the second quarter was a sensational piece of footballing. Shooting outside of left tackle, he shook off about a half-dozen tackles and side-stepped his way down the gridiron for 45 yards and a touchdown."

The game also featured the first cheap shot of the rivalry. John "Tarzan" Taylor threw a punch at Howard "Cub" Buck of the Packers. Buck, who stood 6 feet 3 inches and weighed 250 pounds, declined to retaliate. Instead, he admonished Taylor, who was 5-11, 173, by saying, "You are supposed to be a college graduate and a gentleman, you know."

Three future Pro Football Hall of Famers started for the Staleys that day: Guy Chamberlain at left end, George "Brute" Trafton at center, and Halas at right end. Chicago's other starters were Ralph Scott, left tackle; Taylor, left guard; Russell Smith, right guard; Hugh Blacklock, right tackle; Walter "Pard" Pearce, quarterback; Ed "Dutch" Sternaman, left halfback; Stinchcomb, right halfback; and Ken Huffine, fullback.

The Packers started one future Hall of Famer: Curly Lambeau at quarterback. The other starters were Bill "Gus" DuMoe, left end; Frank Coughlin, left tackle; Emmett Keefe, left guard; Richard "Jab" Murray, center; Joe Carey, right guard; Buck, right tackle; Dave Hayes, right end; Norm Barry, left halfback; Grover Malone, right halfback; and Art Schmael, fullback.

Those were the starters, according to the game summary in the *Press-Gazette*, but whether the information was correct is anyone's guess. Record-keeping was haphazard at best. It's possible that others may have started the game, some perhaps assuming the names of the players listed above.

Several times over the next two decades, the *Press-Gazette* made reference to the fact that several Packers ducked out just a few hours before kickoff and didn't play. But the articles never mentioned any names. Moreover, a week after playing the Staleys, the Packers used three players from Notre Dame in a game against Racine. All three, it was later discovered, played under names other than their own.

16. Bears Win a Playoff
Bears 33, Packers 14
December 14, 1941; Wrigley Field

The Packers players were sitting in the stands at Comiskey Park in Chicago on December 7, 1941, watching the Bears play the Chicago Cardinals, when it was announced over the public address system that the Japanese had bombed Pearl Harbor that morning.

The United States was at war.

Everybody was saying, 'Pearl Harbor? Where the hell is that?'" recalled Tony Canadeo, the Packers' Hall of Fame running back.

World War II would soon have a profound impact, in one way or another, on the lives of all Americans. And professional football players were not excepted. Many of the Bears on the field that day, and the Packers in the stands, would serve their country overseas. "We were extremely depressed because we knew all of us, over a period of time, would be going into the service," said Bears halfback Hugh Gallarneau.

Still, there was a football season to finish. The Packers already had completed their regular season with a 10-1 record. They were at Comiskey Park to watch the Bears, who needed to beat the Cardinals to finish 10-1 and force a first-ever playoff game for the NFL's Western Division title. The Bears won as expected, 34-24, setting up a showdown with the Packers the next week at Wrigley Field.

Green Bay had used a seven-man line to stifle Chicago's powerful T-formation in a 16-14 upset on November 2. The Bears knew the Packers would try the same strategy in the playoff game; this time, they had prepared for the overloaded line.

Led by George McAfee, Gallarneau, and 235-pound rookie fullback Norm Standlee, the Bears piled up 267 yards on the ground. "We just annihilated them," said Bears quarterback Sid Luckman. "That game was unreal. We took the ball and just marched up and down the field, up and down the field. We were so high for that game. George McAfee went crazy . . . Hugh Gallarneau . . . Norm Standlee had the biggest day he ever had. We absolutely destroyed them."

More than five decades later, Luckman still gets animated when he talks about the game. "We'd double-team the inside guard, come across, and block on the end," he said. "We'd fake to McAfee, then give the ball to Standlee, or fake to Standlee and give it to McAfee. The Packers were completely and totally destroyed. I think that game and the Washington Redskins game—73-0—were the two greatest rushing games in the history of football, when two teams were really competing against each other."

The Packers took a brief 7-0 lead. End Ray Riddick recovered Gallarneau's fumble on the opening kickoff. Five plays later, with barely one minute elapsed, Clarke Hinkle crashed over right guard for the touchdown.

"I just about died, because Halas was somewhat unforgiving if you made a mistake like that in a Bear-Packer game," Gallarneau said. "I felt so bad about that fumble. I also was worried my salary would be cut. A few minutes later, happily, I returned a punt eighty-one yards to tie the score."

The Bears broke open the game with twenty-four points in the second quarter and cruised to the convincing victory.

A crowd of 43,425 braved sixteen-degree weather to watch the game. In contrast, the Bears' anticlimatic 37-9 victory over the New York Giants in the NFL title game the next week at Wrigley drew a mere 13,341.

"The thing I remember is that when we played the Packers, we packed the roof," recalled Bears end Ken Kavanaugh. "Then, we got to the championship game and we had about twelve thousand people. Green Bay was always sold out. When we beat the Packers, we only got our regular-season salary. The championship game was the one we'd get all the money, and there was nobody there."

The Bears were paid only $430.94 each for the championship game.

From 1940 until 1943, the Bears had one of the greatest runs in NFL history. They went 37-5-1 in those four seasons and won three league titles. But who knows what their legacy would have been without World War II?

Nine of Chicago's offensive starters in the playoff game against Green Bay spent time in the service.

"Oh, Jesus!" said Luckman. "Forty-one was a team. The '42 team was probably one of the great teams of all time. It's a shame the war came along and broke up that team. All of us were in our early twenties. That was the problem. All of us went into the service."

17. Packers Win First NFL Title
Packers 25, Bears 0
December 8, 1929; Wrigley Field

As the North Western train carrying the triumphant Packers neared Green Bay at 8:30 p.m. on Monday, December 9, the players were concerned to see an eerie red glow in the distance.

Some of the Packers thought the glow emanated from warning lights. Perhaps there had been a bad accident on the line ahead.

The glow, it turned out, came from thousands of fans who lined the tracks and waved red flares to welcome home their conquering heroes. On a bitterly cold night, an estimated twenty thousand cheering fans—

more than half the city's populace—rushed the train as it chugged into the station on Green Bay's west side.

"People were packed in an almost immovable mass around the station," Jack Rudolph wrote in the *Press-Gazette* in 1960. "They were overflowing into the yards and perching on top of roofs, box cars, in every available window—some even climbed telephone poles. The size of the crowd took the police by complete surprise, and if it hadn't been for its good-natured cooperation, things would have been an utter mess. As it was, traffic was at a standstill for blocks in every direction."

As the train neared the station at a crawl, brakemen and volunteers walked ahead of it to clear the right of way. Locomotive and industrial plant whistles blew, joined by the honking horns of nearly six thousand automobiles.

Paul Mazzoleni, a longtime Packers fan who was then sixteen years old, vividly remembers the wild celebration.

"The chief of police allowed the bars to stay open all night," Mazzoleni said. "It was no holds barred. I remember being part of it. You couldn't get close to the railroad station. You were just part of the mob."

The citizens of Green Bay had good reason to be proud. The Packers had beaten the Chicago Bears the day before to complete a 12-0-1 season and win their first NFL championship. They had been playing on the road since late October, winning seven of their final eight games; only a scoreless tie with the Frankford Yellowjackets on November 28 marred their record.

For the season, the Packers recorded eight shutouts and outscored their opponents, 198-22. They shut out the Bears three times by the combined score of 62-0.

The NFL title was a momentous accomplishment for the Green Bay franchise, which had not been accorded big-league status by the other teams in the league. As the circuit had grown, most of the smaller cities had lost their franchises. But Green Bay was a survivor, and by winning the 1929 championship proved its worthiness as a league member.

In the days leading up to the final game against the Bears, a "championship fund" had been launched by the people of Green Bay to reward the players for their successful season. In 1929, there was no championship game or money involved in winning the NFL title.

The drive, updated daily in front-page stories in the *Press-Gazette*, raised $5,073.60.

A Standard Oil company employee took up a collection and raised twenty-four dollars. The students of the Badger Commercial school chipped in $7.50. One young girl sent in a dollar and a note: "Enclosed please find one dollar for our perfect team."

At a lavish victory dinner at the Beaumont Hotel, attended by four hundred fans and broadcast by WHBY radio of Green Bay, each player received a watch and a new leather billfold containing $220.

Halfback Johnny Blood spoke on behalf of the players. "I'm in the greatest town in the world," he said, "and I'm glad to be here—in Green Bay, the home of the perpetual fatted calf."

18. Bart Starr's Final Game
Bears 23, Packers 21
December 18, 1983; Soldier Field

A season-ending victory over the Bears, a berth in the playoffs, perhaps extended life for embattled coach Bart Starr . . . it was all within the grasp of the Packers, who had a 21-20 lead with 90 seconds left in the final game of the 1983 season.

But the Bears drove down the field, and Bob Thomas kicked a 22-yard field goal with ten seconds left, sealing Green Bay's fate . . . and Starr's.

The Packers finished with an 8-8 record; had they won the game, they would have been 9-7 and made the playoffs. Starr was fired the next morning having compiled a 53-77-3 record over nine mostly forgettable seasons.

The Bears finished 8-8 that year also, but would make the playoffs in seven of the next eight seasons and win Super Bowl XX under Mike Ditka. "That was the start of the Bears, in my opinion," said Matt Suhey, who played fullback for Chicago from 1980 to 1989. "We beat a big rival within our division. We drove down the field in the last part of the game, finally won a game in the last minute or two. We went over the hump. Then the next year, '84, we started playing good football."

History might have been different had the Packers' woeful defense been able to stop the Bears on that drive . . . or had Starr had the presence to use his timeouts, which would have given his offense one more chance to score.

Starr was widely criticized for letting the clock run down as the Bears marched inexorably toward victory. After the game, when he was asked why he didn't use any time outs, he snapped, "That's our business."

Looking back now, however, Starr admits he was at fault. "I blame myself totally for that loss," he said. "I should have taken the timeouts. I should have done it, rather than just let a no-decision continue, thinking we could block any kick. We were so good at blocking kicks; that was the decision. But I knew better, and if we had taken a timeout sooner, we might have had a chance to get back down the field and kick one ourselves."

Robert Parins, team president and former Brown County judge, fired Starr the next day. "The judge told me he almost fired him on the plane on the way home and his wife talked him out of it," said Bob Harlan, who succeeded Parins as president in 1989. "I guess she thought the timing was bad, that it wasn't the proper place to do it. All I know is, the next morning, when I got to the office, I was right down the hall from the judge, and he put his coat on the rack and headed straight for Bart's office.

"He came by my door ten minutes later and said, 'Well, it's done. I just fired Bart.'"

Starr had taken the Green Bay job in 1975, with no background as a head coach on any level. He got his experience on the job, but he believes—and many of his former players agree—that he had become a good coach by the time he was fired.

"They were real unfair to Bart," said Ezra Johnson, who played defensive end for the Packers from 1977 to 1987. "He was a hell of a coach, to me. And he was a genuine, real man, a man of his word."

Even Bears quarterback Bob Avellini noticed how much Starr had improved as a tactician. "I thought by '83, he had become a good coach," Avellini said. "I remember in the early years, you'd look across the field, and I didn't think he knew what he was doing."

The biggest problem with the Packers wasn't Starr's coaching, his players said. It was a porous defense that had allowed 439 points that season, or 27.4 per game. Chicago's final drive, when everything was on the line for Green Bay, served to reinforce just how bad the defense was.

"We had a bunch of boneheads running that organization who knew nothing about football," said Greg Koch, a tackle for the Packers from 1977 to 1985. "I'm talking about the guys at the top. I'm talking about the guys who wouldn't pay the money for Bruce Clark. They pay $17 million for Reggie White now, and look where they are. But we're playing with Richard Turner and Daryle Skaugstad at nose tackle, and they think we're going to the playoffs."

The season finale at Soldier Field was played on a bitterly cold day. The temperature that morning had dipped to minus-eleven degrees, a record for Chicago on that date, and only 35,807 fans showed up for the game; there were 29,986 no-shows.

"That was the coldest game I've ever been in," said Packers quarterback Lynn Dickey. "I think the temperature was five below at game time, and the wind chill was 60 below. The whole country seemed to be in a deep freeze."

The Packers took a 21-20 lead with just under four minutes left. About two minutes later, they discovered they had gotten the outside help they needed to make the playoffs when the scoreboard flashed that the Los Angeles Rams had beaten New Orleans, 26-24.

All they needed to do was stop the Bears.

They couldn't do it, even though Walter Payton, who had almost singlehandedly carried Chicago on offense the entire day, was on the bench with a rib injury. Second-year quarterback Jim McMahon picked the defense apart, Thomas kicked the field goal, and it was over.

"All we had to do was hold them and we'd go to the playoffs," recalled Packers center Larry McCarren. "Son of a bitch. They go right down the field, and Bob Thomas kicks a field goal that looks like a whirlybird. It was just a terrible looking kick, and it made it by about this much"—McCarren held his fingers an inch apart—"at the corner of the cross bar.

"Bart gets fired the next day, and history is changed. If we go to the playoffs, would they have fired Bart? I kind of doubt it."

19. The Packers Look In-Vince-able
Packers 49, Bears 0
September 30, 1962; Lambeau Field

The Bears were about to face one of the greatest professional football teams ever assembled, and several of their top players were injured. It was no time to be short-handed.

Halfbacks Willie Galimore and Charles Bivins were hurt, and did not play. Fullback Rick Casares was slowed by a heel injury, and defensive back J.C. Caroline wasn't at full speed, either. The biggest void, however, was left by Hall of Fame linebacker Bill George, who was hospitalized in Chicago with a back injury.

In desperation, coach George Halas had checked George out of the hospital and brought him to the airport—the Bears were flying to Green Bay for the first time—but it was obvious that George was in severe pain.

"Boy, he was pale as a ghost," recalled teammate Fred Williams. "Hell, they had to take him back to the hospital. So we go on up to Green Bay, and they whipped the hell out of us. When we got back to Chicago, Bill was still in the hospital. I'm worried about him. I call him up, and he says, 'Gull dang.' I say, 'Bill, don't worry about hurtin'. We dedicated the game to you.'

"But Halas was going to take him up there. Good God! It just wasn't possible."

Even at full strength, the Bears almost certainly would not have been a match for the Packers, who were on their way to a 13-1 record and their second straight NFL championship. Green Bay outscored its opponents, 415-148, that season, and scored more than thirty points in eight games.

"That was our very best team of all," said Boyd Dowler, a wide receiver for the Packers from 1959 to 1969. "I don't think there is any doubt about it. Some of my teammates say that the first Super Bowl team was the best team. I don't think it was even close. Both offensively and defensively, we were quicker, we were younger, we were faster . . . we were just better."

The Packers proceeded to hand the Bears one of their worst defeats in franchise history. Bart Starr led Green Bay's offense to six touchdowns and 409 total yards. The defense allowed Chicago into Packers territory just three times all day and intercepted five passes; Herb Adderly returned the last one fifty-one yards for a touchdown. Fullback Jim Taylor rushed for 126 yards in seventeen attempts and scored three touchdowns.

"Yeah, that was our dedication game to Bill George," remembered Mike Ditka, then the Bears' second-year tight end. "They just murdered us. What can you say? It was a good undressing. Bill's statement was, 'Never dedicate one to me again.'"

In his classic book, *"Run to Daylight,"* Packers coach Vince Lombardi, who respected and admired Halas, wrote movingly about his regret that the score was so lopsided. He started the book with this passage:

"I have been asleep for three hours and, suddenly, I am awake. I am wide awake, and that's the trouble with this game. Just twelve hours ago

I walked off that field, and we had beaten the Bears 49 to 0. Now I should be sleeping the satisfied sleep of the contented but I am lying here awake, wide awake, seeing myself searching in the crowd for George Halas but really hoping that I would not find him.

"All week long there builds up inside of you a competitive animosity toward that other man, that counterpart across the field. All week long he is the symbol, the epitome, of what you must defeat and then, when it is over, when you have looked up to that man for as long as I have looked up to George Halas, you cannot help but be disturbed by a score like this. You know he brought a team in here hurt by key injuries and that this was just one of those days, but you can't apologize. You can't apologize for a score. It is up there on that board, and nothing can change it now. I can just hope, lying here awake in the middle of the night, that after all those years he has had in this league—and he has had forty-two of them—these things no longer affect him as they still affect me. I can just hope that I am making more of this than he is, and now I see myself, unable to find him in the crowd and walking up that ramp and into our dressing room, now searching instead for something that will bring my own team back to earth."

20. Winning for Jack Vainisi
Packers 41, Bears 13
December 4, 1960; Wrigley Field

It was as much Jack Vainisi's team as it was Vince Lombardi's.

Vainisi had been hired by Packers coach Gene Ronzani in 1950 as a talent scout and administrative aide. Then just twenty-three years old and straight out of Notre Dame, Vainisi became a virtual one-man scouting operation under Ronzani, and later coaches Lisle Blackbourn and Ray "Scooter" McLean. When Lombardi was hired as head coach and general manager in 1959, he made Vainisi his business manager as well as chief scout. Vainisi had a big say, along with Lombardi's predecessors, in drafting the nucleus of the Glory Years teams.

In 1956, the Packers drafted tackle Forrest Gregg in the second round, tackle Bob Skoronski in the fifth, and quarterback Bart Starr in the seventeenth. In 1957, they obtained halfback Paul Hornung with a bonus choice and picked tight end Ron Kramer in the first round.

Then, in 1958, the Packers had what was regarded as one of the greatest drafts in NFL history: linebacker Dan Currie in the first round, fullback Jim Taylor in the second, linebacker Ray Nitschke in the third, and guard Jerry Kramer in the fourth.

Every one of those nine players made at least one Pro Bowl, and five eventually were inducted into the Pro Football Hall of Fame.

"Jack had brought most of the players in there," said Dave "Hawg" Hanner, who was a player, assistant coach, and scout for the Packers for more than forty years. "There were the trades made for Lew Carpenter, Willie Davis, Henry Jordan, Bill Quinlan, and Fuzzy Thurston. But most of the other players, Jack had drafted."

The players felt close to Vainisi. He was an honest man who treated them with dignity when he negotiated their contracts. Over the years, he drove many of the young players back to training camp after they had played in the College All-Star Game—often stopping at his parents' grocery store on the north side of Chicago to pick up fresh fruit and bread.

"He was concerned about you," Gregg said. "If you had a problem, that was the guy you went to. Jack had a way of telling you where you stood. He'd tell you if you were close to not making the team, if you needed to pick it up, or whatever. Jack was really well-liked and respected by the players."

On Sunday, November 28, 1960, Vainisi collapsed in the bathroom of his Green Bay home and was dead by the time a city rescue squad arrived. He was thirty-three years old. Doctors said death was caused by a chronic rheumatic heart condition. He had been treated for the condition for more than a decade.

"We're all deeply shocked," Lombardi told the *Green Bay Press-Gazette*. "I have lost a close personal friend. I had known him several years before I came here. It will be hard to do without him."

On Wednesday, all the Packers players sat together during the funeral mass at Annunciation Church in Green Bay. They had formed a line at the doorway when the coffin was carried into church.

The Packers also dedicated their game against the Bears the following Sunday to Vainisi. It was an important game, too; Chicago had won the first meeting that year, and Green Bay was coming off consecutive losses to the Los Angeles Rams and Detroit.

But the Packers were sky high, and, led by Hornung's twenty-three points—on two touchdowns, two field goals, and five extra points—they crushed the Bears. The victory lifted Green Bay into a three-way tie for the Western Conference lead; the Packers went on to win the conference, then lost to Philadelphia in the NFL championship game.

After Hornung's second touchdown, he flipped the football into the stands—an unprecedented act that infuriated Bears coach George Halas. "I threw the ball in the stands, which was probably the first end zone antics ever," Hornung said. "I know Halas was pissed off. He tried to fine me. Lombardi said, 'Don't worry. If he tries to do something, I'll pay for it.' I don't know why I did it. It was a reflex motion. I scored a touchdown down in those left field bleachers in Wrigley Field, and everybody was hanging over that overhang. One of the guys said, 'Hornung, throw me the ball.' I just flipped it up.

"Halas once told me, 'Jesus Christ, do you realize what you started?' I guess it was the avalanche of end zone antics."

Defensive end Willie Davis got the Packers' big day started by blocking a punt and recovering the ball in the end zone for a touchdown. Starr completed seventeen of twenty-three passes for 218 yards, and Taylor rushed for 140 yards.

Hornung was the star, however, boosting his season point total to 152, which erased Don Hutson's eighteen-year-old record of 138. He would finish the season with 176 points in twelve games, still the NFL record, despite the fact the schedule was expanded to fourteen games the next year and to sixteen in 1978.

"An article a couple years ago in *Sports Illustrated* wrote about the five greatest records in sports, and mine was included in that," Hornung said. "I felt very proud about that. But records are made to be broken. If somebody breaks it, who cares? And, hell, it's going to be broken. We're going to see twenty-game seasons before not too long."

Still, December 4, 1960, was Hornung's day.

And Vainisi's.

(Note: Lambeau Field was known as new City Stadium until 1965. Wrigley Field was called Cubs Park in 1921.)

Legendary coaches Vince Lombardi (left) of the Packers and George Halas of the Bears chat before a game in the most storied rivalry in professional football. (Photo: Vernon J. Biever)

Opposite top: Bellevue Park was the site of the first Packers-Bears game played in Green Bay in 1923.

Opposite bottom: The railroads converted baggage cars into bar cars for Packer fans going to Chicago for a Bears-Packers game.

Below: Ted Fritsch carries the ball against the Bears in a game at old City Stadium in the 1940s. (These photos: Neville Public Museum)

Right: Clarke Hinkle was one of the toughest Packers of all time, playing fullback from 1932 to 1941. (Copyrighted photo, Milwaukee Journal Sentinel)

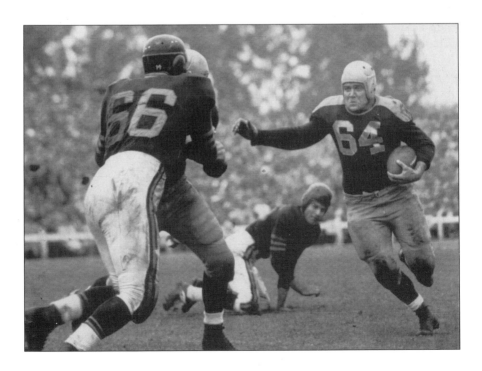

Opposite page: Legendary Bears Bronko Nagurski (*top-left*), Clyde "Bulldog" Turner (*top-right*), and Ed Sprinkle (*bottom-left*). At *bottom-right*, George Halas watches a Bears-Packers game alongside former NFL commissioner Pete Rozelle (at left) during a game at Lambeau Field. (Photo: Vernon J. Biever)

This page, right: James Arness, who played Matt Dillon in the TV series Gunsmoke, is shown in front of the Northland Hotel during the celebration of the opening of Lambeau Field in 1957.

Below: The celebration included festivities at old City Stadium on Saturday. The Bears were repre-sented by this float. (Photos: Neville Public Museum)

Left: Rookie Dick Butkus sneers from the sidelines during a game at Lambeau Field in 1965.
Below: Tight end Mike Ditka of the Bears pulls away from Packer safety Hank Gremminger (46) during a game at Lambeau Field in the 1960s.
Opposite page, top: Walter Payton, the NFL's all-time leading rusher, turns the corner on Packers safety Mark Murphy.
Opposite page, bottom: A Chicago police officer is part of the greeting party as Willie Galimore scores against the Packers in a 1963 Bears victory at Wrigley Field. (Photos on these two pages: Vernon J. Biever)

The Bears' defense dominated the Packers in 1963 at Wrigley Field in one of the biggest games in the history of the rivalry. Waiting for the Packers to break their huddle are Larry Morris (33), Doug Atkins (81), Earl Leggett (71), Bill George (61), Stan Jones (78), Joe Fortunato (31), and Ed O'Bradovich (87). The Bears scored a 26-7 victory and went on to win the NFL championship. (Copyrighted photograph, Milwaukee Journal Sentinel)

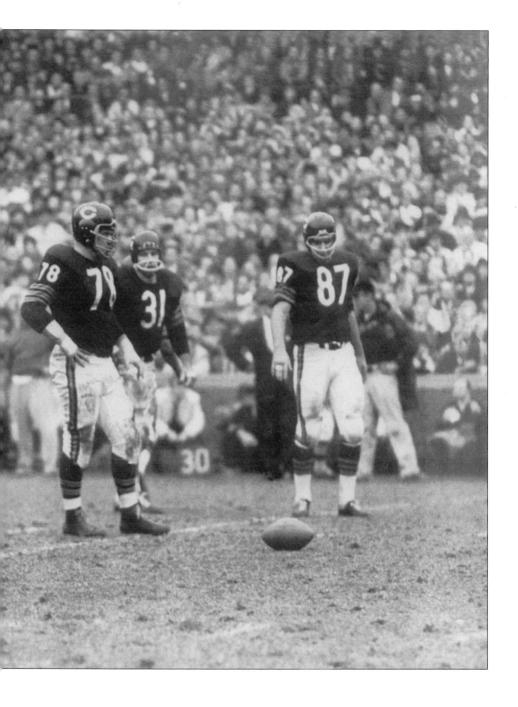

George Halas and Hall of Fame running back Gale Sayers watch intently from the sidelines during a game against the Packers at Wrigley Field. (Photo: Vernon J. Biever)

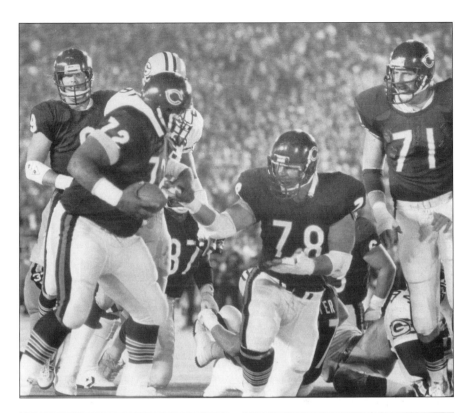

Top: Defensive tackle William "The Refrigerator" Perry scores against the Packers in 1985, and (*above*) greets reporters after the game. (Photos: Vernon J. Biever) The Fridge (*left*) stood 6-foot-2 and his weight often ballooned to more than 350 pounds. (Photo: Mike DeVries/The Capital Times)

Defensive end Richard Dent (95) and defensive tackle Steve McMichael (76) trade high-fives after knocking Green Bay quarterback Randy Wright to the turf in a game at Soldier Field in 1985. (Photo: Vernon J. Biever)

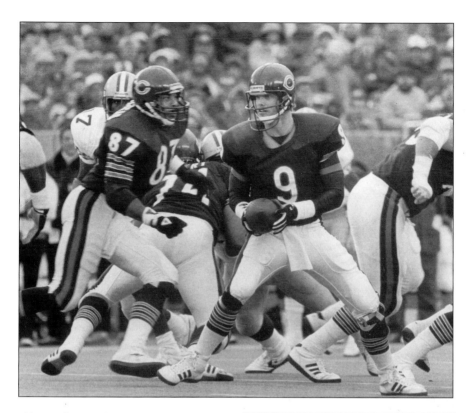

Above: Quarterback Jim McMahon prepares to hand off the ball during a game against the Packers at Soldier Field. McMahon, who was despised by Packers fans when he was with the Bears from 1982 to 1988, spent part of the 1995 season and all of the 1996 season with the Packers. (Photo: Vernon J. Biever) *Right*: Packer fans at Lambeau Field show what they think of the Bears by building this centerpiece for their tailgate party. (Photo: Mike DeVries/ The Capital Times)

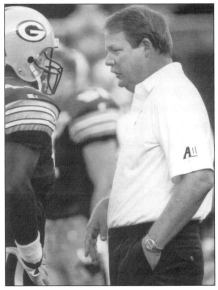

Top: Quarterbacks Brett Favre of the Packers and Erik Kramer of the Bears acknowledge each other as they leave Lambeau Field following the Packers' 35-28 victory in 1995. (Photo: Vernon J. Biever)

Above, left: Safety LeRoy Butler returns an interception against the Bears.

Above, right: Coach Mike Holmgren offers encouragement during a timeout of a Bears-Packers contest. (Photos: Mike DeVries/The Capital Times)

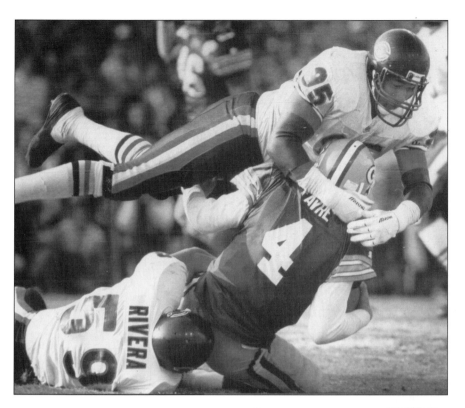

Top: Richard Dent and Ron Rivera smother Brett Favre during the Bears' 30-10 victory in 1992 at Lambeau Field.
Right: Reggie White celebrates the Packers' 28-17 victory over the Bears at Lambeau in 1996, during the Packers' Super Bowl drive. (Photos: Mike DeVries/ the Capital Times)

Coach Mike Ditka watches from the sidelines during a Bears-Packers game.
The Bears won fifteen of twenty games against the Packers during Ditka's
stint as head coach from 1982 to 1992.
(Photo: Mike DeVries/The Capital Times)

Chapter 7

Scores of Anecdotes

When two football teams play each other more than 150 times in a rivalry that involves, over a period of three-quarters of a century, more than 2,000 players . . . well, great stories and fascinating bits of trivia are bound to pile up.

This chapter unpiles them, in chronological order.

THE LEATHER-HELMET ERA

Bobby Cahn, who stood just 5 feet 1½ inches, was the referee in the first two Bears-Packers games. Cahn served as a referee in the NFL from 1921 to 1942. In all, he worked nearly twenty Bears-Packers regular-season games. From 1933 through 1937, he was the referee in ten of eleven games between the two teams.

Tackle Ed Healey was one of the first—if not the first—professional football players to have his contract sold to another team. George Halas purchased Healey from the Rock Island Independents for one hundred dollars in 1922. Halas acquired Healey two days after playing against him and finding it difficult to block him. Had Halas not purchased the contract, Healey's name might adorn the walls of Lambeau Field with the names of other ex-Packers now in the Pro Football Hall of Fame. Healey, a 6-foot-3, 220-pound tackle, played with the Bears from 1922 to 1927 and was inducted into the Hall in 1964.

Years later, Healey told writer Myron Cope, author of *The Game That Was*, that Rock Island had concluded its season when it lost to the Bears. "Green Bay, however, was planning several more games and my own intention was to go up to Green Bay and play the rest of the season for the Packers," said Healey. Instead, he followed instructions and reported to the Bears.

Hall of Famer Red Grange once said of Healey: "He was an absolutely vicious football player."

The first time the Packers beat the Bears was at Bellevue Park on September 21, 1924. The score was 5-0 and the game was listed in the NFL record book until 1974 as being part of the series between the two teams. While the game wasn't billed as an exhibition at the time, it didn't count in the official league standings, either. Thus, the NFL corrected the error after the 1974 season.

One of the more memorable moments of what is now listed as an exhibition game occurred at halftime when the crowd could hear George Halas, then a player-coach, profanely yelling at his backs for misplaying Cub Buck's punts.

The *Green Bay Press-Gazette* reported that one of Papa Bear's players didn't take kindly to the tirade and issued a challenge: "Come back yourself and try when the big fellow kicks. The pigskin looks like a pea in the sky."

Green Bay's victory over Chicago in 1924 was anything but a financial success. In early September, the Packers announced that ticket sales were off about one hundred from the previous year and that they were short about two thousand dollars. The game against the Bears figured to help, but the Packers' board of directors also decided it would be best to protect themselves in the event of bad weather. So they paid an additional premium to increase their rain insurance to three thousand dollars.

As it turned out, the Packers were on the receiving end of a double dose of bad luck. A heavy morning cloudburst kept the size of the crowd down, but, at the same time, it didn't rain enough between 9:00 A.M. and 3:00 P.M., when the Packers' policy was in effect, to collect on the insurance. The policy stipulated that it needed to rain one-tenth of an inch during that six-hour period. More than an inch of rain fell from 6:00 A.M. to 9:00 A.M., but only seven one-hundredths of an inch after that.

Thus, the Packers missed out on collecting a desperately needed three thousand dollars by three one-hundredths of an inch.

The first players ejected from a Bears-Packers game—based on newspaper accounts—were Frank Hanny and Walter "Tillie" Voss. Hanny, the Bears' left end, and Voss, the Packers' right end, were tossed out of the third meeting between the teams on November 23, 1924, for fighting.

"Towards the close of the first half, Hanny paid Tilly (sic) Voss a verbal barrage and Voss came back. The result was that hostilities broke and both players were chased to the sidelines," George Whitney Calhoun reported under his byline "Cal" in the next day's *Press-Gazette*.

Hanny also was ejected from the 1926 game in Chicago for fighting with Dick O'Donnell of the Packers.

Joe Carr, one of the founders of the NFL in 1920 and its president from 1921 to 1939, attended the 1925 Bears-Packers game in Chicago. He was there, in part, because the Packers had lodged a complaint two weeks earlier after losing to the Chicago Cardinals. They claimed that it was nearly impossible for a visiting team to win in Chicago because of biased officials.

Carr, a charter enshrinee in the Pro Football Hall of Fame, continued to frequent Bears-Packers games in both Chicago and Green Bay throughout his tenure. All of Carr's successors—president Carl Storck; and commissioners Elmer Layden, Bert Bell, Pete Rozelle, and Paul Tagliabue—also have attended Bears-Packers games.

Rozelle, commissioner from 1960 to 1989, was on hand in 1969 to help celebrate the Packers' golden anniversary, the launching of their fifty-first season, and the NFL's fiftieth season. Rozelle addressed the fans at Lambeau Field at halftime, but kept his speech brief. "It hasn't taken me one hundred games to realize the last place to be during a Packer-Bear game is in the middle of the field," he said before quickly relinquishing the microphone.

The immortal Red Grange spent his first day with the Bears watching a game against the Packers in Cubs Park, now Wrigley Field. Wearing a stylish raccoon coat, Grange watched from the sideline as the Bears manhandled the Packers, 21-0, in frigid, snowy conditions. Introduced at halftime, Grange received a rousing ovation from the crowd of 6,898.

Grange signed with the Bears the Sunday morning of the game, November 22, 1925, giving the NFL its first big-name attraction. The previous day, he helped the University of Illinois edge Ohio State, 14-9, before 85,000 fans in Columbus, Ohio.

The Bears also announced on Sunday that Grange would make his pro debut against the Chicago Cardinals on Thanksgiving, five days after the Bears-Packers game. The next day, football fans in Chicago stormed The Loop to buy tickets for the game priced at $1.75.

The Bears-Cardinals game drew 36,000 fans, the largest crowd in pro football history up to that point, and kicked off what was in essence a second season for the Bears. The terms of Grange's contract called for the Bears to embark upon a barnstorming tour that would last a little more than two months, cover more than ten thousand miles, and include eighteen games.

Grange played his first game in Green Bay in October, 1927, but as a member of the New York Yankees. The game attracted eleven thousand fans, at that time the largest crowd ever to witness a pro football game in Green Bay. C.C. Pyle, Grange's agent, had formed the Yankees and the American Football League in 1926 when Halas wouldn't give his client a slice of the team. The AFL folded after one season, but the Yankees joined the NFL in 1927. Oddly, Grange tore up his knee that season in a game against the Bears.

With Grange sitting out the 1928 season because of the injury, the Yankees drew poorly and folded at the end of the year. Grange rejoined the Bears in 1929 and played with them in Green Bay for the first time that fall. The game attracted thirteen thousand fans, another record crowd for the Packers.

But Grange never fully recovered from his knee injury. He had more of an impact as a defensive player than an offensive player during the last six years of his career. "Red was like a show horse," said George Musso, a Hall of Fame lineman with the Bears who played with Grange for two seasons. "He was the drawing card. He was a good ballplayer.

He was a ballhawk. But they didn't play him that much. Your drawing card, you're going to protect it."

When the Packers met the Bears on December 9, 1928, in Chicago, they had been on the road, traveling by train, for nearly a month. The Packers departed Green Bay on November 15 for five consecutive road games against the New York Giants, Pottsville Maroons, Frankford Yellowjackets, Providence Steam Roller, and the Bears. They spent the early part of the week, prior to the Bears game, practicing in Atlantic City, New Jersey.

The Packers arrived in Chicago two days before the game and beat the Bears, 6-0. Quarterback Joseph "Red" Dunn threw a long pass to end Dick O'Donnell with less than two minutes to play for the winning touchdown.

Cal Hubbard, a mountain of a man in his day at 6 feet 5 inches and 250 pounds, was ejected in the closing minutes of the Packers' 14-0 victory over the Bears in 1929. Hubbard was tossed for punching Bears lineman Bill Fleckenstein.

This is how *Chicago Tribune* sportswriter Wilfrid Smith described the tiff: "Fleckenstein, with enthusiasm and in quite legal fashion, smacked Hubbard above the eye. On the next play, Hubbard led with his right, which may be poor boxing, but it came close to being taps for Bill."

Hubbard is the only man selected to both the Pro Football Hall of Fame and the National Baseball Hall of Fame. He played tackle in the NFL from 1927 through 1933 and again from 1935 to 1936, spending six of his nine seasons with the Packers. He was selected to the Baseball Hall of Fame for his work as an umpire in the American League after he finished his football career.

It was during a Bears-Packers game that Johnny Blood McNally was given the nickname "The Vagabond Halfback." So claimed the late Oliver Kuechle, a sportswriter with *The Milwaukee Journal* for forty-seven years.

McNally was a free-wheeling, free-spirited halfback, who played with the Packers from 1929 to 1933 and again from 1935 to 1936.

"I happened to give it to him under circumstances that amounted to comic relief in a particularly bitter game between the Bears and Packers in Green Bay some years ago," Kuechle wrote in 1945. "The score was tied, only a couple of minutes remained and the Packers were in the midst of a touchdown drive down near the ten- or fifteen-yard line when time was taken out. A lot of the boys sprawled in exhaustion on the ground and the crowd was tense as only a Packer crowd at a Bear game can be. That is, everybody in the stadium was exhausted or tense except Blood. To Johnny, it was just another game, and while during the timeout, a loud-speaker blared a catchy tune. Johnny pulled off to one side and did a clever jig. Only a vagabond at heart could do that."

McNally was a charter inductee into the Pro Football Hall of Fame in 1963.

Mickey Walker, world middleweight boxing champion from 1926 to 1931, was in attendance at Wrigley Field on November 9, 1930, when the Packers edged the Bears, 13-12. Speaking over the public address system at halftime, Walker told the crowd, "After seeing these two teams play, I don't think my racket is very tough."

Verne Lewellen was one of the Packers' all-time greats and a key to their winning three straight NFL titles from 1929 through 1931. Lewellen played in the backfield, but also was considered the premier punter of his era.

Years later, Francis "Jug" Earpe, a center with the Packers, recalled how in a game in 1930, he and future Hall of Fame tackle William "Link" Lyman of the Bears exchanged words on the field. The Packers were leading by a narrow margin when Lyman, according to Earpe, guaranteed that the Bears were going to rally to win.

Moments later, Lewellen pinned the Bears inside their five-yard line with one of his patented booming punts.

"In running down under the punt," Earpe said almost twenty years later, "I said to Lyman, 'Where are all those scores you were going to get?' And he came back with, 'What would you do without Lewellen?'

"'I don't need to know, Link,' I hollered back to him. 'We've got 'im.'"

The late August "Iron Mike" Michalske played eleven seasons of pro football, including eight with the Packers, and often played the full sixty minutes of a game. Out of those countless plays, one stood out in his memory.

On November 1, 1931, at Wrigley Field, Michalske rambled 80 yards with an interception to score the only touchdown as the Packers beat the Bears, 6-2. Michalske scored in the second quarter after teammate Cal Hubbard batted a Carl Brumbaugh pass in his direction.

Michalske was inducted into the Pro Football Hall of Fame in 1964.

When Hall of Fame quarterback Arnie Herber was involved in an automobile accident on December 7, 1933, three days before the Packers met the Bears at Wrigley Field, he suffered serious injuries, but little damage to his reputation. In today's world, Herber, in all likelihood, would have been arrested by the police, villified by the media, and maybe even suspended by the NFL.

Herber, a future Hall of Famer, was involved in the accident at 4:30 A.M., the Thursday before the game, and was unable to play the following Sunday. Herber dislocated his right hip, injured his right forearm, and sustained a four-inch laceration on the left side of his face when he drove into the rear of a truck near the De Pere city limits.

The *Press-Gazette* carried a story about the accident the day it occurred, but made no further mention of it before the game. There also was no mention in the story about whether Herber might have been driving under the influence of alcohol.

The loss of Herber left the Packers with only seventeen players for the Bears game. Thirteen of them played, including nine who went the full sixty minutes, as the Packers lost, 7-6.

The Bears considered Charles "Buckets" Goldenberg to be one of the Packers' toughest players in the years before World War II. Goldenberg started his career with the Packers in 1933 as a fullback, but later moved to guard and played through the 1945 season.

"Gee, whiz, can that Buckets hit," end Bill Hewitt of the Bears said after the third game between the two teams in 1933. "I'm sure glad this fracas is over with."

Hewitt had played a hero's role in the first two games of 1933. In the first game between the teams in 1934, Hewitt was a standout again. Goldenberg, still playing fullback, also played well, but was knocked out of the game at one point.

"Buckets hit and hit hard, smashed with everything he had until he had to retire late in the game, nearly punch-drunk from a terrific beating taken in the course of his plunges," Arthur W. Bystrom wrote in the *Press-Gazette* the next day.

In 1936, when the two teams met in Green Bay, Goldenberg was side-lined with his foot in a cast. Nonetheless, he and Hewitt were still going at it. After one verbal exchange, Hewitt invited Goldenberg to enter the fray. Goldenberg tersely replied from the sideline, "I wish I could, monkey-face. There's nothing I would like better."

Wayland Becker was the first Green Bay native to play for the Bears. An end, Becker played one season with them in 1934. Later, Becker played three seasons with the Packers, from 1936 to 1938.

A 1934 mid-season exhibition game between the Packers and Bears offered a little bit of everything: a winner-takes-all purse, a historical first, and a bizarre ending.

The game was played at State Fair Park in Milwaukee on October 17, 1934. It was the first night game between the teams and the first meeting between the teams in Milwaukee. It ended with a fan taking a punch at a referee.

Joe Carr, president of the NFL, refused to authorize the game as a league contest because the arrangements were made after the schedule came out. The teams had scaled back to two regular-season games that year after playing three from 1928 through 1933. To hype the game, the Packers and Bears agreed that a thousand dollars would be set aside and divided among the players on the winning team. The players on the losing team would get nothing.

The game drew ten thousand fans and the Bears won, 10-6. It was a typically hard-hitting game, but free of any irrational acts of violence until the two teams were walking off the field. At that point, an unnamed fan delivered the only cheap shot of the night. The fan ran up to head linesman George Lawrie and nailed him with a right to the jaw. Lawrie was sent sprawling to the ground, and the fan disappeared through a gate before anyone took notice.

Al Simmons and Grover Cleveland Alexander, members of the Baseball Hall of Fame, were two notable spectators during the 1930s and 1940s. Simmons, a native of Milwaukee, attended a Bears-Packers game at Wrigley Field in 1935, when he was playing outfield for the Chicago White Sox. Simmons was inducted into the Hall of Fame in 1953. Alexander attended the Packers-Bears game in Green Bay in 1942, four years after he had been inducted into the Hall of Fame. Alexander, who pitched in the majors from 1911 to 1930, had a speaking engagement the next day at nearby Pulaski High School.

Emmet Platten, the Green Bay fan who ran out on the field in 1936 and threw a punch at Ted Rosequist of the Bears, wrote a letter to the *Press-Gazette* that appeared two days after the game. Platten defended his actions, claiming he went on the field to argue with an official, and that Rosequist had gotten in his way.

"For three long years I have battled to get some officials into the league who will not get overly friendly with Mr. Halas, but it is not in the cards," Platten wrote. "I have done everything in my power to bring it to the attention of our directors. Some of the worst officials have been eliminated, but some of the known horse thieves are still assigned to us in the Western Division."

The Bears and Packers played two exhibition games at Gilmore Stadium in Los Angeles following the 1936 season. Both games turned into vicious bloodbaths.

In those days, it was not uncommon for NFL teams to go on postseason tours, playing games to raise money for their coffers. It was unusual, however, for teams to go at each other as savagely as the Bears and Packers did.

The first game was played on January 24, 1937, and ended in a 20-20 tie. Curly Lambeau wrote a byline story about the game for the next day's *Press-Gazette*, and his lead paragraph read: "Yesterday's Packer-Bear football game was one of the roughest I ever witnessed."

Quarterback Arnie Herber had his nose broken after throwing a touchdown pass early in the first quarter. He left the field holding his nose with one hand and using the other to shake a menacing fist at whomever had slugged him. In the second quarter, tackle Lou Gordon of the Packers and halfback Beattie Feathers of the Bears were caught trading punches and banished from the field. Moments later, before the officials were able to restore order, tackle Joe Stydahar of the Bears left the bench and took a swing at Gordon. Later, Buckets Goldenberg of the Packers took a swing at Jack Manders of the Bears.

In addition to Herber's broken nose, running back Johnny Sisk of the Bears suffered a dislocated and badly broken thumb that required surgery after the game.

"Physical! You aren't kidding," said Chester "Swede" Johnston, one of the Packers' fullbacks at the time. "Sisk broke his thumb right off tackling somebody. It was the damndest thing you ever saw. It was just dangling there."

Herm Schneidman, another of the Packers' backs, said the players later heard that Halas had approached Lambeau before the game, requesting that the Packers, who had just won the NFL championship, take it easy on his team and that Lambeau had agreed to do so. But Halas, Schneidman said, double-crossed Lambeau and told his players just the opposite—that the Packers were out to embarrass them.

"So they were all heated up," said Schneidman. "I know on the first three plays, we had a guy knocked out. We were wondering, 'What the hell is going on?' We decided this is for real. Then, we played them again the next week. I think between the two games there were something like twenty guys treated in the hospital."

The Los Angeles fans clamored for a rematch after the first game and the two teams arranged to play again on January 31. This time, the Packers prevailed, 17-14; and, again, both teams suffered a number of casualties.

One was Bronko Nagurski, who suffered a deep gash on his leg. "They brought the ambulance right out on the field," recalled Johnston. "They took him to the hospital and sewed him up. In the second half, he was back out there."

The Bears had three Hall of Fame linemen who all played from the mid-1930s to mid-1940s. George Musso played tackle and guard from 1933 to 1944. Dan Fortmann played guard from 1936 to 1943. Joe Stydahar was a tackle from 1936 to 1942 and again from 1945 to 1946.

Musso was a bull at 6 feet 2 inches and 270 pounds, recalled Tom Greenfield, who broke in with the Packers as a center in 1939. Greenfield stood 6 feet 4 inches, but weighed a mere 209. He faced Musso for the first time in his second game as a pro.

"I centered the ball back to Clarke Hinkle, our fullback, and, hell, I knocked him down," said Greenfield. "Hinkle said, 'What the hell are you doing back here?' I said, 'You're not playing against Musso.' Musso knocked me so hard, it was pitiful."

Fortmann was undersized at 6 feet, 210, but a master of the submarine block. He also was one of the few Bears that the Packers never squawked about.

"Now, there was a gentleman," said Hal Van Every, a halfback with the Packers in 1940 and 1941. "Everyone liked him."

At 6 feet 4 inches and 230 pounds, Stydahar was another large lineman for that era. He also was the most despised of the three, in part because of the two exhibition games in California. Bob Snyder, who joined the Bears two years later and eventually served as an assistant coach under Curly Lambeau, said the Packers blamed Stydahar for breaking Arnie Herber's nose in the first of the two games.

"Joe threw a forearm and hit him and really cut his face bad," said Snyder. "I think the bad blood started at that time. But he wasn't dirty. Joe was just a great tackle."

George McAfee, a great breakaway runner for the Bears, returned a kickoff ninety-three yards for a touchdown in the first quarter of his first game against the Packers in 1940. The touchdown sparked a 41-10 victory. McAfee also ran nine yards for another touchdown and passed for a third.

McAfee was a nemesis to the Packers throughout his eight-year career, which was interrupted by World War II.

"I've made the statement several times. I think he's the greatest all-around football player I ever saw," said Clyde "Bulldog" Turner, a Hall of Fame lineman who played with the Bears from 1940 to 1952. "He was like a ghost out there. You couldn't get a hold of him."

McAfee was inducted into the Pro Football Hall of Fame in 1966.

Three days before the Packers and Bears opened the season against each other in Green Bay in 1943, Don Hutson's father died in Pine Bluff, Arkansas. Hutson also learned at the same time that his brother, Robert, had been reported as killed in action in the South Pacific. After learning of the two deaths in a phone conversation with his mother, Hutson decided to play that Sunday before heading home.

A grief-stricken Hutson caught two passes for forty yards, including a 26-yard touchdown in the fourth quarter that allowed the Packers to tie the Bears, 21-21.

Funeral services for Roy Hutson, Don's father, were held the following day.

Hall of Fame quarterback Sid Luckman was a surprise participant for the Bears when they played in Green Bay in 1944, at the height of World War II. It was the Bears' season opener, and the Packers' second game. Luckman, an ensign in the United States Merchant Marine, was stationed at Sheepshead Bay, New York. He gained permission to play from his commanding officer and flew to Chicago just in time to catch the train to Green Bay the day before the game.

Rusty from inactivity, Luckman had a miserable day. He threw three interceptions as the Bears lost, 42-28.

"I'll tell you something," said Luckman, "that was the most awful beating I've ever taken. They were screaming on the sidelines that I was a draft dodger. Whew! The fans got on me. And I looked at the Packers and thought, 'What the hell are they all doing here?' I was in the service. But they got on me and they beat the hell out of us that day."

The next day, Luckman had to return to his base. But six weeks later, he was again on hand as the Bears gained revenge with a 21-0 victory over the Packers. This time, Luckman's return wasn't the result of last-minute planning, although it no doubt was tied to the Green Bay game.

He also played the week before against the Cleveland Rams after returning from a 7,500-mile voyage on a Navy tanker.

When Curly Lambeau learned two days before the first game in 1944 that Sid Luckman would be playing quarterback for the Bears, his only comment was, "I wish I had Tony Canadeo."

Lo and behold, when the Packers and Bears met again on November 5, Canadeo was in uniform, on leave from the army. Canadeo had returned from the service in mid-October for the birth of his oldest son and wound up playing in three games, the last of which was against the Bears.

"I wouldn't have made all three of those games if Ruthie hadn't had a convenient relapse after having the baby," Canadeo was quoted as saying years later. "Dr. R.M. Cowles was a good friend of the coach, Curly Lambeau, and he said, 'You can't go back yet. Your wife is too ill.' And he called the Red Cross to get my furlough extended."

After the game in Chicago, Canadeo went straight to the railroad station and headed to Fort Bliss, Texas. From there, he was sent to England, where he said he learned about the Packers winning the 1944 NFL title by reading it in *Stars and Stripes.*

THE POST-WAR YEARS

The name Cliff Aberson, starting left halfback for the Packers when they played at Wrigley Field in 1946, is the answer to an obscure trivia question. He played with both the Packers and the Chicago Cubs. Aberson played just that one season with the Packers. He played 63 games, mostly as an outfielder, for the Cubs from 1947 to 1949.

Pid Purdy was a back for the Packers from 1926 to 1927. He also played outfield for the Chicago White Sox in 1926.

A brief ceremony was held before the 1946 Bears-Packers game in Wrigley Field to honor Young Bussey. A backup quarterback for the Bears in 1940 and 1941, Bussey was the Bears' only casualty in World War II. He was killed in the Phillipines in March, 1945. Taps were blown in honor of Bussey just before kickoff.

Howard Johnson, who played with the Packers in 1940 and 1941, was killed in action at Iwo Jima. He was the Packers' only casualty of the war.

Jim Thorpe, considered by many to be the greatest athlete of all time, watched from the stands at Wrigley Field in 1947 when the Bears edged the Packers, 20-17. Thorpe was living in California at the time. He died in 1953.

Gene Ronzani played for the Bears for eight seasons in the 1930s and 1940s, and also served as an assistant coach for three years under George Halas. So he had first-hand knowledge of how the Bears operated when he became head coach of the Packers in 1950.

As a result, paranoia dictated his every move.

He wouldn't even give his players a playbook out of fear that it might wind up in Chicago.

"It was the most ridiculous thing I ever heard," said Fred Cone, a fullback with the Packers from 1951 to 1957. "When we went to training camp and he was putting in the offense, we'd put in maybe twenty plays in one meeting at night. The way he did it, he had a great big plexiglass sheet and he'd hold it up. He'd have the name of the play on top and hold it up for about ten seconds, just long enough for a guy to see what his assignment was. He'd get that and that's all he'd get. You'd never see that play written down again. In case you got traded, he didn't want you to know the plays. He just wanted you to know your assignment."

Before the Packers played the Bears, Ronzani also would take extra precautions at practice. The Packers worked out at the time at Joannes Stadium, a minor-league baseball park located across from old City Stadium. The park had a wooden fence along the first- and third-base lines.

"Because Ronzani was highly suspicious of Halas, he'd have all the hurt guys stand in front of the knotholes and the splits in the fence," said Cone. "And they couldn't move the whole practice."

If Ronzani didn't have extra players available for the assignment, he would do it himself. "He wouldn't even be around," said Deral Teteak, a linebacker with the Packers from 1952 to 1956. "He'd be plugging up holes in the walls, looking outside; looking here, looking there; an airplane would fly over, he'd stop practice. He was really paranoid. He used to say, 'They're around here somewhere, I know they are. They always did it when I was there.'"

Ronzani also resorted to gimmicks more than any other coach in the history of the rivalry. Ronzani coached the Packers from 1950 until the final two games of the 1953 season, a stretch when their talent was appreciably inferior to that of the Bears.

When the Packers opened the season against the Bears in 1951, Ronzani unveiled an offense in which only the quarterback and fullback lined up in the backfield. The halfbacks split out as receivers. The Packers unleashed thirty-eight passes in the game, but lost, 31-20. Tony Canadeo, a Hall of Fame halfback, never carried the ball from scrimmage.

"Gene sprang a surprise on us," coach George Halas said with a wry smile after the game. "It was a good one. We were ready for his double flanker, but not his flanker plus the fullback in motion."

In 1951, when the Packers invaded Wrigley Field, Ronzani employed a one-back, spread offense. Quarterback Tobin Rote lined up four yards behind the center, while both halfbacks and the fullback spread wide, similar to today's shotgun formation.

Rote, as one would expect, had a busy day. He rushed for 150 yards in fourteen carries and completed ten of thirty-three passes for eighty-eight yards. He accounted for all but twenty-three of the Packers' 261 total yards. However, he also had two costly fumbles in the second half and, again, the Packers lost, 24-13.

Ronzani had another surprise for the Bears in the 1952 game at Wrigley Field. He alternated Tobin Rote and Babe Parilli at quarterback, hoping to keep the Bears' defense off balance. Rote was more of a running threat and deep passer, whereas Parilli was more adept at quick throws and pitchouts.

This time the strategy paid off. The Packers stunned the Bears by driving eighty yards for a touchdown on their first possession—Rote guided the offense over the first forty-nine yards and Parilli the last thirty-one—and went on to register a 41-28 victory.

Before the Packers played host to the Bears in the 1952 season opener, Art Daley of the *Press-Gazette* noted in his column: "Real bear meat will be served at Town and Country club for noon lunches before

Sunday's game. Proprietor Danny Griffin got the meat from a hunting friend up north—not in Chicago."

Hall of Fame running back Tony Canadeo played eleven years with the Packers, most of them after their fall from power. He joined the Packers in 1941, when they were one of the dominant teams in the league. By the time he retired in 1952, the Packers hadn't had a winning record in five seasons.

But Canadeo cried tears of joy after his final Packers-Bears game. The Packers won, 41-28, in Wrigley Field and he was given the game ball after leading them in rushing with sixty-one yards in eleven carries. Standing in the locker room, with blood and tears running down his face, Canadeo said between sobs, "Well, I said we were going to beat 'em today—my first year and my last year."

The Packers' victory that day was their first in Wrigley since Canadeo's rookie season. In between, he had been part of nine losing efforts and had missed one other game while he was in service.

Canadeo, who grew up on the northwest side of Chicago, retired after the season with George Halas' blessing. "To me, Canadeo is just tremendous and it's a pleasure to see him go," said Halas. "He's the greatest competitor I know."

In the early 1950s, the trains that left Green Bay for Chicago the weekend of the Bears-Packers game were usually jampacked with fans. "There would be as many as three thousand fans going to Chicago for a game," said Lee Remmel, who covered the Packers for the *Press-Gazette* at the time. "They'd leave early Sunday morning and arrive back after midnight—it was at least a five-hour trip each way—but nobody ever complained."

Sometimes, the fans and players would mingle in the bar car on the way back, but Remmel remembered only one time when there was a problem.

"I remember a confrontation between Dick Afflis and a fan," Remmel said. "A fan got obnoxious, and Dick Afflis was nobody to get obnoxious with. He broke off a beer bottle on the bar and said, 'OK, come after me.' Of course, that ended that discussion abruptly."

Afflis, a burly six-foot, 252-pound lineman, played with the Packers from 1951 to 1954, before going onto greater fame as a pro wrestler with the stage name Dick the Bruiser.

When the Bears lost to the Packers, 41-28, at Wrigley Field on November 9, 1952, they scored their first two touchdowns on kickoff returns. Leon Campbell, a second-year fullback from Arkansas, returned one eighty-six yards for a touchdown in the first quarter. Eddie Macon, a second-round draft pick that year out of the College of Pacific, returned another eighty-nine yards for a touchdown in the third quarter.

Only twice in club history have the Bears returned two kickoffs for touchdowns in the same game. Both times, they did it against the Packers. The other time was September 22, 1940, when George McAfee and Ray Nolting scored on returns of ninety-three and ninety-seven yards, respectively.

When Gene Ronzani resigned under fire with two games remaining in the 1953 season, many Packers fans felt the move was long overdue. In fact, when the Packers' executive committee hired Ronzani, it wasn't a popular decision. The people in Green Bay refused to embrace someone as Curly Lambeau's successor who had played and coached for the Bears.

"Green Bay never got along with Gene Ronzani," said former linebacker Deral Teteak. "They had other people in mind to be the coach other than an ex-Bear. If they wanted to hire someone there were a lot of ex-Packers around."

Ronzani didn't improve his popularity by hiring almost all ex-Bears—Ray Nolting, Dick Plasman, Tarzan Taylor, Scooter McLean and Chuck Drulis—as assistant coaches during his four-year tenure.

Ronzani also regularly picked up ex-Bears off the waiver wire. "Every time the Bears cut somebody, we'd bring them in," said former defensive tackle Dave Hanner. "We had as many ex-Bears as we did Packers: Ray Bray, Washington Serini, Jim Keane, among others."

Veryl Switzer broke the Packers' team record for longest punt return against the Bears on November 7, 1954. He returned a punt ninety-three yards for a touchdown as the Packers dropped a 28-23 decision at Wrigley Field. Almost twenty years later to the day, Steve Odom broke Switzer's record when he returned a punt ninety-five yards against the Bears. Odom's return sparked a 20-3 victory for the Packers on November 10, 1974, at Milwaukee County Stadium.

One of the wildest games in the history of the rivalry took place on November 6, 1955, at Wrigley Field. The Bears led, 45-3, with thirteen minutes, thirty-three seconds left in the game. The final score was Bears 52, Packers 31. The eighty-three points still stands as the series record for most combined points.

Some of the more fascinating statistics from the game included the following: the Bears rushed for 406 yards, still the second-highest one-game total in club history; fullback Rick Casares and halfback Bobby Watkins of the Bears each rushed for 115 yards; the Bears recovered four fumbles; the Packers intercepted five passes; and the Bears never punted.

The gamesmanship between the Bears and Packers has rarely been inspired by rational thinking and fair play.

Before games in 1954 and 1955 at City Stadium, the Packers asked that the Bears wear white jerseys with their white pants. The reason for the request was that the Packers had switched from green to navy blue jerseys, the same color as the Bears. Both years, Halas refused to cooperate.

"There was quite a rhubarb about that, but Halas was the big boss in those days and if he said 'no,' that's the way it went," said former Packers linebacker Deral Teteak. "We both wore the same colored jerseys, but we had different colored helmets."

The advent of television finally lent some reason to the dispute, forcing the teams to wear contrasting colors.

The first Packers-Bears game to be televised in Green Bay was played on November 11, 1956, at Wrigley Field. The first game in the rivalry telecast back to Chicago was the first game ever played in what is now Lambeau Field in 1957.

It has been more than forty years since the Packers' Al Carmichael returned a kickoff 106 yards against the Bears, but he still shares the NFL record. Two players have matched Carmichael's record, but nobody has broken it. Noland Smith of Kansas City returned a kickoff 106 yards in 1967 and Roy Green of the St. Louis Cardinals did it in 1979.

Carmichael set the record on October 7, 1956, in the last Packers-Bears game ever played at old City Stadium. Carmichael's return tied the score, 7-7, but the Bears went on to win, 37-21.

"I remember it very well because I was late getting to the stadium that day and we were always instructed not to run the ball out of the end zone under any circumstances," said Carmichael. "Ironically, I had a fairly big argument with Lisle Blackbourn (the Packers' head coach at the time) just prior to running on the field. So I told the other receiver that I didn't care where the ball was, I was going to run it out. He kept cautioning me not to. I said, 'I don't care.' So it all really began in a moment of anger more than anything."

Forrest Gregg, then a rookie lineman, threw the key block that sprang Carmichael free around the twenty-yard line.

The same day that the Packers christened what is now Lambeau Field, the New York baseball Giants played their final game at the Polo Grounds. The date was September 29, 1957. The Polo Grounds was the home of the Giants for sixty-eight years, and was one of the most storied ballparks in the history of the major leagues.

A capacity crowd of 32,132 watched the Packers beat the Bears, 21-17, that day. A crowd of 11,605 said good-bye to the Polo Grounds as the Pittsburgh Pirates beat the Giants, 9-1. The next year, the Giants moved to San Francisco.

Moments after the opening kickoff of the 1958 Packers-Bears game at what is now Lambeau Field, field announcer Clair Stone had some horrifying news for Norm Buckman, a fan from nearby Seymour.

"Norm Buckman, you are asked to go home immediately. Your house is on fire," Stone announced over the PA system.

In 1958, the Packers played the Bears one week after suffering the most lopsided loss in their history, a 56-0 thrashing at the hands of the Baltimore Colts. The loss left the Packers with a 1-4-1 record on the way to a 1-10-1 finish, their worst ever.

Coach Scooter McLean, in the days leading up to the game against the Bears, confessed that he had been too easy on his players and that they were taking advantage of him. He also vowed to get tough. "Quite a few of them stopped playing ball as soon as they had the squad made," McLean said. "They now know where they stand and what the results will be if they don't come through. New rules have been established."

The Packers gave a better effort against the Bears, but lost, 24-20. Still, it was enough for McLean to relax his new get-tough policy. After the game, Paul Hornung and Max McGee talked him into letting them stay over Sunday night in Chicago.

"Scooter said, 'All right. I'm going to let you guys stay, but I don't want to hear one thing about you getting in trouble,'" said McGee. "So we went to the Chez Paree where 'The Adorables' were the dancing group. Christ! Pretty soon, they're introducing us and it got into Kup's column that Hornung and McGee weren't too good in the game, but they were pretty good dancing with The Adorables. So we get back and Scooter fined us. Scooter was a heckuva guy, but getting tough was not his deal."

The Bears and Chicago Cardinals may have been crosstown rivals for four decades, but their rivalry never compared to Bears vs. Packers. The Bears-Cardinals rivalry started in 1920, making it the oldest in pro football. From 1933 through 1949, the Bears and Cardinals were in the same division and played each other twice a year. They battled it out for the Western Division title in 1947 and 1948.

It didn't matter. The Bears-Packers game was bigger.

"Oh, it was much bigger," Hall of Fame quarterback Sid Luckman said. "There was no comparison. The Cardinals beat us all the time because we didn't pay any attention to them. They were always a lousy team."

In truth, the Bears dominated the series when the two teams were in Chicago. They held a 45-19-6 advantage when the Cardinals moved to St. Louis in 1960.

THE LOMBARDI YEARS

Vince Lombardi did more than just change the fortunes of the Packers on the football field after taking over as head coach in 1959. He also turned a penurious franchise into a prosperous one.

One of the consequences was that it speeded up the inevitable. The train rides that added as much flavor to the Bears-Packers rivalry as the donnybrooks on the field became a thing of the past. In Lombardi's first season, the Packers rode a train to Chicago, but returned to Green Bay for the first time on a United Airlines charter. By 1962, both teams were flying to and from games in the respective cities.

After three decades of headquartering at the Knickerbocker Hotel during their annual excursions into Chicago, the Packers also upgraded their hotel accommodations. In Lombardi's second year, they moved to the luxurious Drake Hotel, a short walk across the street from the Knickerbocker.

One of the most exciting finishes in the rivalry occurred in the season opener in 1960, when John Aveni kicked a sixteen-yard field goal with thirty-five seconds remaining to give the Bears a 17-14 victory over Lombardi's Packers. The Bears scored all seventeen of their points in the fourth quarter to erase a 14-0 deficit.

While it was a rewarding victory for George Halas, he admonished the people of Green Bay for allowing a high school football game to be played in a heavy rain the Friday night before the game.

Halas said the field was in "deplorable condition." He also urged the city fathers to review their policy and cancel future high school games in the event of bad weather. "It would be like building a beautiful home and putting sawdust on the floors for carpeting," Halas said.

Lombardi expected—make that demanded—that his players play with pain. But even Lombardi was surprised when defensive tackle Dave Hanner declared himself fit to play in the first Packers-Bears game in 1961.

Hanner had undergone an appendectomy just twelve days prior to the October 1 meeting. But on Thursday, three days before kickoff and just nine days after his surgery, Hanner was hitting dummies on the practice field and itching to play.

Rookie Ron Kostelnik started at defensive tackle, but was replaced by Hanner when the Bears picked up two first downs on their first possession. Hanner stayed in the game and played admirably as the Packers shut out the Bears for the first time since 1935, 24-0.

"We played next to each other," said Willie Davis, the Packers' Hall of Fame defensive end. "I thought he was crazy at the time, but he played well. He was a football player extraordinaire."

Mike Pyle, who played center for the Bears for nine years, also has vivid memories of that game, his third as a professional. His twist to the story was that he was surprised when he discovered Hanner wasn't at his usual position.

"I was in total awe of the defensive team of the Packers," said Pyle. "Here I'm a rookie and it's early in the game, and I'm thinking I've got Henry Jordan on my left, Hawg Hanner on my right, and Ray Nitschke in front of me. I get over the ball and I hear this guy say, 'Hey, rook. Don't you dare come out after me. I'm going to kill you.' I'm afraid to look. I think it's Hawg Hanner. He wasn't my man, so I went after Nitschke or Jordan, but as soon as the play was over, I turned around to see who it was. I'm looking through my face mask and here it was Ron Kostelnik, another rookie."

When the 1961 season started, Bart Starr was still an untested quarterback in the eyes of some of his teammates. Drafted in the seventeenth round in 1956, Starr had taken over as the starting quarterback during the previous season and had helped guide the Packers to the NFL championship game. But he had displayed only flashes of the potential that would allow him to become a Hall of Fame quarterback.

The doubts were erased when the Packers shut out the Bears, 24-0, the third game of the season.

"Bill George was still playing middle linebacker for the Bears," said Jerry Kramer, who joined the Packers in 1958 and became a perennial all-pro guard. "Bart was kind of an unknown quantity to most of us. Very quiet, very polite, invisible almost. We didn't know what the hell Bart was made of. He just never said anything. He didn't kid much, didn't joke much; he was very private. So you never knew what kind of fire he had, what kind of competitor he was.

"We're playing the Bears and Bart threw a long pass down field. The ball was way down the field and we were both standing there watching it. The defensive tackle was standing there watching it. The play at the line of scrimmage was over. But Bill George came through intentionally and hit Bart in the face with a forearm. Knocked him on his ass and said, 'That ought to take care of you Starr, you pussy.' I looked over at Bart and his upper lip was split clear up into his nose. He gets up, sticks a finger out and says, 'Fuck you, Bill George! We're comin' after you!'

"Of course, that was the only time in my life I heard Bart use the F-word. I tell people he said bleep. The word bleep—Bart invented it. Anyway, he comes back to the huddle. We go, 'You better get that looked at.' He's bleeding all the way down the front of his jersey. He says, 'Huddle up.' He got loud, showed authority and took the club down for a score. Then, he went to the sidelines and got his face sewed up right there: six, eight stitches. They put a wrap over the stitches, patted him on the ass, and he went back in the ballgame. From that point on, I kinda said, 'Don't worry about Bart. He's got it. He'll be there.'"

October 1, 1961, was a memorable day in sports history. Roger Maris hit his sixty-first home run to break Babe Ruth's single-season record.

The following day, the editors of the *Chicago Tribune* ran the story about Maris' feat on the front page of the paper. In football-crazed Green Bay, the story wasn't even played on the front page of the sports section. It appeared on page two.

The entire front page of the sports section was devoted to the Packers-Bears game, except for a two-paragraph filler about a Lebanon Valley college football player who had died that weekend.

When the Packers beat the Bears, 31-28, on November 12, 1961, it gave them their first sweep of the series since 1935. They had beaten the Bears in the first game in Green Bay, 24-0.

In the second game, Paul Hornung kicked a 51-yard field goal in the third quarter to give the Packers a 31-7 lead before the Bears scored the final twenty-one points of the game.

Middle linebacker Ray Nitschke was given a weekend pass to play that Sunday. He had been called into active duty with the Army ten days earlier and was stationed at Fort Lewis, Washington. After the game, Hornung and wide receiver Boyd Dowler had to report to active duty: Hornung to Fort Riley, Kansas, and Dowler to Fort Lewis.

The three, however, received weekend passes the rest of the season, except on a handful of occasions, and continued to play a key role as the Packers won their first NFL championship since 1944.

It was after a trip to Green Bay that George Halas started having mandatory pre-game meals on Sunday mornings. Walking back from St. Willebrord Church to the Northland Hotel, Halas peeked in the window of Chili John's Restaurant, famous for its hot, greasy chili, and a popular haunt for visiting NFL players. Chili John's, at the time, was located in downtown Green Bay, just down the street from the Northland.

"He saw J.C. Caroline eating at Chili John's for breakfast," said Stan Jones, former Bears lineman. "That was the beginning of pre-game meals at the hotel. I'm serious. Before that we always ate on our own."

Halas, the master psychologist, met his match when Vince Lombardi became coach of the Packers. No longer was Papa Bear able to artfully win the mind games against the Packers' coaches that he had in the past. In fact, the tables were completely turned.

Soon after Lombardi arrived, Halas' players began to openly grumble that they were being out-coached in their twice-a-year battles. They even created their own code word, albeit not a very imaginative one, for their arch-rivals.

"A lot of guys on the team thought the coaches choked up before the Green Bay game," said Bob Wetoska, who played tackle for the Bears from 1960 to 1969. "They didn't want to get the coaches excited, so they used to call it 'Red Bay' instead of Green Bay."

No player was more outspoken about the supposed inadequacies of the Bears' coaches than was Hall of Fame defensive end Doug Atkins, who played with the Bears from 1955 to 1966. "When I got there, football was starting to pass the Bears by. Same old people, same old thing," said Atkins. "Halas had the same speech and everything. We had some good personnel, but if you don't put the round ones in the round ones and the square ones in the square ones, like Lombardi did, you've got problems. Our coaches couldn't compare with him. There was no way. I mean, we were out-coached from the time the game started until it was over."

The players might have called Green Bay, Red Bay. But Halas, too, had his own pet phrase to describe the Packers.

"With Halas, it was always the 'Packer pricks,'" said Wetoska. "That's what he used to call 'em."

Atkins was legendary for more than his talents on the football field. He had a reputation for hard living that was as gargantuan as his 6-foot-8, 275-pound frame.

Former Packers guard Jerry Kramer will attest to that after spending a night with Atkins in a Los Angeles watering hole before a Pro Bowl in the early 1960s. "Doug challenged Ron Kramer and I to a drinking contest," said Kramer. "Doug was just flapping his gums, teasin', givin' us bullshit, so we actually decided to have a drinking contest. Ron Kramer, Doug Atkins and I, and Tommy Davis, the kicker for the 49ers. We went to a bar at maybe 3:30 in the afternoon. Doug orders a martini. I said, 'I ain't going for that. Give me a scotch and water.' Ron Kramer said, 'I'll have the same thing.' Tommy says, 'I'm not gettin' in the contest, but I'll keep score.'

"So we sit there until 8:30, 9 o'clock and we had like twenty-seven drinks. Doug is having martinis. He'd get two or three behind and he'd go, 'Oh, bullshit. Gulp, gulp, gulp,' and catch up. About 9 o'clock, I say to Ron, 'I'm done. That's enough. I'm outta here.' Ron says, 'Me too.' So we awarded Doug the championship, but he stayed there another two hours.

"The next day we went to practice and everything was fine. Then, after practice, Doug went out to a race track. He was standing at the window, ready to make a bet, and he collapsed. He lost consciousness. They brought an ambulance, took him to the hospital and the doctor told him if he had another drink in the next year, he might die. We went down to see him and he gave us a big cussin.' 'You sons of bitches, now I can't even have a beer.'"

The Bears scored one of the greatest coups in franchise history during the week before the Bears-Packers game at Wrigley Field in 1964. The NFL draft was held the weekend before the game and the Bears used two of their three first-round picks to select future Hall of Famers Dick Butkus and Gale Sayers.

The draft was held during the season, in part because the NFL and rival American Football League were competing for players. But the Bears managed to sign both Butkus and Sayers over the next five days. Sayers spurned an offer from the AFL's Kansas City Chiefs, owned by millionaire Lamar Hunt. Butkus had been drafted by what were then the cash-poor Denver Broncos, but also entertained an offer from the New York Jets, which had acquired his AFL bidding rights.

Paul Hornung was one of Vince Lombardi's favorite players and also one of his favorite whipping boys. Hornung drew both Lombardi's wrath and a steep fine the night before the Packers played the Bears in Chicago in 1964. And it was all over a glass of water.

"There was a rule, we weren't allowed to sit at a bar. A stupid rule, but that was a Lombardi rule," said Hornung. "Anyway, I had a date in Chicago, a very attractive girl. I was meeting Ron Kramer and his wife for dinner, and we were going over to the Red Carpet. A friend of mine owned it. When we went in, they had this bar that seated about six people, an intimate little bar, and nobody was there. My date said, 'What a cute little bar, let's sit at the bar.' Well, I didn't want to explain to her that I couldn't sit there. Here I am, twenty-eight years old or something, and I've got to play kiddie time again.

"So I didn't say anything and, lo and behold, about ten minutes later in walks Lombardi with his whole entourage. He screamed and hollered, said I was suspended and fined. The girl didn't know what to think, but we had dinner, anyway. The next day, coach came up to me and said, 'I want to apologize for last night, but goddamnit, you better have a good day.'"

Hornung scored the first touchdown and kicked a field goal as the Packers beat the Bears, 17-3. And he did so with a clear head. The glass that was sitting in front of him when Lombardi walked in was filled with nothing but water.

"I wasn't drinking that night," said Hornung. "But the rule was you couldn't sit at the bar."

The first time the Bears and Packers played a regular-season game on a day other than Sunday was December 5, 1964. The two teams met in a nationally televised Saturday afternoon game at Wrigley Field, following a blizzard that dropped twelve inches of snow on Chicago.

Hall of Fame safety Willie Wood returned punts sixty-four and forty-two yards to set up touchdowns, and returned an interception twenty-eight yards to set up a field goal as the Packers won, 17-3.

Green Bay running back Jim Taylor also made history that day, gaining eighty-nine yards in twenty-one carries to become the first player in NFL history to rush for a thousand yards in five straight seasons.

Sid Luckman, Hall of Fame quarterback and longtime assistant coach with the Bears, witnessed countless tirades by George Halas. In fact, he observed so many of them, he finds it difficult to sort them out in his mind. Luckman holds a more vivid memory of an outburst by Vince Lombardi after the Packers beat the Bears, 23-14, at Lambeau Field in 1965.

The Packers built a 20-0 halftime lead, then sputtered to a 23-14 victory. Although they were never in serious danger of losing the game, the Packers were outgained by the Bears, 309 yards to 113, in the second half.

At the time, both the home and visiting locker rooms at Lambeau Field were located in the team's administration building at the north end of the stadium. So the teams were within earshot of one another. "Lombardi closed the door and we could hear him screaming and yelling," Luckman said. "I don't want to use the words he used, but he went on about what a terrible display they had put on in the second half. Oh, Jesus! He was screaming and yelling. After they had won! He really got on them."

Moments before his outburst, Lombardi had evicted reporters from the hallway outside the locker room and stood up the CBS television announcers, who were waiting for him to appear on a post-game show. Lombardi eventually met with reporters, but fed them nothing but terse answers. "Satisfied?" Lombardi snapped at one question. "How could I be satisfied? I guess we felt we had a couple of touchdowns and could just take a vacation out there."

CBS never did get its interview.

One of the CBS representatives nudged an assistant at one point and said, "Go get Lombardi for the post-game show." The assistant responded, "You want to go knock on the door and get him, go ahead. I'm not going in there after him."

It was in that same game in 1965 that Gale Sayers got his first pro-longed test as an NFL running back. After the Bears fell behind, 23-0, Sayers scored their two touchdowns: one on a six-yard run late in the third quarter, the other on a sixty-one-yard pass from quarterback Rudy Bukich.

Sayers, one of the most electrifying runners in the history of the NFL, had been a huge disappoinment up until then.

Chosen for the College All-Star Game, a summer exhibition that matched the defending NFL champions against the league's top rookies, Sayers landed in the doghouse of the team's coach, Hall of Fame quarterback Otto Graham. In a scrimmage against the Bears in Rensselaer, Indiana, Sayers limped off the field after running just a few plays. The medical staff found nothing wrong with him.

"This boy has as great a natural talent as any athlete I've seen," Graham said of Sayers at one point that summer. "But unless he changes his attitude, he'll never make the Bears because George Halas won't have him."

After joining the Bears, Sayers displayed flashes of brilliance in an exhibition game against the Los Angeles Rams, but played sparingly in the first two regular-season games. He entered the game against the Packers with just sixty-two yards in thirteen carries.

"Little known fact," said Stan Jones, who spent twelve years with the Bears as a player and another twenty-seven as an assistant coach in the NFL, "but after his first two games, they were thinking of trading him. I know this because I was a player-coach in '65 and I was in the coaches' locker room. George Allen was the head of personnel and George Halas said to him, 'Scout around and see what you can get for him.'"

Sayers finished the season with 867 yards in 166 carries, a 5.2 average. He scored twenty-two touchdowns, which still stands as an NFL record for rookies. He also was named the league's rookie of the year.

The Bears, in turn, rebounded from their 0-3 start and finished 9-5. One of their victories was a convincing 31-10 romp over the Packers in the seventh week of the season.

"This is a better Chicago Bears team than the Bears who won the 1963 National Football League championship," Lombardi said after the rematch in Wrigley Field.

Sayers wasn't the only young running back who caused the Packers fits in 1965. Andy Livingston, a six-foot, 234-pound fullback who signed with the Bears in 1964 when he was nineteen years old, following a brief stay at an Arizona junior college, rushed for 110 yards in just eleven carries in the two games in 1965.

Cooper Rollow of the *Chicago Tribune* went so far as to write after the second Bears-Packers game that Livingston "some day will be billed as the league's new Jim Brown." Greatness, however, eluded Livingston. He suffered a knee injury and didn't play in 1966. After playing sparingly in 1967 and early in the 1968 season, he was suspended by the Bears after deserting an October practice. He was subsequently traded to the New Orleans Saints and led them in rushing in 1969, but he lasted just one more season.

"Andy Livingston could have been a great, great back," said Ronnie Bull, a fellow running back with the Bears. "He just didn't have his head screwed on completely right. Then he got hurt and everything seemed to go downhill. He had a lot of talent, though. I saw him at 255 pounds run like a 4.5-second forty. Just unbelievable."

Most reporters assumed Lombardi was joking when he said with a smirk, "I thought they were lousy," when he was quizzed about his defense following a 17-0 victory over the Bears at Wrigley Field in 1966.

While the Packers held the Bears to six first downs and eighty-nine total yards, and Sayers to a mere twenty-nine yards rushing, Lombardi apparently wasn't kidding.

"We get in the locker room and we're all happy," said Dave Robinson, a linebacker with the Packers from 1963 to 1972. "But Vince came in and kicked a trash can across the room. He said the defense quit on him. He said, 'I'm going to have a whole new defense next week.' He just ripped us a new asshole."

What apparently upset Lombardi was that he wanted to take a good look at his two high-priced rookie running backs, Donny Anderson and

Jim Grabowski, and didn't get that chance because Willie Wood returned an interception for a touchdown early in the fourth quarter and the Bears' offense spent most of the time on the field. When asked about his pre-game plans after the game, Lombardi's terse response to a reporter was, "I had every intention of playing them, but like many good intentions, they just remained intentions."

Grabowski and Anderson played, but combined for only four carries.

Lombardi also may have had another motive for his outburst. The Packers were scheduled to play the Atlanta Falcons, a first-year expansion team, the following Sunday and Lombardi may have been thinking ahead, guarding against a letdown. As it turned out, either he had nothing to fear or his tongue-lashing produced the desired results; the Packers buried the Falcons, 56-3.

"Who knows what his reasons were?" said Robinson. "That's how he was. You never knew how he was going to react."

Ed McCaskey, the chairman of the board of the Bears, joined the organization in 1967 as vice president and treasurer. If he didn't know already, he quickly learned that his father-in-law, George Halas, and his brother-in-law, Mugs Halas, took nothing to chance in running the franchise.

"True story," said McCaskey. "My first day on the job, Mugs Halas called me into his office and said, 'What do you know about the National Football League?' I said, 'I know they play football and the Bears are in it.' He said, 'What do you know about the disaster plan?' I said, 'I never heard of it.' He said, 'Well, we have a disaster plan. Dad and I will always fly on the team plane. I want you to always fly commercial. Now, if the plane goes down, you are allowed to take any assistant coach as your head coach. Take Phil Bengtson of Green Bay. You are allowed to take any backup quarterback as your quarterback. Take Zeke Bratkowski of Green Bay. Now, each of the teams in the league has to give you three players. Just take whatever they give you because the rest of them don't matter. But here's the important thing: the week the plane goes down, you won't be able to play. Make sure you make up that game at the end of the year.'

"I said, 'Mugs, what if my plane goes down?' He said, 'Then, we don't have any problem.'"

The NFL realigned its teams into four divisions in 1967 and placed its four Midwest franchises—Chicago, Green Bay, Detroit, and Minnesota—in the Central Division of the Western Conference. The NFL and American Football League had agreed to a merger in 1966, but the two leagues retained separate identities until 1970.

Under the new format, the Packers and Bears settled the first Central Division title on November 26, 1967, at Wrigley Field. The Packers won, 17-13, and mathematically eliminated the Bears with three games left in the season.

Vince Lombardi, enjoying a rare moment of satisfaction, said after the game, "It feels great, frankly. It feels great." Veteran defensive end Willie Davis proclaimed, "We wanted this game as bad as any we have ever played."

Only Hall of Fame defensive tackle Henry Jordan sensed that the euphoria would be short-lived; that Lombardi wouldn't tolerate complacency with three weeks remaining in the regular season. "When we walk in there Tuesday," Jordan said, "Lombardi will glare at us like we're losers."

What made the victory so special was that it gave the Packers a chance to make history.

"It gave us a chance to win our third straight world championship," said former wide receiver Boyd Dowler. "Our goal for those three years, starting in 1965, then '66, then '67, was to win three in a row. Nobody in league history had won three in a row and nobody has since."

After finishing the regular season 9-4-1, the Packers went on to win their third straight NFL title and second straight Super Bowl. The Packers of 1929, 1930, and 1931 had won three straight championships, but that was before the NFL had division play and a league championship game.

The Lombardi Packers are still the only team to have won three straight titles since 1933, the year the NFL split into Eastern and Western divisions.

NO FRILLS, NO THRILLS FOOTBALL

Following the 1967 season, Vince Lombardi resigned as head coach of the Packers—he remained with the team one more year as general manager before taking over as head coach of the Washington Redskins—

and hand-picked Phil Bengtson, his longtime defensive assistant, as his successor.

Four months later, George Halas retired as head coach of the Bears. He chose Jim Dooley, one of his assistants and a former Bears receiver, as his replacement.

Over the next seventeen seasons, until the Bears climaxed the 1985 season by winning Super Bowl XX, the two teams were mediocre at best, but usually downright woeful. During that span, the Bears finished better than .500 three times. The Packers had four winning seasons. The rivalry suffered as a result.

There were fans who became turncoats to the point where the most thunderous boos at Soldier Field were directed at the Bears, rather than at the hated Packers, and vice versa when the teams played at Lambeau Field. Other fans simply were turned off. Three times in the 1970s, Soldier Field was nearly half-empty for Bears-Packers games. The no-show count in each case was more than twenty-three thousand. There were more than nine thousand no-shows for a game at Lambeau Field in 1975.

Newspapers in both cities began to downplay the games and often lampooned them. After the Bears lost to the Packers, 21-3, at Wrigley Field in 1969 and fell to 1-12, Cooper Rollow of the *Chicago Tribune* started his game story with a bogus dateline: "Dullsville, U.S.A." Before the 1973 game at Soldier Field, a *Tribune* headline read: "Stupor Bowl— Bears vs. Pack." The *Tribune* dubbed the second game in 1975 the "Cellar Bowl." In Green Bay, the *Press-Gazette* labeled it "The Basement Bowl."

The only saving grace was that whenever the two teams met, they continued to play smash-mouth football, although it was rarely a pretty sight. "You wouldn't say it was a display of talent," said Dick Corrick, a member of the Packers' scouting department from 1971 to 1987. "It was just old-fashioned football. That's all either one could do."

Throughout Phil Bengtson's three-year tenure as head coach, the Packers' kicking game was a disaster. The Bears were the beneficiaries of those woes on two occasions in Bengtson's first year: in the Midwest Shrine exhibition game and the first regular-season meeting.

The Packers lost to the Bears, 10-7, in the Shrine game when Fernando Souza, a soccer player from Brazil, missed two field goals, one from twenty yards out, and Wade Traynham missed a third from thirty-seven yards in the final two minutes. Within the next week, both kickers were waived.

On November 3, the Packers lost again to the Bears, 13-10. The goat was Errol Mann, who missed field goal tries from forty-four and twenty-nine yards. Complaining of a stiff leg after his second miss, Mann removed himself from the game, leaving the kicking chores to backup fullback Chuck Mercein. He, in turn, missed a twenty-two-yard attempt with a little more than three minutes left in the game.

"It just gets worse and worse," bemoaned Bengtson in his post-game interview. Three days later, the Packers signed Mike Mercer to replace Mann. In all, Bengtson tried six different kickers over his three seasons as coach, and countless others in training camp. "We used to have kicking cavalcades every Monday. About twenty new guys out there," said former all-pro guard Gale Gillingham. "Jesus Christ! It was terrible."

The Bears and Packers celebrated the hundredth anniversary of their rivalry in their December 15, 1968, meeting at Wrigley Field. Fourteen of the fifteen living Hall of Fame members from both teams were saluted at halftime.

The list of immortals present for the ceremony included Dan Fortmann, Red Grange, Ed Healey, Link Lyman, Bronko Nagurski, Joe Stydahar, George Trafton, and Bulldog Turner of the Bears; and Arnie Herber, Clarke Hinkle, Cal Hubbard, Don Hutson, Johnny Blood McNally, and Mike Michalske of the Packers. George Halas was the only one missing. He was in a London hospital recovering from hip surgery.

In the years since, however, the NFL has revised its record book. The league no longer counts the 1941 playoff game that the Bears and Packers played for the Western Division title in the series standings. The game is listed in a separate post-season category. A 1924 meeting played in Green Bay also no longer is listed as a regular-season game.

The NFL now recognizes the game played on December 14, 1969, as the one hundredth in the rivalry.

Halas' retirement as the Bears coach in 1967 apparently didn't end the espionage that had earmaked the rivalry in years past.

Before the two teams met in the season opener in 1969, assistant coach Wayne Robinson of the Packers spotted two men on the Wednesday before the game taking pictures outside the team's Oneida Street practice field. The men edged their way through a gate in the fence to take pictures with still cameras equipped with telescopic lenses.

A Green Bay police officer was instructed to escort the two from the premises. After doing so, he returned to the practice area. "Do you know where they're from?" he asked. He then answered his own question, "Chicago," before snickering and adding, "But they told me, 'We're not Bear fans.'"

The Northland Hotel, from the mid-1930s until it was converted into a home for low-income people in the late-1970s, was the hub of activity in downtown Green Bay the night before a Packers-Bears game.

The Bears were one of the last visiting NFL teams to stay there before it closed. They didn't always get a good night's sleep because rabid, not to mention inebriated, Packers fans would march through the halls in the wee hours of the morning, pounding on doors, blowing horns, and ringing the fire alarms to keep them awake.

There was a reason, however, that the Bears didn't move into plusher, quieter accommodations. To do so would have been sacrilegious, columnist Robert Markus of the *Tribune* wrote the day after the Bears opened the season in Green Bay in 1969.

"Are you kidding?" Markus wrote. "That would be like ordering a hamburger and Coke in Maxim's. The Northland is where the action is. It's always been that way. A Bear-Packer game in Green Bay is a college weekend. The game is going to be great, and don't forget the party.

"A group checked into the Northland yesterday carrying five quarts of booze. Suddenly, catastrophe. A full quart of Early Times went crashing to the floor in front of the registration desk. The man did not blink an eye. He peeled a bill off a big roll and handed it to his companion. 'Run out and get another quart.'"

Former Bears quarterback Virgil Carter holds one distinction in the Bears-Packers rivalry. He conducted the most contemptuous, most memorable, and most costly post-game interview in its history after he had been yanked as the Bears' quarterback in a 21-3 loss to the Packers at Wrigley Field in 1969.

Carter, a fifth-round draft choice in 1967, was surprised to learn from a Chicago sportswriter the Monday before the game that he would be the starter. But by game time, he was under the impression he would play the entire game.

Coach Jim Dooley, after watching Carter complete just two of ten passes for seventeen yards in a scoreless first half, decided to change quarterbacks. Bobby Douglass replaced Carter in the second half and completed six of thirteen passes for twenty-six yards with two interceptions.

"That's the third time they screwed me and that'll be the last," Carter said afterward in what the *Tribune* described as "a macabre scene" in the Bears' locker room. "I won't give them another chance. It said in the papers this week I would be the quarterback for the whole game and that Douglass was not going to play. I would consider that being a liar."

When asked how Dooley had explained the decision to him, Carter responded, "He didn't have the guts to tell me anything. All he said was Douglass was starting and for me to stand next to him on the sidelines." Carter added that he would ask to be traded the first thing Monday morning.

The next day, owner George Halas announced that Carter had been fined a thousand dollars for conduct detrimental to the ball club. The fine, at that point, was the steepest in Bears history. On Tuesday, Dooley declared that Carter also had been dismissed from the team and would not suit up for the final game of the season against Detroit.

Carter never played again for the Bears, but he discovered he had plenty of supporters among the team's fans.

Frank Diamond, a Chicago-area advertising salesman, initiated a fund drive that week to raise the thousand dollars to pay Carter's fine. His slogan was "Dollars for Virgil," and he opened two bank accounts in the Chicago area to handle donations.

The Bears and Packers frequently have picked up each other's castoffs over the years. More than sixty players have played for both teams. But trades between the two teams have been rare.

One of the few significant deals they consummated occurred in January, 1970. The Packers sent linebacker Lee Roy Caffey, a starter on their two Super Bowl teams; reserve running back Elijah Pitts; and center Bob Hyland, a former number one draft pick, to the Bears for the second pick in that year's NFL draft. The Packers used the choice to select Notre Dame defensive tackle Mike McCoy.

Rudy Kuechenberg, a journeyman linebacker but a demon on special teams, delivered a pre-game speech before the Packers played the Bears in Lambeau Field in 1970 that would have made a sailor blush. It was X-rated from start to finish. Kuechenberg had recently joined the Packers after playing three years with the Bears.

"We had our pre-game talks, and I think Gale Gillingham, Bart Starr, Willie Wood, and Carroll Dale said their things, all the guys we looked up to," said Larry Krause, who at that time was a rookie running back. "Then, Rudy Kuechenberg goes, 'Daaah, can I say something coach?' He was so psyched up that he rattled on for like ten minutes of straight profanity. Everybody is kind of looking at each other like, 'What the hell is he talking about?' Nobody could understand anything but his swearing.

"Then on the opening kickoff—I think we had to kick over because we were offsides—we were running up the field and Rudy is just jawin' at Butkus, 'Oh, Dick, I missed you the last time, but I'm going to kick the crap out of you, kill you, do this.' Dick never looked sideways and says, 'Rudy, you're crazy.'"

One of Bart Starr's last hurrahs as a quarterback occurred in 1970 in the Packers' 20-19 victory over the Bears at Lambeau Field. He scored the winning touchdown on a three-yard rollout with three seconds left to play, climaxing an eighty-yard drive that took one minute, thirty-seven seconds.

Starr ran untouched into the end zone when tight end John Hilton, his intended receiver, was knocked down at the line of scrimmage.

"Only one in three million quarterbacks could do what Starr did," linebacker Doug Buffone of the Bears said. "He's a classic."

Starr was thirty-six years old at the time and had played little in the previous month because of a shoulder injury.

However, over the course of his career, Starr had his problems against the Bears' defense. His lifetime passing rating against the Bears was 66.1, while his overall career rating was 80.5. He also threw twenty-four interceptions against the Bears compared to sixteen touchdown passes.

The Packers and Bears played each other for fifteen straight years, from 1959 through 1973, in the Midwest Shrine exhibition game at Milwaukee County Stadium. During the George Halas-Vince Lombardi era, the teams went at each other almost as fiercely as they did during the regular season. Players were ejected for fighting. The two coaches kept their starters in for most of the game. But by the 1970s, the games were usually more boring than entertaining, reflecting the sad state of both teams.

In fact, if there was one game that typified the ineptitude of the Bears and Packers more than any other during this era, it was the 1971 game. The Bears won, 2-0, when the Packers' Frank Patrick, a 6-foot-7, second-year quarterback who had been drafted as a tight end, lost track of where he was and stepped out of the end zone for a safety in the third quarter.

The teams combined that night for 218 total yards, but were penalized a total of 200 yards.

Not everyone, however, agrees that the game was lacking in technical merit. Some old Bears and Packers would take their good old slugfests over today's fast-break aerial shows any day.

"It was the greatest game," Doug Buffone, who played linebacker with the Bears from 1966 to 1979, said of that 2-0 contest. "There was nothing fancy about the game. You just stood out there and beat the shit out of each other."

There might not have been another head coach in the history of the rivalry who worked himself into more of an emotional lather than Abe Gibron.

Not George Halas. Not Curly Lambeau. Not Mike Ditka. Not Forrest Gregg.

Like Halas and Ditka, pumpkin-shaped Abe also had played for the Bears. He stormed the sidelines, most notably on Bear-Packer Sundays, from 1972 to 1974 as the team's head coach.

"Abe is Lebanese," said Gary Kosins, a backup running back for the Bears during Gibron's three years as coach. "He's emotional to begin with. That's in his blood. But when we were playing the Packers, he was almost livid at times."

Former linebacker Dave Robinson said the Packers derived amusement watching Gibron's sideline tirades from across the field.

"We used to joke—in those days the commissioner was worried about uppers in the league—that the only guy taking uppers in the Packer-Bear game was Abe," said Robinson.

Unfortunately for Gibron, he was judged by his record—11-30-1—not by whether his teams beat the snot out of the Packers. But after at least one of those thirty losses, a 23-17 setback against the Packers in 1972, he claimed a moral victory.

"They went off the field like flies," Gibron said of the Packers. "We just beat the waste water out of them."

If Sid Luckman typified the Monsters of the Midway and Bart Starr the Lombardi Packers, then Bobby Douglass and Lynn Dickey typified the play of their respective teams during this era of futility.

Douglass was a linebacker in quarterback's cleats. At 6 feet 4 inches and 225 pounds, he could punish opponents, but he couldn't consistently beat them. He was too unbridled, too erratic, and too prone to making bonehead mistakes throughout his seven years with the Bears.

Douglass had one of his best games as a pro against the Packers in 1973, passing for 108 yards, rushing for 100, and scoring four touchdowns in a 31-17 victory at Lambeau Field. But in six games against the Packers, he completed a mere forty-seven percent of his passes and threw for just one touchdown.

"Bobby Douglass had tremendous talent, but he had no brains," said former teammate Mac Percival. "Bobby could have played any position on the field, but he just wasn't a good quarterback. He was one of those guys who threw the ball to you the same speed if you were five yards away or fifty-five."

Dickey was just the opposite. He was a cerebral quarterback with great touch on the ball, but he was too brittle to get the Packers over the hump. During his ten years with the Packers, he was healthy and able to play in only nine games against the Bears. And when he did play, he often took a brutal beating.

In fact, the first time he played against them, he sustained a season-ending shoulder separation when he was hit from behind and slammed to the turf at Soldier Field by defensive end Roger Stillwell. The hit by Stillwell occurred after Dickey had the wind knocked out of him on two occasions by what he claimed were blatant cheap shots.

"It was Jim Osborne," Dickey said in reference to one of the Bears' defensive tackles. "It happened twice. I threw a pass and I was starting to walk down the field. The next thing I knew, I just dropped to my knees. He just walked by me, saw I wasn't looking, and just gave me a shot in the stomach. I lost all my air, but I couldn't really tell who it was. Then, it happened later in the game. I doubled over again, not as bad, but I saw who it was."

Osborne said he didn't recall ever sucker-punching Dickey, but he remembered hitting him once with all his force.

"I just unloaded on him," said Osborne. "It was probably one of the hardest hits I made on someone. The thing I remember most was that I knocked him out of his shoe. If you can believe this. You know how your shoes are laced up and everything, I knocked him out of his shoe, totally out. But it wasn't a dirty shot."

One of the reasons the Packers and Bears had lousy football teams during this period was because they had lousy quarterbacks.

Some of the forgettable names who played quarterback for the Packers in games against the Bears during this seventeen-year span: Frank Patrick, Rick Norton, Don Milan, Carlos Brown, Randy Johnson, Brian Dowling, and Rich Campbell. Two no-name quarterbacks who played for the Bears against the Packers were Kent Nix and Rusty Lisch.

Most of the other quarterbacks who participated in the rivalry during this period weren't much better, but they stuck around long enough to deserve the tag of journeymen. On the Packers' side, the list included Don Horn, Scott Hunter, Jerry Tagge, David Whitehurst, and Randy Wright. Ex-Bears who belong in the same category were Virgil Carter, Jack Concannon, Gary Huff, Bob Avellini, Mike Phipps, and Vince Evans. Bobby Douglass played for both teams.

Douglass played for the Packers in 1978. Jack Concannon also played for them one season. So did ex-Bears wide receiver Dick Gordon. And, of course, we can't forget Rudy Kuechenberg.

"You know, every ex-Bear we ever had, they all had a screw loose in a fun kind of way," said Larry McCarren, who played center for the Packers from 1973 to 1984. "Jack gets in a wreck one night, hits a bridge abutment or something, and the next day his face is swollen about a time-and-a-half. He squeezes his helmet on and goes out and practices. Bobby D—he had that gun. I remember him throwing balls at buckets in practice: 'Watch me get this thing. Grrrrrrr.' They were all nuts."

One of the more bizarre events in the history of the Bears-Packers rivalry occurred on July 25, 1974. Twenty veteran players from the two teams were arrested outside Lambeau Field for picketing a rookie scrimmage.

The NFL Players Association had called a strike before training camp opened, but the owners were determined to proceed with their pre-season games, playing draft choices and free agents. The scrimmage, hastily scheduled just a week in advance to replace the Packers' annual intra-squad game, was viewed nationally as a test run of what might happen two days later, when the exhibition season was scheduled to begin with the annual Hall of Fame game in Canton, Ohio.

Of the twenty players arrested at Lambeau Field that night, fourteen were Packers, four were Bears and another was an ex-Bear.

"We decided we'd join forces with them," said kicker Mac Percival, the Bears' player representative. "We'd walk around the stadium with our signs. Of course, the Packer guys had cold beer and some food, and we thought this would kind of make a fun deal. Come to find out the police said we had to get back out in the street. The Packer players said, 'No, we're going to stay here.' I said, 'No, let's be safe. I don't want to go to jail.'

"Anyway, we started marching right near the stadium. The next thing I knew we were surrounded by ten or twelve police cars. I thought, 'Oh my gosh.' The policemen came up and said, 'We've got to take you to jail.' So they took us down to the station, finger-printed us, and threatened us with our lives. Then, when the game was over, they let us go. They were just getting us out of the way."

The arrests were made after Packers officials acquired a restraining order against their own players. The scrimmage attracted 36,210 fans, a coup for the owners.

Ed McCaskey, chairman of the board of the Bears, can carry a tune. He sang with dance bands for three years before enrolling in college in 1940. So he was caught off guard, but not ill-prepared, by a surprise request from Packers coach Dan Devine when he visited Green Bay before the 1974 rookie scrimmage. At the time, McCaskey was the Bears' vice president and unofficial troubleshooter.

"Mugsy (Halas) said, 'I want you to go up there and advance the game. See what's going on. Find out anything you can,'" said McCaskey. "So I went up and went to St. Norbert College, where the Packers trained. Dan Devine was the coach and he made me feel very welcome. Then, after practice, they had a team meal. And you know how they have rookies get up and sing their school song. So all of a sudden, Devine announced they had a special guest and that we'd love to hear his song: 'Bear Down, Chicago Bears.' Devine made me get up on a chair and sing the damn thing."

The day after the Packers lost to the Bears, 10-9, in October, 1974, Dan Devine agreed to one of the most lopsided trades, not only in Packers history, but in NFL history. He traded five high draft picks, including two firsts and a second, to the Los Angeles Rams for thirty-four-year-old quarterback John Hadl.

The Packers had started Jerry Tagge at quarterback against the Bears in a Monday night game and couldn't muster a touchdown in the second half, despite starting drives at Chicago's 29-, 37- and 36-yard lines. However, it wasn't Tagge's performance that precipitated the trade, according to Bill Tobin, who at that time was director of pro scouting for the Packers.

A deal already had been consummated the week before. But Tobin expected the new Packers quarterback to be a youthful Archie Manning, not an over-the-hill John Hadl. "We already had agreed on the trade with the New Orleans Saints, for two ones and two twos," said Tobin. "Archie Manning was coming to Green Bay. He was young. He was talented. He just hadn't made it work down there."

To make a long story short, the Saints were playing in Atlanta the day before the Bears-Packers game and Tobin went there to finalize the deal. The Saints started their backup quarterback, Bobby Scott, and everything was going according to plan until Scott tore up his knee. Manning had to finish the game, and the Saints reneged on the trade.

On Tuesday, Devine, desperate to salvage the season and save his job, swung the trade for Hadl without consulting anyone else in the organization.

Dave Roller was an emotional, roly-poly defensive tackle of marginal ability, but he was a fan favorite in Green Bay during his four years with the team. Roller fueled the rivalry in the second game in 1976 by threatening to maim Bears quarterback Bob Avellini. He said he planned to even the score for the cheap shots that had been leveled at Lynn Dickey in the first game that year.

"I'm going to take it out on Avellini the next time we play," Roller said on a radio talk show in Milwaukee. "It's one for one and it's gonna be Mr. Avellini's time when we get them up here. As far as I'm concerned, I'm gonna throw out the rulebook when we play in Green Bay."

As it turned out, Roller lost his starting job that week because of an ankle injury and played sparingly. The next year, Roller was hampered by a torn muscle in his leg, but was still popping off.

"I don't like Avellini," Roller said before the first game. "It's a personal thing. It's something he said about me at a banquet in the off-season. It was an off-color remark in front of eight hundred people."

Twenty years later, Avellini and Roller still don't mince words when they speak about each other. "He wasn't even good, but he probably was the best they had," Avellini said of Roller. "To me, he was an average defensive tackle and the only reason you knew he was there was because he opened up his mouth."

And what does Roller think of Avellini?

"He was kind of cocky, like nothin' stunk about him," said Roller. "I don't think he had the arm to go deep. I don't think he had the smarts to read the defenses as well as he thought. Just hand it off to Walter Payton. It doesn't take a rocket scientist to do that."

Payton rarely, if ever, involved himself in the trash talking that went on between the two teams during his Hall of Fame career. But during an appearance at a suburban Chicago shopping mall before the first meeting between the Bears and Packers in 1978, he made the mistake of belittling the Packers' early season success. After five straight losing seasons, the Packers had won four of their first five games.

"I've been surprised Green Bay has done so well," Payton told the *Woodstock Daily Sentinel.* "Everyone has, I think. But the only real good team they've played has been Oakland. After they lose on Sunday, they'll have to regroup and put things back together, and I don't think they'll be able to do this."

Mike Young, a Packers fan living in Crystal Lake, Illinois, called a reporter with the *Green Bay Press-Gazette* and read him the quote. After the paper ran Payton's comments in its Sunday edition, they were posted on a bulletin board in the Packers' locker room.

The Packers limited Payton to eighty-two yards in nineteen carries and won, 24-14.

No player was more despised by the Packers during the late 1970s than was former Bears safety Doug Plank. The Packers regarded Plank as a cheap-shot artist who would spear unsuspecting receivers, but shy away from head-on contact.

"He's pathetic," former backup wide receiver Ron Cassidy said in 1979 after the Packers lost to the Bears, 15-14. "I don't like the way he acts on the field. I don't care much for him or the way he plays."

Buddy Ryan, the Bears' former defensive coordinator, disagreed that Plank was a dirty player. "He wasn't a real good tackler," said Ryan, "but he was a great hitter."

Eddie Lee Ivery might be remembered to this day as the greatest running back in the history of the Packers if it hadn't been for two ill-fated games on Soldier Field's artificial turf.

Drafted in the first round in 1979, Ivery led the Packers in rushing and receiving during the pre-season that year. But he suffered ligament and cartilage damage to his left knee in the season opener against the Bears. Two years later, Ivery again sustained ligament damage to the same knee, again at Soldier Field.

Ivery played seven years with the Packers and was a reliable, steady running back, but he never again displayed the flashes of brilliance that people saw during that first pre-season. "Eddie, man, he had a lot of promise," said former Packers defensive end Ezra Johnson. "I thought he would have been a great player. I think he would have ranked up there with a guy like Walter Payton."

Kevin Gilbride, head coach of the San Diego Chargers, wasn't the first person Buddy Ryan ever attacked on a sideline. When Ryan and Gilbride were assistants together in Houston, television cameras caught Ryan throwing a jab at Gilbride's chin. Former Packers tackle Greg Koch said he was assaulted once by Ryan, when Ryan was the Bears' defensive coordinator.

"We ran a screen pass and I ran my guy out of bounds," said Koch. "He and I and Buddy all go down in one heap. Buddy gets up and kicks me in the stomach. Buddy Ryan! If I could have gotten to him, I'd have killed him."

When the Packers beat the Bears, 31-28, on December 4, 1983, at Lambeau Field, Bart Starr apologized to his players after the game for not exerting his authority as head coach. The Packers won on a 19-yard field goal by Jan Stenerud as time expired after blowing a 28-14 lead in the final six minutes. The momentum had shifted when Packers offensive coordinator Bob Schnelker called a halfback option pass on third-and-one that the Bears intercepted.

"You know what kind of confidence I have in Bob Schnelker," said Starr. "He's a brilliant, brilliant coordinator. But I should have overruled it because ultimately I have to take responsibility."

The next day, Schnelker, who was more stoic, but just as bullheaded and independent as Bears defensive coordinator Buddy Ryan, told the offense in a team meeting: "I'd call it again."

Quarterback Rich Campbell, the sixth player taken in the 1981 draft, had one fleeting moment of glory in his four years with the Packers. In 1984, at Soldier Field, on the one occasion when a Forrest Gregg team beat the Bears, Campbell threw a 43-yard touchdown pass to wide receiver Phillip Epps in the final seconds for a 20-14 victory.

Campbell, the Packers' third-string quarterback, came off the bench in the second quarter after Randy Wright was injured. Lynn Dickey, the starting quarterback, also was sidelined with an injury. Campbell, who played in only seven games with the Packers, said after the game that he was hopeful it would serve as a turning point in his career.

Many of his teammates, however, shook their heads in disbelief. His touchdown pass was badly underthrown. The play succeeded only because Bears reserve cornerback Terry Schmidt slipped and lost track of Epps.

"Rich Campbell threw just a godawful pass and the stupid Bear defensive back fucked up," recalled center Larry McCarren, who missed the game because of a neck injury. "I remember Campbell saying afterwards, 'I guess that shows I can play in this league.'

"I remember thinking, 'This is stupid. That was a terrible pass. It was the grace of God. Let's not get carried away here.' The Bear defensive back got all discombobulated because the ball was so underthrown, and Campbell is going, 'I guess this shows all my detractors.' I thought, 'Holy Christ.'"

SPANNING TWO SUPER BOWLS

The odyssey that took Jim McMahon from starting quarterback with the Bears in Super Bowl XX to backup quarterback for the Packers in Super Bowl XXXI was one of the most implausible developments in the history of this storied rivalry.

As the Bears' starting quarterback during the Mike Ditka era, McMahon triggered the rage of Packers fans every time he played at Lambeau Field. Cocksure and irreverent, he symbolized everything Packers fans despised about the Bears. Worse yet, he beat the Packers eight times in nine starts as the Bears' quarterback.

After being traded by the Bears before the start of the 1989 season, McMahon played with five other teams before joining the Packers late in 1995. He appeared in only six regular-season games with the Packers, including a token appearance against the Bears in 1996 at Soldier Field, but, over time, Packers fans grudgingly accepted his status as the team's number two quarterback behind Brett Favre.

But he wasn't welcomed with open arms when he first arrived. "He had a hard time with it, as he told me," said Ron Wolf, general manager of the Packers. "In fact, he refused to bring his family up here because he had gotten some letters: 'Keep your ass out of here.'

"Before the first game he played here at Lambeau Field, I had occasion to walk down the pathway behind the private boxes. I didn't really know what was happening, but I heard people say, 'There he is. There he is. He's wearing number 9.' It didn't hit me until I knew who they were talking about, but they were going, 'Can you believe he's wearing a Packer uniform? Can you believe that? The Packers put him in our uniform.' People were disappointed."

The players in Green Bay warmed up to McMahon and Steve McMichael, another ex-Bear, more readily. McMichael, a defensive tackle, played with the Packers in 1994 after thirteen seasons with the Bears.

"Jim is a crazy, crazy guy," said former tackle Ken Ruettgers. "Steve is the same way, but a different crazy. Steve was more a tough-guy crazy. Jim was more of a quarterback loony, crazy kind of guy. But we loved having them in Green Bay."

It was rather remarkable during the Mike Ditka-Forrest Gregg era of the rivalry that there weren't more crippling injuries, considering the number of cheap shots that were exchanged. As fate would have it, the most serious injury occurred on a routine, open-field tackle.

Tim Lewis, a promising young cornerback with the Packers, was forced to retire after sustaining a spinal injury in 1986 at Lambeau Field. Lewis was injured when he lowered his head to tackle wide receiver Willie Gault on the final play of the third quarter. Lewis was treated on the field for about five minutes and was removed in a wheelchair. He announced his retirement three days later after doctors advised him that he risked permanent paralysis if he continued playing.

Lewis, a number one draft pick in 1983, intercepted sixteen passes in forty-two career starts.

Former wide receiver Johnny Morris retired from the Bears in 1967 and became a network broadcaster, but whenever he ventured to Green Bay on assignment for CBS-TV, he was made to feel unwanted.

"Forrest Gregg wouldn't let me come to their practices," said Morris. "We'd come up on Saturday, and I couldn't get in practice because he thought I was going to give information to the Bears. Even Bart Starr was a little wary of me. He was nice enough, but he didn't want me to come to practice. That shows you about the rivalry. I'm an analyst for the game and they thought I'd take information back to the Bears."

Mike McCaskey, president and CEO of the Bears, almost felt at home when he arrived at Lambeau Field before a game in the mid-1980s and peered out the back window of the press box.

"I saw this water tower," said McCaskey. "Some iron workers who were constructing the darn thing had painted in big, bold letters: 'Go Bears.' They printed it on the water tower facing the field."

The Bears, for most of Mike Ditka's tenure as coach, seemed to thrive on turmoil, whether they were feuding with the Packers or squabbling among themselves. A case in point was the 1987 game at Soldier Field.

In the days leading up to the game, wide receiver Dennis McKinnon criticized Vince Tobin's defensive schemes. McKinnon claimed the Bears' defense had turned soft since Buddy Ryan's departure as defensive coordinator. He urged Tobin to start challenging offenses by blitzing more.

Tobin lashed back. "First off," he said, "I think Dennis McKinnon has got a big mouth, and there's only one thing worse than having a big mouth, and that's if you don't have the facts to back up your mouthy statements."

The following Sunday, the Bears beat the Packers by a comfortable 23-10 margin in their final game against a Forrest Gregg-coached team.

"If there was not a controversy going on, we were not the Bears," said McKinnon. "We thrived on that more than anything else."

When Walter Payton retired after the 1987 season as the NFL's all-time leading rusher, he had gained more yards against the Packers than against any other team. In twenty-four games against Green Bay, Payton gained 2,484 of his 16,726 yards. He had thirteen games of one hundred yards or more, including a 205-yard performance in 1977.

Unlike many of his teammates, Payton commanded the utmost respect of the Packers during his thirteen seasons in the league.

"Payton was such a fluid running back, and his leg strength was second to none," said John Meyer, a defensive coordinator for the Packers under Bart Starr. "You'd think during the game, he wasn't doing that much. Then, you'd sit down after the game and go, 'Oh God!' You'd add up all the yards and it was staggering. He never had the breakaway speed to go sixty, seventy yards, but he'd eight-, ten-yard you to death."

Payton also was a class act, when a lot of classless things were taking place in the rivalry. In fact, he was such a class act, according to former linebacker Mike Douglass, that it gave him an additional psychological edge whenever he played against the Packers.

"Walter always played the apology-type thing," said Douglass. "After a good play, he'd apologize, pick you up, pat you on the butt. People talk about Michael Jordan now—I heard a coach say he treats the other players in the league so well that nobody plays hard against him—but that was almost the same approach Walter had on the football field. When he came at you, he'd try to break your neck when he hit you. But you're thinkin' easy and he'd run right through you. I guarantee you because of the respect players had for Walter, they'd ease up. Walter was so great and gracious, and he used that to his advantage."

The Illinois-Wisconsin border is the Mason-Dixon Line of pro football. Cross it, if you're a Bears fan, and you are in enemy territory; and vice versa, if you are a Packers fan. But every summer since 1984, the Bears have held their training camp in Platteville, a city of nine thousand, located in the southwestern corner of Wisconsin.

Improbable as it may seem, they have been warmly received. Their practices regularly attract anywhere from one to five thousand people, many of them their own fans, who drive up from Illinois. But, no doubt, the Bears also have won a few converts in the Packers' home state.

"There are a lot of Packer fans there, but it's a four-hour drive from Green Bay and it's three hours from Chicago," said Bryan Harlan, director of public relations for the Bears. "And I think the fans in that whole tri-state area are a little bit split among Green Bay, Minnesota, and Chicago. So I think we went to an area where the fans weren't quite as loyal to any one team as the rest of the state. And I think we developed a really big following there. That's changed a little bit since we've gotten worse and Green Bay has gotten better. But it has worked out well, even though it is in the enemy state, so to speak."

The Bears headquarter at the University of Wisconsin-Platteville. They also trained in Wisconsin from 1935 to 1943 at St. John's Military Academy in Delafield, located west of Milwaukee.

Bryan Harlan is the son of Bob Harlan, president of the Packers. As a youngster growing up in Green Bay, Bryan worked as a ball boy for the Packers and later served as an intern in their public relations department. He was hired by the Bears in 1984.

Only occasionally, he said, has he caught any grief about his connections to the Packers. "A couple of coaches on Ditka's staff, Johnny Roland and Steve Kazor, would say when I walked out to practice, 'Hey, you're not spying.' I'd say, 'Yeah, I'm spying. We've beaten 'em like eight straight times. I must be doing a helluva job spying for them.'"

After Forrest Gregg stepped down as coach of the Packers following the 1987 season, it didn't end the ill will that existed between the two teams.

The Bears won the first game in the Mike Ditka-Lindy Infante era, 24-6, at Lambeau Field and the two coaches ran off the field without shaking hands and steaming over what transpired in the closing minute of the game.

With fifty-six seconds remaining, the Bears had the ball when Infante elected to call a timeout. On the next play, Ditka ordered quarterback Mike Tomczak to throw deep—the pass fell incomplete—for what could have been a rub-it-in-their face touchdown.

Ditka declined comment when asked what he thought about the timeout. "That's none of of your business," he said. Infante responded, "I mean, if anybody wants me to quit, they're looking at the wrong guy."

Earlier in the fourth quarter, Ditka and trash-talking Packers line-backer Tim Harris engaged in a heated and unusually lengthy shouting match in front of the Bears' bench. That spat extended to the next season when Ditka said on his radio show that Harris would never get the recognition he deserved because of his big mouth. "Sometimes God blesses people with talent and takes away their brains," Ditka said in reference to Harris.

Harris' response: "If Ditka's going to take a low blow at me, fine. He can do whatever he wants. I don't respect his opinion, whatsoever, on me anyway."

An unnamed Bears fan might hold the distinction for paying the highest tab ever to watch a Bears-Packers game. The fan paid five thousand dollars for a luxury box seat to watch the 1988 game at Lambeau Field.

"The people in Chicago are crazy," the late Gene Sladky, then a member of the Packers' board of directors, told the *Chicago Tribune*. "I don't think they know what money is."

It took the Packers three seasons before they wrote off tackle Tony Mandarich as one of the biggest busts in the history of the NFL draft. Mike Ditka passed judgment on Mandarich, the second player selected in 1989, well before then.

Ditka called Mandarich a "Bozo," before the first Bears-Packers game in 1990. After a lengthy holdout, Mandarich sat on the bench his rookie year. Before the next season, he taunted the Bears in a commercial for McDonald's that appeared on Chicago TV.

"Tony Mandarich—he was an enigma coming out," said Ditka. "You can't stick that needle in your ass and then all of a sudden pull the needle out and be the same football player. Basically, steroids made a him a lot better than he was."

Ditka said he sensed from the start that Mandarich would be a bust. "You know what gave me the first clue about that was the way he talked," said Ditka. "Great players don't talk. They don't have to pump any air into the fact they're a good player. That will show through. And that's what bothered me about him. He kept talking about how great he was and how he was going to do this and that. He was a joke."

Running back Brent Fullwood, another of the Packers' first-round busts, pulled what was perhaps the most cowardly stunt in the history of the Bears-Packers rivalry in 1990 at Soldier Field. Here is the story as told by former linebacker Brian Noble.

"We come out at halftime and the offense is on the field. All of sudden, we've got no tailback. Everybody goes, 'Where the hell is Fullwood? Where the fuck is Fullwood?' Domenic Gentile, our trainer, comes down and says he won't come out. 'What do you mean he won't come out?' 'He's got stomach cramps.' Fullwood had just decided he wasn't coming out, showered, and then came out dressed in street clothes. That bothered everybody in itself. Then, we get back to Green Bay after getting our ass kicked and who is the first person out in the bars that night? Brent. The next day, we heard about it. So we come in to watch film and a couple of guys went in to see Lindy and said, 'Lindy, we need to have a team meeting before we watch the films.' Lindy walks out, the other coaches walk out; and then Tim Harris, Keith Woodside, Herman Fontenot, a lot of guys aired some dirty laundry. They really got into it. They tore him a new asshole. Brent apologized for letting the team down, for doing what he did. But, needless to say, that was the end of Brent Fullwood in Green Bay."

Two days after the Packers' 27-13 defeat, Fullwood was traded to Cleveland for a seventh-round draft pick. "It was a fire sale, to be right up front with you," Tom Braatz, the Packers' vice president of football operations, said at the time.

The Brett Favre era in Green Bay officially began four days before the Packers played the Bears at Lambeau Field in 1992. Favre, who was in his second year but his first with Green Bay, after being acquired in a trade with Atlanta, had replaced an injured Don Majkowski a month earlier against Cincinnati with electrifying results. He led a fourth-quarter rally that gave the Packers a 24-23 victory.

Majkowski was declared fit to play against the Bears, but first-year coach Mike Holmgren, after wavering on a decision early in the week, declared Favre his starter.

The Packers lost that Sunday, 30-10, but Favre has had the Bears' number ever since. Going into the 1997 season, his record as a starting quarterback against them was 8-2 and his passing rating was 100.2.

Favre's success, according to Holmgren, stems from a comfort level he hasn't attained against some of the Packers' other opponents. "I think quarterbacks, in general, have teams where they feel pretty good about going in and playing them due to their defensive scheme or their personnel," said Holmgren "Conversely, I don't think he has felt that against Minnesota and Dallas.'

One of the more tense, as well as touching, moments in the history of the Bears-Packers rivalry occurred in 1992. Linebacker Brian Noble lay motionless on the Lambeau Field turf for nearly ten minutes after tackling running back Brad Muster on a goal-line play in the third quarter. Noble lost feeling in his legs and was taken off the field strapped to a stretcher.

"The interesting thing was my coach (Holmgren) didn't come over there, but Mike Ditka did," said Noble. "Mike Singletary came over there. I'll never forget Mike Singletary—one of the best linebackers of all time—came over, grabs my hand, looks me in the eye and says, 'We'll say a prayer for you.' Neal Anderson did the same thing. Mark Bortz. Tom Thayer. Jay Hilgenberg. There was a sincerity in their looks that goes beyond the game of football. I can't put into words—I played against those guys, what, sixteen times—how I felt looking into their eyes and seeing fear in their eyes. That will stick with me the rest of my life."

X-rays showed that Noble suffered nothing more than a back contusion, and he returned to the lineup after missing only two games.

Dave Wannstedt, hired as the Bears' head coach in 1993, was drafted by the Packers in the fifteenth round in 1974, but never played for them. Wannstedt, an offensive tackle, injured his neck late in the pre-season and underwent surgery to repair a damaged lymph node.

After being placed on injured reserve, he went home to Pittsburgh, still hoping to play that season. "I came back seven, eight games into the season," said Wannstedt. "Dan Devine was the coach and I said, 'I'm ready to go.' He says, 'OK, good, you're cut.' And that was it."

Wannstedt began his coaching career the next season as an assistant at the University of Pittsburgh, his alma mater.

The first time he played against the Bears after signing with the Packers as a free agent, defensive end Reggie White registered two sacks to set an NFL record for career sacks. White sacked quarterback Jim Harbaugh twice in the Packers' 17-3 victory on October 31, 1993, to surpass Lawrence Taylor's sack total of 132½.

When the Bears and Packers met at Soldier Field on December 5, 1993, it marked the first time in thirty years that both teams had winning records going into one of their matchups in the second half of the season. The Packers were 7-4 and tied for first in the NFC Central. The Bears were 6-5.

The Packers won, 30-17, and qualified for the playoffs for the first time in eleven years with a 9-7 record. The Bears finished 7-9.

It isn't just the football fans of Wisconsin who want blood when the Bears travel north across the state line. Ex-Bears offensive linemen Mark Bortz and Jay Hilgenberg claim even the law is hostile toward them. Bortz, a native of Pardeeville, Wisconsin, said he became convinced of that after the Packers beat the Bears, 40-3, at Lambeau Field in 1994.

"We get our asses kicked," said Bortz. "We're leaving the stadium and, normally, when you leave a stadium, they have a police escort that'll take you out of there. These escorts—sometimes, it's downright dangerous—they'll ride on the shoulder of the road, get you off on the median to ride between lanes with these big buses. Well, up in Green Bay, they have a state trooper and what he's doing is actually waving cars in front of us to keep us in traffic longer. Finally, Tim LeFevour, he's like our vice president of operations, gets out and tells the trooper, 'Leave us. We'll get to the airport. We don't need help.'"

Hilgenberg told the *Green Bay Press-Gazette* in 1988 that he felt as though every radar gun in the state was pointed at him when he ventured into Wisconsin. "I grew up in Iowa and we traveled to Wisconsin a lot," he said. "We never had trouble driving through Wisconsin. Since I've been in Chicago and had Illinois plates on, it seems like the state troopers in Wisconsin always pick me up."

Quarterback Brett Favre's six-week stay in a substance abuse treatment clinic in 1996 raised suspicions that he had played on more than just adrenalin and guts when the Packers beat the Bears, 35-28, on November 12, 1995, at Lambeau Field. Favre was admitted to the Menninger Clinic in Topeka, Kansas, in May, 1996, for an addiction to Vicodin, a common painkiller. Favre played against the Bears seven days after leaving a game against the Minnesota Vikings on crutches with a badly sprained left ankle. Defensive end Reggie White also played against the Bears that day, despite spraining the medial collateral ligament in his right knee against the Vikings.

Coach Mike Holmgren insists that the medical treatment Favre received from the team and Favre's addiction were not related. "There was a feeling that was a game he had to have taken something," said Holmgren. "He did not practice all week. Then, before the game, he was wrapped so tight, he couldn't run. He couldn't do a lot of the things he does. But he threw five touchdown passes that game. Reggie White, the same thing. Reggie was hurt and nobody talks about him. But prior to a game, the medication Brett was taking, that was not what he was taking after the game."

The 1995 game was not the first time Favre played against the Bears after making a remarkable recovery from an injury. He separated his left shoulder prior to the second game in 1992 and admitted he took painkillers in order to play. He also was listed as questionable before the second game in 1993 with a thigh bruise and the first meeting in 1995 with a sprained left ankle.

Jim Flanigan played linebacker for the Packers from 1967 to 1970. His son, Jim Flanigan, currently plays defensive tackle for the Bears. Even though Jim Sr., still resides in the Green Bay area, he said his allegiances weren't divided when the Bears and Packers met.

"I always root for my son," he said. "The Packers haven't sent me a check in a long time."

When the 1996 NFL schedule was released, Packers president Bob Harlan expected an outcry in Green Bay. In 1995, the Packers stopped playing part of their home schedule in Milwaukee, but also decided to split their season-ticket package. Milwaukee fans would receive tickets to the team's second and sixth home games. Green Bay ticket-holders would get tickets to the other six.

The Bears game was the sixth home game in 1996. The only other time in the history of the rivalry that Green Bay fans were deprived of tickets to the Bears game was in 1974, when it was played in Milwaukee County Stadium. At that time, the Packers were swamped with calls and letters from outraged fans.

This time, Harlan said no more than a handful of fans complained. "I think it's very fair, but it hasn't alarmed people like I thought it would," said Harlan. "But one guy wrote and said, 'It's the day I look forward to all year.'"

There are fans, and others, who fear the Bears-Packers rivalry won't hold the same significance for future players because of free agency. The theory is that the players won't stick around long enough to acquire the same hatred for the other team that previous generations of players held. But it didn't take long for linebacker Bryan Cox, a high-priced free agent signed by the Bears before the start of the 1996 season, to vent his hostilities in the rivalry.

In his first game against the Packers, Cox was penalized and subsequently fined $87,500, or one game's pay, for making an obscene gesture at an official following a 50-yard touchdown pass by quarterback Brett Favre at the end of the first half. The touchdown propelled the Packers to a 37-6 victory, something else that didn't sit well with Cox.

"Heart, heart, heart, heart," he bellowed in the locker room after the game. "We've got to get some damned heart. It's a line in 'The Wizard of Oz.' Some of our guys have to go see the Wizard because we don't have a lot of heart."

Bears vs. Packers broke new ground in May, 1997, spilling over into the world of professional wrestling. Steve McMichael, who spent thirteen years with the Bears before finishing his career with the Packers in 1994, tangled with Packers defensive end Reggie White in a pay-per-view World Championship Wrestling Slamboree in Charlotte, North Carolina.

The event was billed as a Bears-Packers grudge match, and White even wore a green jersey with his number 92. McMichael, who has found a second career as a pro wrestler, won the match when he hit White, a novice in the ring, over the head with a briefcase.

"The Green Bay Packer cheesehead ain't no match for a Monster of the Midway," McMichael crowed.

Jim McMahon couldn't resist one last act of irreverence.

McMahon, who announced his retirement after serving as the Packers' backup quarterback in the 1996 season, donned a Bears jersey in the East Room of the White House moments before the Packers met President Bill Clinton in May, 1997.

The Packers were Clinton's guests of honor for winning Super Bowl XXXI.

McMahon's intention was to honor the Bears who won Super Bowl XX. That year, 1986, the Bears were not invited to the White House because of the tragedy of the space shuttle Challenger, which exploded just after takeoff on January 28, two days after the Super Bowl.

Still, the image of McMahon in his navy-and-orange jersey didn't sit well with Packers general manager Ron Wolf or coach Mike Holmgren. According to witnesses, both were beside themselves with anger.

Chapter 8

Like a River: It Ebbs and Flows

With klieg lights on, cameras and tape recorders rolling, and the pens of Chicago's sports reporters and columnists poised to record his every word, Rick Mirer stepped to the podium to be introduced as the Chicago Bears' new quarterback at a news conference in early 1997.

The Bears had traded a first-round draft pick for Mirer, a former Notre Dame star whose career never got untracked with the Seattle Seahawks. Mirer, the second player chosen in the 1993 draft, was expected to help turn the Bears into playoff contenders.

There were many questions to be answered that day. How much did he know about the Bears' offense? What were the terms of his contract? Why did his career stall in Seattle? What did he think of the talent level on his new team, and its prospects to reach the playoffs?

Seconds after the floor was opened for questions, Les Grobstein of WSCR radio got right down to the nitty-gritty.

"How important is it," Grobstein asked, "to beat the Green Bay Packers?"

Mirer smoothly gave the politically correct reply. He said there was plenty of incentive to beat the Packers, because they were the defending Super Bowl champions, and division opponents, as well.

"My impression," said Grobstein, "was, 'Wrong answer.'"

A lot of other people in Chicago felt the same way.

"I could tell by the looks of the media's faces," said Bryan Harlan, the Bears' director of public relations. "Some people wanted him to say, 'That's all that matters. If we go 2-14 and beat Green Bay twice, it's a great season.'"

Mirer couldn't be blamed for not knowing that the Bears-Packers rivalry transcends the National Football Conference Central Division race. Soon enough, Bears fans hoped, Mirer would learn that Green Bay is to Chicago what Southern Cal is to Notre Dame. Maybe then, he'd get it.

Mirer's predecessor, Erik Kramer, had never endeared himself to the fans, in part because he had not been able to beat the Packers and also because he didn't seem to lose any sleep over it. "The fans certainly don't like it if the players don't get involved in the rivalry," said Doug Buffone, a Chicago sportscaster who played linebacker for the Bears from 1966 to 1979. "I remember when we were playing the Packers in 1995 and Erik Kramer called it just another game. There was an uprising. There was a total uprising. The fans were saying, 'How could you say something like that? That's blasphemy.'"

The truth be known, Kramer isn't the only contemporary player who takes a businesslike approach to professional football's oldest rivalry. In the second half of the 1990s, it is mostly the fans who are keeping the fire burning and the antipathy simmering.

The dynamics within and between the teams have changed, and by extension, so has the rivalry. From an organizational standpoint, the mutual scorn has diminished noticeably since Mike Ditka was fired as Chicago's coach after the 1992 season.

The current coaches, Mike Holmgren in Green Bay and Dave Wannstedt in Chicago, do not have longstanding ties to their franchises, so they have no history of contempt upon which to draw. In addition, they are fairly close friends—as close as two coaches within the same division can be—and together have organized Christian coaches' breakfasts at league meetings. That's a striking contrast to what occurred in the mid-1980s, when the only thing Ditka and Forrest Gregg organized was mayhem.

"That comes up every year, how Ditka and Gregg hated each other, and how the fact that Dave Wannstedt and I don't hate each other takes away from the rivalry," Holmgren said. "Believe me, you know how competitive I am, and I can tell you Dave is just as competitive. There's a mutual respect there, but we go at it."

That respect is reflected in the fact that the players on both sides no longer spout off before games or trade insults and cheap shots during them. Bulletin board material is nearly non-existent, and neither Holmgren nor Wannstedt would stand for any sort of thuggery on the field.

"I think with Mike and Dave, there is a dignity back with this game that it deserves," said Packers general manager Ron Wolf. "There is a special feeling afforded this game, but it hasn't become a knock-down, drag-out brawl, which is what it was."

Another factor that has seemingly diminished the intensity of the rivalry is that, going into the 1997 season, Green Bay had won six straight games against Chicago, and eight of the last ten. During that span, the Bears often have lost by lopsided scores—33-6 and 40-3 in 1994, 37-6 in 1996—which suggests that they don't approach the game the same way the Packers did as underdogs during the Ditka-Gregg era. Hopelessly overmatched then, Green Bay always battled and brawled until the final gun.

"The coaches in Chicago just don't get it," Grobstein said. "They try to keep their team on an even keel every week. That doesn't work in this rivalry. Gregg's teams were always outmanned, but he got them to play a certain way, maybe even dirty, and they almost pulled off a couple of upsets."

Also worth noting is that in Green Bay, other opponents have taken the Bears' place—at least temporarily—on the high end of the hate meter. The Packers have lost eight straight games to the Dallas Cowboys since 1991, and under Holmgren, they have a 3-7 record against the Minnesota Vikings, another division rival. It's safe to say that the Packers get wired tighter for those two opponents these days than they do for the Bears.

"Talking to these guys now, the Bears are almost like a homecoming game," said former Packers linebacker Brian Noble, who retired after the 1993 season. "These guys don't understand. Their Chicago game is the Dallas Cowboys. That's their rivalry.

"But for me, the Chicago game was what you played Pop Warner for; that was what you played high school ball for—that rivalry. It was that one game a year that you wanted to play the best game of your life in. That's what the Chicago Bear game was."

Ask the players on both rosters about the rivalry today, and you get a mixed bag of answers. Some of the players who have been around a few years, such as Green Bay safety LeRoy Butler and Chicago defensive end Alonzo Spellman, recognize its importance.

"This goes on and on," said Butler, a second-round draft pick in 1990 and, going into the 1997 season, the Packers' senior member in terms of years with the franchise. "When I got here, that was the first thing I was told: 'Beat the Bears. Beat the Bears. We don't care about anybody else.' I think the rivalry will remain strong. Chicago is only four hours away. The fans really love it. That will never die."

Spellman, a first-round draft pick in 1992, broke in at the tail end of the Ditka era. He saw how much the rivalry meant to veteran teammates such as Richard Dent, William Perry, and Steve McMichael. "There is no game—*no* game—that compares to the game between the Bears and the Packers," Spellman said. "Records don't matter. There's three times a year when we have to get it up another notch: the two Packer games, and the playoffs."

Some of the younger players, however, seem to take Kramer's approach to the rivalry. If the game is significant beyond its ramifications on the division race, they either don't see it, or they don't understand it. "We have a big rivalry with Dallas, because we haven't been able to beat them," said Packers guard Aaron Taylor, a first-round draft choice in 1994. "I don't know . . . the Bears is just another game. I think the media and fans get caught up in it more than the players do."

John Jurkovic, a nose tackle for the Packers from 1991 to 1995 and a native of the Chicago area, pointed out that the dearth of competitive games in recent years has hurt the rivalry as much, if not more, than anything else. "The problem is, we'd beaten them so many times," said Jurkovic, who now plays for Jacksonville. "Pretty soon, you start taking them for granted a little. It's like you're playing Tampa Bay."

Jurkovic has a point, and it's one that Wannstedt readily acknowledges.

"You really don't have a rivalry unless the games are real, real meaningful," Wannstedt said. "A rivalry is when both teams are damned good, and the game is meaningful. How meaningful was the game in getting to the Super Bowl in the 1980s? You know, Ditka and Forrest Gregg screaming at each other was probably more meaningful to the fans than who the hell was going to the Super Bowl. The Bears were a hell of a lot better team."

Wannstedt's pragmatic view may be accurate, but pragmatism goes out the window, from the fans' perspective, anyway, when the subject turns to Bears vs. Packers. Those fans wouldn't mind seeing a little more acrimony—and a little less harmony—between today's opposing players and coaches, because that's what they feel. The fans still hold a grudge. They still lob insults back and forth over the state border.

They still live and die with this game, twice a year.

"I hear, 'It's just another game,' from some of the players and coaches in Chicago now," said Bill Tobin, the vice president and director of football operations for the Indianapolis Colts, and a former member of the Bears' front office. "When I hear that, I think, 'The fans don't feel that way about it. You better get in tune with it.'"

In Racine, Wisconsin, a blue-collar city of ninety thousand just sixty miles north of Chicago, but definitely within the boundaries of Packer Country, the fans' loyalties play out in an interesting scenario each fall.

Two taverns—one a hangout for Packers fans, the other a haven for Bears fans—have established their own border war. Separated by a city block, both bars are jammed with overflow crowds on game days. They set up tents outside and pipe in the game on big-screen TVs. Fans walk back and forth between the bars to swap taunts and insults, and to toast the opposing team's misfortune. The turnouts have gotten so large, the Racine Police Department has asked the bars to take out a parade permit.

That's just one example of fan involvement in this series. It's a phenomenon that goes back decades and shows absolutely no signs of abating any time soon.

However, no matter how passionately the fans feel about Bears vs. Packers, there are reasons for concern that the rivalry may never again be the same. Primarily, free agency has changed the way NFL teams are structured. In the mid-1980s, for example, it would have been inconceivable that Steve McMichael and Jim McMahon—the respective heart and soul of the Bears—would someday wear the Packers' green and gold. In the mid-1990s, it happened.

"That is where football is lost," said Tobin. "Geez! I'm in the business, and I have to get out a program to find out who is where. Which Jones is this? Oh, that's the Jones who started out in Seattle, went to Tampa, to St. Louis, to New England, and now is down in Jacksonville. That kind of stuff."

Realignment also is a possibility, because the NFL almost certainly will continue to expand. It is extremely doubtful that the Bears and Packers ever would be split up by the league, but stranger things have happened.

"I think it would be highly unlikely, but in the age of change, I don't think you ever put the words 'never happen' on it," said Mike McCaskey, the president and CEO of the Bears since 1983. "It's highly unlikely, simply because the fans in both cities care so much about the rivalry."

While there are a number of young owners in the NFL who seem to have little or no appreciation for tradition, there are others who still cherish the importance of Bears vs. Packers and other longstanding rivalries. "I know tradition seems to be a word of antiquity," said George Young, general manager of the New York Giants. "But I don't believe it should be. We ought to maintain those good rivalries. The fans get lost in this. They get lost enough in free agency. They can't be lost in this thing. As long as there is an NFL there ought to be that rivalry."

Still, in 1950 when the old All-America Football Conference was absorbed by the NFL, one of the proposals for realignment had the Bears and Packers playing in opposite divisions. The idea was nixed by then-commissioner Bert Bell.

Until the Bears settle their stadium situation, the possibility exists, however remote, that they could move out of Chicago. To be sure, the rivalry would lose something if and when the team left historic Soldier Field. But it would lose a lot more if the Bears left the City of Chicago.

"If they put them in Cleveland and made them the Cleveland Bears, that would certainly affect it," Wolf said. "The Gary Bears? They're the Chicago Bears. That would be like us moving to Cleveland, so we could have more money. The Cleveland Packers? It doesn't sound right."

Another disturbing development is that some ex-Bears from the more violent days of the rivalry openly rooted for the Packers in Super Bowl XXXI. "I was one of those guys who was pulling for the Packers," admitted Jim Osborne, who played defensive tackle for Chicago from 1972 to 1984. "The thing I admire is the way they rebuilt their organization. I have a lot of respect for Holmgren. I just think they've done it the right way putting a class organization together."

While there are forces at work that seem to be shaping Bears vs. Packers into a kinder, gentler rivalry, it is worth noting that this is a series that has a history of emotional peaks and valleys. Certainly, there are no guarantees that there will never again be an era comparable with the Ed Sprinkle or Ditka-Gregg years. Just imagine one of Ditka's ex-players someday coaching the Bears, or one of Gregg's players coaching the Packers. Instant fireworks.

Besides, the contempt hasn't completely disappeared. Wolf, for instance, senses an arrogance about the Bears, and he doesn't understand or appreciate it. "They have no reason to be arrogant," he said. "They haven't accomplished anything. What have they done? They accomplished dick shit. The Chicago Bears. They had football's team in the '80s. To win only one title with that team? Know what I mean?"

In Chicago, former Bears defensive end Dan Hampton remains as blunt and outspoken as he was during his playing days. Hampton, who called the Bears' games for WGN Radio in 1995 and 1996, doesn't think the Super Bowl champion Packers should be classified as a great team.

"Everybody wants to rave about the Packers," Hampton said. "But take Brett Favre off that team and you've got an 8-8 ballclub. I believe that in my heart. You tell me why the Packers win more than eight games if Favre isn't on that team. The offensive line? I don't think so. The running game? Nah. Receivers? Nah. Reggie White? He and Sean Jones took more plays off than anybody I've ever seen. Tell me why they win. I'm telling you, it's Brett Favre.

"And if that kid gets hurt, they've got big problems."

As long as a few people, such as Wolf and Hampton, are willing to throw some salvos at the other organization, and as long as the teams continue to play twice a year, the possibility remains that the bitterness will re-surface. In the meantime, the series continues to be extended in terms of history and tradition.

"I think this is a rivalry that will stand the test of time as long as they stay in Chicago, because we're always going to be in Green Bay," said Holmgren. "They're two of the teams that started the league, and because of Lombardi, Halas, Ditka, Gregg, Starr, all the great players—and because of the contrast in the two cities and their proximity—I don't think you have to worry about the rivalry changing."

Holmgren probably is correct. The only way the rivalry would wither is if the fans lose interest—which simply isn't going to happen any time soon—or if the games are not competitive for an extended period.

It's interesting to note that Bears fans are losing their patience with Wannstedt because of his inability to beat the Packers. "Wannstedt has not been as vocal as the fans think he should be, and that is always thrown back at him," said Terry Boers, a broadcaster for WSCR in Chicago and a former sportswriter for the *Chicago Sun-Times.* "He has been charged with that—not really understanding the rivalry. And nothing bugs the fans more than that, other than maybe his entire team."

Dennis McKinnon, who played wide receiver for the Bears from 1983 to 1988, believes the Monsters of the Midway have lost their identity, and can regain it only by beating the Packers. "The Packers have taken something from the Bears that we held sacred," McKinnon said. "And until the players understand that—that, in order to win the Central Division, you've got to beat Green Bay—then we're going to be second fiddle."

Certainly, the franchises are overdue for a period when they battle for conference or division supremacy. It has been three decades since the Bears rose up to challenge the Lombardi Packers on occasion, and more than five decades since the teams fought for NFL championships on an annual basis.

"When the Bears were really good, like in '85, the Packers weren't so good," said John Madden, the Fox network football analyst and former coach of the Oakland Raiders. "Now, the Packers are one of the elite teams, and the Bears aren't that good.

"If they ever get to where the Packers are the Packers, and the Bears are like the Dallas Cowboys are now, then you'd see the damn rivalry back—and forget Forrest Gregg and Mike Ditka."

Appendix

Game-by-Game Results

1. Staleys (Bears) 20, Packers 0; November 27, 1921; at Cubs Park—Half-back Pete Stinchcomb, quarterback Pard Pearce, and end George Halas scored the Staleys' three touchdowns.
2. Bears 3, Packers 0; October 14, 1923; at Bellevue Park—Dutch Sterna-man kicked the decisive field goal in the second quarter.
3. Bears 3, Packers 0; November 23, 1924, at Cubs Park—Joe Sternaman kicked the decisive field goal in the third quarter.
4. Packers 14, Bears 10; September 27, 1925; at City Stadium—Quarterback Charlie Mathys passed to halfback Verne Lewellen on fourth-and-goal from the six-yard line early in the fourth quarter for the winning touchdown.
5. Bears 21, Packers 0; November 22, 1925; at Cubs Park—Halfback John Mohardt, quarterback Joe Sternaman, and fullback Oscar Knop scored the Bears' touchdowns.
6. Bears 6, Packers 6; September 26, 1926; at City Stadium—Right halfback Laurie Walquist passed to left halfback Paddy Driscoll for a Bears touch-down to tie the score in the fourth quarter. Fullback Carl Lidberg scored the Packers' touchdown in the third quarter.
7. Bears 19, Packers 13; November 21, 1926; at Cubs Park—Paddy Drsicoll returned a Packers fumble for the winning touchdown in the fourth quarter.
8. Bears 3, Packers 3; December 19, 1926; at Soldier Field—Paddy Driscoll kicked the tying field goal for the Bears with about five minutes remain-ing in the game. Pid Purdy was credited with a 50-yard dropkick for the Packers' field goal.
9. Bears 7, Packers 6; October 2, 1927; at City Stadium—Pid Purdy missed an extra point after the Packers had scored on a one-yard run by Verne Lewellen with 1:48 remaining in the game. Running back Bill Senn scored the Bears' touchdown on a one-yard run in the second quarter.

10. Bears 14, Packers 6; November 20, 1927; at Wrigley Field—Paddy Driscoll threw a 31-yard scoring pass to Bill Senn in the fourth quarter for the Bears' clinching touchdown. Senn also scored the Bears' other touchdown, taking a short pass from Driscoll and running 52 yards in the second quarter.

11. Bears 12, Packers 12; September 30, 1928; at City Stadium—Verne Lewellen scored two second-half touchdowns to erase a 12-0 deficit and give the Packers a tie. Harry O'Boyle of the Packers missed a field goal in the closing seconds. Dick Sturtridge returned a punt 80 yards for the Bears' second touchdown.

12. Packers 16, Bears 6; October 21, 1928; at Wrigley Field—The Packers picked up only one first down in the second half, but sealed the victory when guard Bruce Jones scored on an interception return in the fourth quarter.

13. Packers 6, Bears 0; December 9, 1928; at Wrigley Field—Quarterback Red Dunn threw a long touchdown pass to end Dick O'Donnell with less than two minutes remaining for the winning touchdown.

14. Packers 23, Bears 0; September 29, 1929; at City Stadium—Fullback Hurdis McCrary, end Tom Nash, and fullback Bo Molenda scored touchdowns and the Packers held the Bears to five first downs.

15. Packers 14, Bears 0; November 10, 1929; at Wrigley Field—Hurdis McCrary scored the Packers' touchdowns on a 15-yard pass reception from Red Dunn and on an interception return from near midfield.

16. Packers 25, Bears 0; December 8, 1929; at Wrigley Field—Halfback Eddie Kotal scored two touchdowns on spectacular running catches, and Verne Lewellen scored one touchdown and passed for another as the Packers clinched their first NFL title.

17. Packers 7, Bears 0; September 28, 1930; at City Stadium—Verne Lewellen scored the only touchdown on a one-yard run in the second quarter. Lewellen had runs of 8, 10, and 23 yards on the winning drive.

18. Packers 13, Bears 12; November 9, 1930; at Wrigley Field—Verne Lewellen scored the go-ahead touchdown on a 21-yard pass from Red Dunn early in the fourth quarter. After Laurie Walquist scored for the Bears later in the fourth quarter, Walt Holmer missed the extra point.

19. Bears 21, Packers 0; December 7, 1930; at Wrigley Field—The Bears intercepted six passes and end Luke Johnsos scored two of their three touchdowns as they snapped the Packers' seven-game winning streak in the series.

20. Packers 7, Bears 0; September 27, 1931; at City Stadium—Verne Lewellen scored the only touchdown on a one-yard run in the second quarter after end Lavvie Dilweg had recovered a fumble at the Bears' 22-yard line.

21. Packers 6, Bears 2; November 1, 1931; at Wrigley Field—Guard Mike Michalske scored the Packers' touchdown on an 80-yard interception return in the second quarter.

22. Bears 7, Packers 6; December 6, 1931; at Wrigley Field—The Bears intercepted six passes and halfback Joe Lintzenich scored their only touchdown in the first quarter. Red Dunn missed what would have been the tying extra point in the second quarter.

23. Bears 0, Packers 0; September 25, 1932; at City Stadium—Each team punted 13 times and combined for just 13 first downs in a fierce defensive struggle. A bad snap from center foiled a Bears field goal attempt after they reached the Packers' 23-yard line late in the fourth quarter.

24. Packers 2, Bears 0; October 16, 1932; at Wrigley Field—Tom Nash blocked Dick Nesbitt's punt out of the end zone in the second quarter for a safety.

25. Bears 9, Packers 0; December 11, 1932; at Wrigley Field—Fullback Bronko Nagurski scored on a 56-yard run in the fourth quarter to clinch the victory on a snow-covered field.

26. Bears 14, Packers 7; September 24, 1933; at City Stadium—End Bill Hewitt scored the winning touchdown when he blocked an Arnie Herber punt and returned it for a touchdown on the final play from scrimmage. The Bears scored all 14 of their points in the final three minutes.

27. Bears 10, Packers 7; October 22, 1933; at Wrigley Field—The Bears scored all 10 of their points in the final four minutes on a touchdown reception by Luke Johnsos and a field goal by Jack Manders.

28. Bears 7, Packers 6; December 10, 1933; at Wrigley Field—Back Keith Molesworth threw a touchdown pass to halfback Gene Ronzani in the second quarter for the Bears' touchdown. Lineman Joe Zeller blocked Roger Grove's extra-point try after the Packers scored on an 88-yard punt return by Bob Monnett in the fourth quarter to preserve the Bears' victory. Fullback Clarke Hinkle returned the opening kickoff 92 yards, but was tackled by end Bill Karr at the four-yard line and the Packers failed to capitalize on the opportunity.

29. Bears 24, Packers 10; September 23, 1934; at City Stadium—Bronko Nagurski scored on runs of 1 and 34 yards in the fourth quarter to break a 10-10 tie. Nagurski gained 90 yards in 14 carries, his single-game high against the Packers.

30. Bears 27, Packers 14; October 28, 1934; at Wrigley Field—Rookie halfback Beattie Feathers starred for the Bears by rushing for 155 yards in 15 carries and scoring two touchdowns, including one on a pass reception.

31. Packers 7, Bears 0; September 22, 1935; at City Stadium—The Packers scored on the first play from scrimmage: an 83-yard pass from tailback Arnie Herber to end Don Hutson.

32. Packers 17, Bears 14; October 27, 1935; at Wrigley Field—Arnie Herber threw two touchdown passes to Don Hutson covering 65 and 3 yards in the final two-and-a-half minutes as the Packers overcame a 14-3 deficit.

33. Bears 30, Packers 3; September 20, 1936; at City Stadium—Gene Ronzani, Bill Hewitt, quarterback Carl Brumbaugh, and Bill Karr scored the Bears' four touchdowns.
34. Packers 21, Bears 10; November 1, 1936; at Wrigley Field—Clarke Hinkle rushed for 109 yards in 13 attempts and scored the go-ahead touchdown in the second quarter on a 59-yard run.
35. Bears 14, Packers 2; September 19, 1937; at City Stadium—The Bears scored both of their touchdowns over a seven-play span in the third quarter: one on a short run by halfback Ray Nolting and the other on a 45-yard pass from quarterback Bernie Masterson to halfback Jack Manders.
36. Packers 24, Bears 14; November 7, 1937; at Wrigley Field—The Packers scored on a 78-yard pass from Arnie Herber to Don Hutson to spark a 17-point flurry in the second quarter. Back Eddie Jankowski scored the Packers' other second-quarter touchdown on a 27-yard interception return.
37. Bears 2, Packers 0; September 18, 1938; at City Stadium—Consecutive bad snaps by center Darrell Lester in a game played in mud and rain led to the Bears' safety. The first snap sailed over the head of Arnie Herber for a 27-yard loss to the Green Bay five-yard line; the second produced a Bears safety when Packers guard Tom Jones fell on the ball in the end zone. Clarke Hinkle missed a field goal from the 37-yard line in the closing seconds.
38. Packers 24, Bears 17; November 6, 1938; at Wrigley Field—Fullback Bert Johnson fumbled twice in the first three minutes and the Packers converted both turnovers into touchdowns: one on a pass from Bob Monnett to Clarke Hinkle and the other on a Monnett to Don Hutson pass. Back John Howell preserved the victory when he tipped a fourth-down pass by quarterback Ray Buivid at the goal line with less than one minute to play.
39. Packers 21, Bears 16; September 24, 1939; at City Stadium—After trailing 13-0 at halftime, the Packers scored three touchdowns in the third quarter on an 11-yard run by tailback Cecil Isbell, a one-yard run by Clarke Hinkle, and a fumble recovery in the end zone by center Tom Greenfield.
40. Bears 30, Packers 27; November 5, 1939; at Wrigley Field—Fullback Bill Osmanski scored the winning touchdown on a four-yard run late in the fourth quarter in a game where the lead changed hands six times. Osmanski's touchdown was set up by a 45-yard pass from quarterback Sid Luckman to halfback Bob MacLeod.
41. Bears 41, Packers 10; September 22, 1940; at City Stadium—Halfbacks George McAfee and Ray Nolting each returned a kickoff for a touchdown to trigger the rout. McAfee returned his 93 yards and Nolting raced 97 yards. The Packers outgained the Bears, 333 yards to 290, but turned the ball over nine times.

42. Bears 14, Packers 7; November 3, 1940; at Wrigley Field—Running back Gary Famiglietti broke a 7-7 tie when he scored on a seven-yard run in the second quarter. The Packers reached the Bears' 20-yard line three times in the fourth quarter, but were stymied by the Bears' defense.

43. Bears 25, Packers 17; September 28, 1941; at City Stadium—George McAfee scored the go-ahead touchdown on a 13-yard run in the third quarter. Bob Snyder sealed the victory with a 34-yard field goal with three minutes left.

44. Packers 16, Bears 14; November 2, 1941; at Wrigley Field—The Packers handed the Bears their only loss of the season as Cecil Isbell and halfback Lou Brock scored touchdowns, and Clarke Hinkle kicked a field goal.

45. Bears 44, Packers 28; September 27, 1942; at City Stadium—After the Bears had trailed 21-13 at halftime and 28-27 after the third quarter, Frank Maznicki scored the go-ahead points on a 17-yard field goal. Gary Famiglietti scored three touchdowns for the Bears.

46. Bears 38, Packers 7; November 15, 1942; at Wrigley Field—The Bears scored their first two touchdowns on a 45-yard fumble recovery by linebacker Bulldog Turner and a 54-yard interception return by Sid Luckman. Don Hutson caught 10 passes, his highest total ever against the Bears, for 117 yards.

47. Bears 21, Packers 21; September 26, 1943; at City Stadium—A 26-yard touchdown pass from halfback Tony Canadeo to Don Hutson midway through the fourth quarter gave the Packers a tie.

48. Bears 21, Packers 7; November 7, 1943; at Wrigley Field—Halfback Scooter McLean scored the Bears' first touchdown and tied the game on a 66-yard run, and halfback Harry Clarke scored what proved to be the winning touchdown on a 38-yard pass from Sid Luckman in the third quarter.

49. Packers 42, Bears 28; September 24, 1944; at City Stadium—After the Bears scored 14 points in the fourth quarter to tie the game, 28-28, Lou Brock scored on a 42-yard run and back Ted Fritsch returned an interception 50 yards for a touchdown in the closing minutes to give the Packers a victory.

50. Bears 21, Packers 0; November 5, 1944; at Wrigley Field—Sid Luckman passed for two touchdowns—a 31-yarder to Scooter McLean and a 24-yarder to end George Wilson—and scored on a quarterback sneak to lead the Bears. The Bears' defense limited the Packers to eight first downs and a mere 49 yards rushing.

51. Packers 31, Bears 21; September 30, 1945; at City Stadium—Fullback Don Perkins scored on a two-yard run late in the fourth quarter to seal the victory. Perkins set up the touchdown with a 47-yard run after the Packers had nearly blown a 17-0 third-quarter lead.

52. Bears 28, Packers 24; November 4, 1945; at Wrigley Field—The Bears cut the difference to 24-21 with two seconds left in the first half on a 24-yard pass from Sid Luckman to end Ken Kavanaugh, climaxing an 88-yard drive, and took the lead early in the third quarter when fullback Jim Fordham scored on a one-yard run, climaxing a 71-yard drive. Halfback Bob Margarita rushed for 116 yards in 16 carries for the Bears.

53. Bears 30, Packers 7; September 29, 1946; at City Stadium—Sid Luckman passed for two touchdowns in the first half, covering 33 yards to Scooter McLean and 23 yards to Ken Kavanaugh, as the Bears built a 17-0 lead and coasted to victory. The Bears outgained the Packers, 432 yards to 114.

54. Bears 10, Packers 7; November 3, 1946; at Wrigley Field—The Bears never advanced beyond Green Bay's 22-yard line, but scored 10 points in the third quarter when end Ed Sprinkle returned a Ted Fritsch fumble 30 yards for a touchdown and Frank Maznicki kicked a 28-yard field goal.

55. Packers 29, Bears 20; September 28, 1947; at City Stadium—Quarterback Jack Jacobs passed for two touchdowns and ran for a third, and also intercepted two passes to lead the Packers to victory. The Packers intercepted five passes in all.

56. Bears 20, Packers 17; November 9, 1947; at Wrigley Field—After the Packers took a 10-0 lead early in the second quarter, the Bears quickly erased it with a 31-yard touchdown pass from Sid Luckman to end Jim Keane and an eight-yard touchdown run by halfback Hugh Gallarneau following a Don Kindt fumble recovery. With 20 seconds left in the game, halfback Noah Mullins preserved the victory by blocking a 29-yard field goal attempt by Ward Cuff.

57. Bears 45, Packers 7; September 26, 1948; at City Stadium—Rookie back Johnny Lujack intercepted three of Jack Jacobs' passes in the first half, setting up two touchdowns, as the Bears built a 31-0 lead. The Packers had the ball for eight plays in the first half, and lost the ball four times on interceptions and twice on fumbles.

58. Bears 7, Packers 6; November 14, 1948; at Wrigley Field—The Bears scored in the third quarter on a 34-yard pass from quarterback Bobby Layne to Ed Sprinkle. After the Packers scored late in the fourth quarter, Ed Cody's extra point try went wide right.

59. Bears 17, Packers 0; September 25, 1949; at City Stadium—Quarterback Johnny Lujack, after being knocked out of the game in a scoreless first half, returned in the second half to kick a field goal and throw two touchdown passes. The Packers didn't complete a pass in 13 attempts and had four intercepted.

60. Bears 24, Packers 3; November 6, 1949; at Wrigley Field—Johnny Lujack passed for 177 yards to set up three touchdowns and the Bears limited the

Packers to one field goal on four drives that advanced beyond the Chicago 20-yard line.

61. Packers 31, Bears 21; October 1, 1950; at City Stadium—Back Wally Dreyer returned an interception 28 yards for a touchdown, defensive back Rebel Steiner returned another interception 94 yards for a touchdown, and Billy Grimes returned a punt 68 yards for a touchdown as the Packers used big plays and five turnovers to pull off a victory.

62. Bears 28, Packers 14; October 15, 1950; at Wrigley Field—Johnny Lujack scored on runs of 25, 1, and 7 yards. The Packers scored the first touchdown of the game in the first quarter on a 73-yard run by halfback Billy Grimes.

63. Bears 31, Packers 20; September 30, 1951; at City Stadium—Johnny Lujack passed for 160 yards and rushed for a game-high 54 yards, and the Bears scored all four of their touchdowns on short runs.

64. Bears 24, Packers 13; November 18, 1951; at Wrigley Field—Quarterback Tobin Rote rushed for 150 yards in 14 attempts, but blew two scoring opportunities for the Packers by fumbling in the third quarter at the Chicago 11-yard line and in the fourth quarter at the Chicago three. Fullback John Dottley rushed for 117 yards in 17 attempts to lead the Bears.

65. Bears 24, Packers 14; September 28, 1952; at City Stadium—After end Bob Mann of the Packers dropped a sure touchdown pass with his team trailing 10-7 in the fourth quarter, the Bears exploded for 14 quick points, their final touchdown coming on a 45-yard run by John Dottley.

66. Packers 41, Bears 28; November 9, 1952; at Wrigley Field—Fullback Fred Cone scored two touchdowns, including a 38-yard pass reception that gave the Packers a 24-7 lead in the third quarter, and kicked a field goal and five extra points to spark the victory. Leon Campbell returned a kickoff 86 yards for the Bears' first touchdown and Eddie Macon returned another one 89 yards for the Bears' second touchdown.

67. Bears 17, Packers 13; October 4, 1953; at City Stadium—Quarterback George Blanda threw a 16-yard pass to end Jim Dooley for the winning touchdown with three-and-a-half minutes left. The touchdown pass climaxed a six-play, 51-yard drive following an interception by rookie defensive back George Figner.

68. Bears 21, Packers 21; November 8, 1953; at Wrigley Field—Quarterback Babe Parilli threw a 23-yard touchdown pass to end Billy Howton with 1:15 remaining to give the Packers a tie. The Packers took a 14-0 lead in the first six minutes of the game, but Don Kindt of the Bears narrowed the gap by scoring later in the first quarter on a 67-yard interception return.

69. Bears 10, Packers 3; October 3, 1954; at City Stadium—Former Packers tackle Paul Lipscomb recovered a fumble at the Green Bay nine-yard line,

setting up a five-yard touchdown pass from quarterback George Blanda to halfback Billy Stone in the fourth quarter that gave the Bears the victory on a muddy, sloppy field.

70. Bears 28, Packers 23; November 7, 1954; at Wrigley Field—Linebacker Wayne Hansen returned a fumbled punt 14 yards for a touchdown and George Blanda threw a seven-yard touchdown pass to end John Hoffman as the Bears erased a 23-14 deficit in the final 10 minutes 10 seconds of the game. Switzer, who fumbled the punt that Hansen recovered, scored on a 93-yard return for the Packers in the second quarter.

71. Packers 24, Bears 3; October 2, 1955; at City Stadium—Tobin Rote threw two touchdown passes, covering 32 yards to end Bill Howton and 29 yards to end Gary Knafelc, and fullback Howie Ferguson rushed for 153 yards in 15 carries as the Packers scored an easy victory. The Packers forced six turnovers.

72. Bears 52, Packers 31; November 6, 1955; at Wrigley Field—Fullback Rick Casares rushed for 115 yards in 16 carries and halfback Bobby Watkins rushed for 115 yards in 14 carries to lead the Bears. The Bears led after the third quarter, 38-3, before the two teams combined for six touchdowns and 42 points in the fourth quarter. Howie Ferguson of the Packers also exceeded the 100-yard rushing mark with 117 yards in 17 attempts.

73. Bears 37, Packers 21; October 7, 1956; at City Stadium—Rick Casares rushed for 139 yards in 24 carries to star for the Bears in the final game of the rivalry played at old City Stadium. Quarterback Ed Brown of the Bears passed for two touchdowns and scored another. Al Carmichael of the Packers set an NFL record by returning a kickoff 106 yards for a touchdown.

74. Bears 38, Packers 14; November 11, 1956; at Wrigley Field—End Harlon Hill caught a 70-yard touchdown pass, end Bill McColl caught a 69-yard touchdown pass, and defensive back J.C. Caroline returned an interception 52 yards for a touchdown as the Bears won on big plays.

75. Packers 21, Bears 17; September 29, 1957; at new City Stadium—In the first game ever played at what is now named Lambeau Field, the Packers pulled out a victory on a six-yard touchdown pass from Babe Parilli to Gary Knafelc with 8:21 remaining in the game.

76. Bears 21, Packers 14; November 10, 1957; at Wrigley Field—Rick Casares scored the winning touchdown on a nine-yard run with 1:01 remaining in the game after the Packers failed to convert a fourth-and-one situation at the Bears' 31-yard line. With the score tied, 14-14, late in the third quarter, one of the most controversial plays in the history of the rivalry occurred when halfback Joe Johnson caught a pass from quarterback Bart Starr at the one-yard line and fell into the end zone for what appeared to be a Packers touchdown, but the officials ruled it was an incomplete pass.

77. Bears 34, Packers 20; September 28, 1958; at new City Stadium—Half-back Willie Galimore scored three of the Bears' touchdowns on runs of one and eight yards, and a pass reception of 79 yards.

78. Bears 24, Packers 10; November 9, 1958; at Wrigley Field—Rick Casares rushed for 113 yards in 15 carries and scored on a 64-yard run to lead the Bears.

79. Packers 9, Bears 6; September 27, 1959; at new City Stadium—Fullback Jim Taylor scored on a nine-yard run in the fourth quarter and defensive tackle Dave Hanner tackled Bears quarterback Ed Brown in the end zone for a safety later in the quarter as the Packers pulled out a victory in Vince Lombardi's debut as head coach.

80. Bears 28, Packers 17; November 8, 1959; at Wrigley Field—The Bears converted two fumbles by halfback Paul Hornung into their first two touchdowns. Halfback Merrill Douglas scored on a six-yard run after Hornung fumbled at the Packers' 12-yard line on the second play of the game. Later in the first quarter, Rick Casares scored on a five-yard run after Hornung's second fumble to give the Bears a 14-0 lead.

81. Bears 17, Packers 14; September 25, 1960; at new City Stadium—John Aveni kicked a 16-yard field goal with 35 seconds remaining to climax a fourth-quarter comeback. The Bears scored all of their points in the fourth quarter. Willie Galimore scored the first touchdown on an 18-yard run early in the quarter and Rick Casares scored the second, one minute 55 seconds later, on a 23-yard run.

82. Packers 41, Bears 13; December 4, 1960; at Wrigley Field—Bart Starr completed 17 of 23 passes for 227 yards, including nine of 10 in the second half when the Packers scored 28 of their points. Paul Hornung scored 23 points on two touchdowns, two field goals, and five extra points to give him 152 points after 10 games, a new NFL single-season scoring record. Jim Taylor of the Packers rushed for 140 yards in 24 carries.

83. Packers 24, Bears 0; October 1, 1961; at new City Stadium—The Packers registered their first shutout against the Bears since 1935. Linebacker Dan Currie led Green Bay's defense by intercepting two passes and sacking quarterback Ed Brown for a 13-yard loss on fourth-and-goal from the Green Bay one the first time the Bears had the ball. Jim Taylor rushed for 130 yards in 19 attempts.

84. Packers 31, Bears 28; November 12, 1961; at Wrigley Field—The Packers built a 31-7 lead in the third quarter and registered their first sweep of the Bears since 1935. Paul Hornung scored the Packers' final 10 points on a leaping, 34-yard touchdown pass from Bart Starr and a 51-yard field goal. Rookie tight end Mike Ditka caught nine passes for the Bears, including touchdown receptions of 47, 15, and 29 yards

85. Packers 49, Bears 0; September 30, 1962; at new City Stadium—Jim Taylor rushed for 126 yards in 17 carries and scored three touchdowns as the Packers scored their most lopsided victory in the history of the series.
86. Packers 38, Bears 7; November 4, 1962; at Wrigley Field—Fullback Jim Taylor rushed for 124 yards in 25 attempts and scored four short-yardage touchdowns.
87. Bears 10, Packers 3; September 15, 1963; at new City Stadium—Chicago's defense never allowed the Packers to penetrate beyond its 33-yard line and held them to 150 total yards. Fullback Joe Marconi broke a 3-3 tie in the third quarter, scoring on a one-yard run
88. Bears 26, Packers 7; November 17, 1963; at Wrigley Field—Roger Leclerc kicked two field goals and Willie Galimore scored on a spectacular 27-yard run as the Bears built a 13-0 lead in the first quarter. Leclerc kicked four field goals in all and Galimore led the Bears with 79 yards rushing in 14 carries. The victory gave the Bears a one-game lead over the Packers in the Western Division race with four games to go. The Bears' defense forced seven turnovers, including two interceptions by safety Roosevelt Taylor.
89. Packers 23, Bears 12; September 13, 1964; at new City Stadium—Paul Hornung booted a 52-yard field goal on a free kick on the final play of the first half to give the Packers a 17-3 lead. Hornung kicked three field goals in all and rushed for 77 yards in 15 carries in his first regular-season appearance after being suspended for the entire 1963 season.
90. Packers 17, Bears 3; December 5, 1964; at Wrigley Field—Safety Willie Wood set up two touchdowns with punt returns of 64 and 42 yards, and also set up the Packers' field goal with an interception return.
91. Packers 23, Bears 14; October 3, 1965; at Lambeau Field—The Packers built a 23-0 lead before rookie running back Gale Sayers scored two second-half touchdowns on a six-yard run and a 65-yard pass reception in his first extended appearance as a pro.
92. Bears 31, Packers 10; October 31, 1965; at Wrigley Field—The Bears scored 17 points in the second quarter after the Packers had scored a touchdown on the game's opening drive. The Bears intercepted Bart Starr three times, including two in the second quarter by defensive end Doug Atkins and cornerback Bennie McRae that set up touchdowns.
93. Packers 17, Bears 0; October 16, 1966; at Wrigley Field—The Packers limited running back Gale Sayers to 29 yards in 15 attempts and registered their first shutout over the Bears in Chicago since 1932. The Packers scored all of their points in the second half, including a touchdown on a 20-yard interception return by Willie Wood midway through the fourth quarter.
94. Packers 13, Bears 6; November 20, 1966; at Lambeau Field—Reserve quarterback Zeke Bratkowski replaced an injured Bart Starr late in the first

quarter and sparked the victory with two touchdown passes to wide receiver Carroll Dale, including the game-winner on a 32-yard pass late in the fourth quarter.

95. Packers 13, Bears 10; September 24, 1967; at Lambeau Field—Don Chandler kicked the game-winning field goal from 46 yards out with 1:03 remaining. Fullback Jim Grabowski led the Packers with 111 yards in 32 attempts. The Bears lost despite forcing eight turnovers.

96. Packers 17, Bears 13; November 26, 1967; at Wrigley Field—Halfback Donny Anderson scored the go-ahead touchdown in the second quarter on a one-yard run, following a 69-yard kickoff return by Travis Williams, as the Packers clinched the Central Division championship with three games to go. This was the last Bears-Packers game for Hall of Fame coaches George Halas and Vince Lombardi.

97. Bears 13, Packers 10; November 3, 1968; at Lambeau Field—Mac Percival kicked a 43-yard field goal on a free kick with 32 seconds left to give the Bears the victory. Gale Sayers rushed for 205 yards in 24 carries.

98. Packers 28, Bears 27; December 15, 1968; at Wrigley Field—Third-string quarterback Don Horn engineered the victory—Bart Starr was sidelined with a rib injury and Zeke Bratkowski injured his ribs late in the first quarter—by completing 10 of 16 passes for 187 yards, including a 67-yard touchdown to Jim Grabowski. Linebacker Ray Nitschke intercepted a Jack Concannon pass at the Green Bay 35 with 1:07 remaining to thwart the Bears' final threat and deprive them of the Central Division title.

99. Packers 17, Bears 0; September 21, 1969; at Lambeau Field—Halfback Travis Williams rushed for 67 yards in 18 carries and caught a 31-yard touchdown pass from Bart Starr to spark the Packers' victory.

100. Packers 21, Bears 3; December 14, 1969; at Wrigley Field—Travis Williams scored on a 39-yard run and a 60-yard pass from Don Horn to again lead the Packers to victory.

101. Packers 20, Bears 19; November 15, 1970; at Lambeau Field—Bart Starr engineered an 80-yard drive that started with 1:40 left in the game and scored the winning touchdown on a three-yard rollout with three seconds showing on the clock. Starr, who was 36 years old at the time, completed 23 of 35 passes for 220 yards.

102. Bears 35, Packers 17; December 13, 1970; at Wrigley Field—Quarterback Jack Concannon completed 21 of 34 passes for 338 yards and four touchdowns to lead the Bears to victory in the last game played between the two teams at Wrigley Field.

103. Packers 17, Bears 14; November 7, 1971; at Soldier Field—Dave Hampton returned a kickoff 62 yards to set up a 22-yard, game-winning field goal by Lou Michaels with 59 seconds remaining. Quarterback Bobby

Douglass had scored on a one-yard run with 3:18 remaining to tie the score after linebacker Dick Butkus had recovered a fumble by Hampton at the Green Bay 11.

104. Packers 31, Bears 10; December 12, 1971; at Lambeau Field—Quarterback Scott Hunter threw a 77-yard touchdown pass to Carroll Dale on the first play from scrimmage to propel the Packers to victory on "Ray Nitschke Day."

105. Packers 20, Bears 17; October 8, 1972; at Lambeau Field—Rookie kicker Chester Marcol booted the game-winning field goal from 37 yards out with 30 seconds remaining. Mac Percival of the Bears missed a 51-yard field goal attempt with five seconds left.

106. Packers 23, Bears 17; November 12, 1972; at Soldier Field—Chester Marcol kicked a 51-yard field goal in the first half as the Packers built a 17-7 lead and two more, both from 21 yards out, in the second half.

107. Bears 31, Packers 17; November 4, 1973; at Lambeau Field—Bobby Douglass rushed for 100 yards in 19 carries and scored four short-yardage touchdowns, including three in the second half, as the Bears overcame a 17-10 halftime deficit.

108. Packers 21, Bears 0; December 16, 1973; at Soldier Field—Fullback John Brockington rushed for 142 yards in 22 attempts and halfback MacArthur Lane gained 101 yards in 19 carries—the first time in history two Packers running backs surpassed 100 yards in the same game—as the Packers won despite completing only three passes.

109. Bears 10, Packers 9; October 21, 1974; at Soldier Field—The Bears scored all of their points on their first two possesions as Mirro Roder kicked a 24-yard field goal and wide receiver Charlie Wade caught a 57-yard touchdown pass from quarterback Gary Huff. In the second half, the Packers started drives from the Chicago 29-, 37-, and 36-yard lines, following turnovers, but had to settle for three field goals.

110. Packers 20, Bears 3; November 10, 1974, at Milwaukee County Stadium—Steve Odom returned a punt 95 yards for a touchdown to break a 3-3 tie in the second quarter.

111. Bears 27, Packers 14; November 9, 1975; at Soldier Field—Running back Walter Payton climaxed a 71-yard drive by scoring on a five-yard run with 51 seconds left in the first half to give the Bears a 17-7 lead, and safety Craig Clemons returned an interception 76 yards for a touchdown to pad the margin in the second half.

112. Packers 28, Bears 7; November 30, 1975; at Lambeau Field—John Brockington rushed for 111 yards in 26 attempts and scored three touchdowns to lead the Packers.

113. Bears 24, Packers 13; November 14, 1976, at Soldier Field—Chicago converted two Green Bay fumbles into touchdowns in the first quarter and Walter Payton, then in his second year, surpassed the 100-yard mark for the first time against Green Bay with 109 yards in 18 carries.

114. Bears 16, Packers 10; November 28, 1976; at Lambeau Field—Bob Thomas kicked three field goals and Walter Payton rushed for 110 yards in 27 carries as the Bears prevailed in six-degree weather with a minus-14 wind chill.

115. Bears 26, Packers 0; October 30, 1977; at Lambeau Field—Walter Payton rushed for 205 yards in 23 attempts as the Bears piled up 375 yards rushing and won in a cakewalk despite completing only four passes.

116. Bears 21, Packers 10; December 11, 1977; at Soldier Field—Walter Payton surpassed the 100-yard mark for the fourth straight time against the Packers, gaining 163 yards in 32 carries.

117. Packers 24, Bears 14; October 8, 1978; at Lambeau Field—Safety Steve Luke recovered a fumble to set up a Chester Marcol field goal and returned an interception 63 yards for a touchdown as the Packers won despite being outgained 357 yards to 166.

118. Bears 14, Packers 0; December 10, 1978; at Soldier Field—The Bears scored on a one-yard run by Walter Payton in the second quarter and on a 35-yard pass from quarterback Mike Phipps to wide receiver James Scott in the third quarter to prevent the Packers from clinching a playoff berth.

119. Bears 6, Packers 3; September 2, 1979; at Soldier Field—Bob Thomas kicked two first-half field goals from 25 and 19 yards out, and the Bears sacked Packers quarterback David Whitehurst six times.

120. Bears 15, Packers 14; December 9, 1979; at Lambeau Field—Linebacker Tom Hicks intercepted a Lynn Dickey screen pass and returned it 66 yards for a touchdown early in the fourth quarter to give the Bears a 12-7 lead. Bob Thomas kicked a 44-yard field goal less than two minutes later to make it 15-7.

121. Packers 12, Bears 6 (ot); September 7, 1980; at Lambeau Field—Chester Marcol ran 25 yards for the winning touchdown 5 minutes, 53 seconds into overtime after defensive tackle Alan Page blocked his 34-yard field goal attempt.

122. Bears 61, Packers 7; December 7, 1980; at Soldier Field—Quarterback Vince Evans completed 18 of 32 passes for 316 yards and Walter Payton rushed for 130 yards in 22 attempts as the Bears gained 594 total yards in their most one-sided victory in the history of the rivalry.

123. Packers 16, Bears 9; September 6, 1981; at Soldier Field—The Packers took a 13-0 lead in the first half and escaped with the victory when fullback Matt Suhey lost a controversial fumble—the Bears' contention was

that he was down before the ball popped loose—at the Green Bay one-yard line with 32 seconds remaining.

124. Packers 21, Bears 17; November 15, 1981; at Lambeau Field—David Whitehurst threw three touchdown passes, including a 39-yarder to running back Harlan Huckleby for the go-ahead score in the second quarter.

125. Packers 31, Bears 28; December 4, 1983; at Lambeau Field—Jan Stenerud kicked a 19-yard field goal as time expired. The field goal was set up by a 67-yard pass from Lynn Dickey to wide receiver James Lofton. The Bears had tied the score with 1:50 left on a 59-yard punt return by Dennis McKinnon.

126. Bears 23, Packers 21; December 18, 1983; at Soldier Field—Bob Thomas kicked a 22-yard field goal with 10 seconds remaining.

127. Bears 9, Packers 7; September 16, 1984; at Lambeau Field—Bob Thomas kicked three field goals, including a 28-yarder with 11:11 remaining, after the Packers had taken a 7-6 lead into the fourth quarter. The Bears ran 72 plays to the Packers' 45 and held a 40:50 to 19:10 edge in time of possession.

128. Packers 20, Bears 14; December 9, 1984; at Soldier Field—Backup quarterback Rich Campbell threw a 43-yard touchdown pass to wide receiver Phil Epps with 34 seconds remaining after the Bears had taken a 14-13 lead early in the fourth quarter. The Packers scored their second touchdown on a 97-yard kickoff return by Del Rodgers.

129. Bears 23, Packers 7; October 21, 1985; at Soldier Field—After the Packers took a 7-0 lead in the first quarter, the Bears scored 21 points in the second quarter on three short touchdown runs. Walter Payton scored two of them behind blocks by defensive tackle William Perry, who lined up in the backfield, and Perry scored the other.

130. Bears 16, Packers 10; November 3, 1985; at Lambeau Field—Defensive tackle Steve McMichael tackled quarterback Jim Zorn for a safety with 12:18 left in the game and the Bears drove 49 yards following the Packers' free kick to score the winning touchdown on a 27-yard run by Walter Payton. The game was marred by 15 penalties, including five unsportsmanlike conduct calls.

131. Bears 25, Packers 12; September 22, 1986; at Lambeau Field—Trailing 12-10 in the third quarter, the Bears scored the final 15 points of the game on a 52-yard field goal by Kevin Butler, a safety by Steve McMichael, a 42-yard pass from quarterback Steve Fuller to wide receiver Keith Ortego, and a 27-yard field goal by Butler.

132. Bears 12, Packers 10; November 23, 1986; at Soldier Field—Kevin Butler kicked the game-winning field goal from 32 yards out with 2:37 remaining after safety Dave Duerson recovered a fumble on the Green Bay 34.

133. Bears 26, Packers 24; November 8, 1987; at Lambeau Field—Kevin Butler kicked a 52-yard field goal as time expired to give the Bears the victory. After the Packers scored on a 47-yard field goal by Al Del Greco with one minute left, quarterback Jim McMahon completed two passes, covering 41 yards, to set up Butler's winning kick.

134. Bears 23, Packers 10; November 29, 1987; at Soldier Field—After the Packers had taken a 10-7 lead in the second quarter, the Bears rallied to win behind three field goals by Kevin Butler. He converted from the 21-, 27-, and 52-yard lines.

135. Bears 24, Packers 6; September 25, 1988; at Lambeau Field—After turning the ball over on their first three series and falling behind 6-0, the Bears scored 17 points in the second quarter on 45- and three-yard touchdown runs by halfback Neal Anderson and a 35-yard field goal by Kevin Butler. The Bears ran the ball on 51 of 72 offensive plays. Anderson finished with 105 yards rushing in 20 carries.

136. Bears 16, Packers 0; November 27, 1988; at Soldier Field—Neal Anderson gained 139 yards in 17 carries, including an 80-yard touchdown run. The Packers had only 11 rushing attempts for a mere 22 yards.

137. Packers 14, Bears 13; November 5, 1989; at Lambeau Field—Quarterback Don Majkowski threw a controversial 14-yard touchdown pass to wide receiver Sterling Sharpe with 32 seconds remaining as the Packers snapped an eight-game losing streak against the Bears. The officials on the field ruled that Majkowski had crossed the line of scrimmage before delivering the pass, but the replay official reversed the call.

138. Packers 40, Bears 28; December 17, 1989; at Soldier Field—Don Majkowski and running back Keith Woodside accounted for all four of Green Bay's touchdowns. Majkowski completed 21 of 36 passes for 244 yards and a touchdown, and also ran for two touchdowns. Woodside rushed for 116 yards in 10 attempts, including a 68-yard run for the first touchdown of the game.

139. Bears 31, Packers 13; September 16, 1990; at Lambeau Field—Backup quarterback Anthony Dilweg, starting his second game following a 45-day holdout by Don Majkowski, was sacked six times, fumbled three times, and threw an interception as the Bears' defense dominated the game.

140. Bears 27, Packers 13; October 7, 1990; at Soldier Field—Neal Anderson rushed for 141 yards in 21 carries and Kevin Butler kicked field goals of 50 and 51 yards to lead the Bears.

141. Bears 10, Packers 0; October 17, 1991; at Lambeau Field—The Bears limited the Packers to five first downs and 138 yards total yards, and scored their only touchdown in the second quarter on an eight-yard pass from quarterback Jim Harbaugh to tight end James Thornton.

142. Bears 27, Packers 13; December 8, 1991; at Soldier Field—Jim Harbaugh threw two touchdown passes to wide receiver Wendell Davis, covering 20 and 35 yards, after the Packers had taken a 10-7 lead in the second quarter. Running back Brad Muster also scored two touchdowns on runs of eight and six yards. The victory was Mike Ditka's 100th in regular-season play as a head coach.

143. Bears 30, Packers 10; October 25, 1992; at Lambeau Field—A 43-yard pass from punter Chris Gardocki to running back Mark Green on a controversial play—league officials later declared that the Bears sent more than two players in motion on the play—sparked a 17-point outburst by the Bears in the second quarter. Before the fake punt, Green ran onto the field, then headed back, stopping just short of the sideline and running a pass route. League officials also declared that Green had not come within five yards of the Bears' huddle and was an ineligible player.

144. Packers 17, Bears 3; November 22, 1992; at Soldier Field—Running back Edgar Bennett rushed for 107 yards in 29 attempts in his first pro start to the lead the Packers to victory. The Packers scored the go-ahead touchdown in the second quarter on a 49-yard touchdown pass from quarterback Brett Favre to wide receiver Sterling Sharpe.

145. Packers 17, Bears 3; October 31, 1993; at Lambeau Field—Brett Favre engineered a 17-play, 91-yard touchdown drive in the fourth quarter that sealed the victory. Running back Darrell Thompson climaxed the drive with a 17-yard touchdown run.

146. Bears 30, Packers 17; December 5, 1993; at Soldier Field—Cornerback Jeremy Lincoln took a lateral from linebacker Dante Jones following an interception of a Brett Favre pass and ran 80 more yards for one touchdown; Jones recovered a Favre fumble and returned it 32 yards for another touchdown; and safety Mark Carrier returned another interception off Favre for a 34-yard touchdown to lead the Bears.

147. Packers 33, Bears 6; October 31, 1994; at Soldier Field—Edgar Bennett rushed for 105 yards in 26 carries and Brett Favre scored on a 36-yard run as the Packers won in a driving rain and 45-mile per hour winds.

148. Packers 40, Bears 3; December, 11, 1994; at Lambeau Field—Edgar Bennett rushed for 106 yards in 22 attempts and Brett Favre threw three touchdown passes, including two to Sterling Sharpe.

149. Packers 27, Bears 24; September 11, 1995; at Soldier Field—Brett Favre threw three touchdown passes in the first half, including a 99-yarder to wide receiver Robert Brooks, as the Packers built a 24-7 lead, and defensive end Reggie White forced an Erik Kramer fumble with two minutes left to seal the victory.

150. Packers 35, Bears 28; November 12, 1995; at Lambeau Field—Brett Favre completed 25 of 33 passes for 336 yards and five touchdowns, including the game-winner on a 16-yard screen pass to Edgar Bennett in the fourth quarter. With two minutes left, safety LeRoy Butler preserved the victory by intercepting an Erik Kramer pass in the end zone.

151. Packers 37, Bears 6; October 6, 1996; at Soldier Field—Brett Favre threw four touchdown passes, including a 50-yard "Hail Mary" to wide receiver Antonio Freeman on the final play of the first half, and Don Beebe returned a kickoff 90 yards for a touchdown as the Packers exploded for 34 points in the second and third quarters.

152. Packers 28, Bears 17; December 1, 1996; at Lambeau Field—Desmond Howard returned a punt 75 yards for a touchdown to give the Packers a 14-7 lead in the third quarter, and two fourth-quarter touchdowns by running back Dorsey Levens and Brett Favre sealed the victory.

The Bears have won 81 games, the Packers have won 65, and there have been six ties entering the 1997 season.

Bibliography

Chicago Bears media guides, 1966 to present
Chicago Tribune, 1921 to present
The Game That Was, by Myron Cope
Green Cathedrals, by Philip J. Lowry
Green Bay Packers media guides, 1956 to present
Green Bay Packers and NFL game programs, 1952 to present
Green Bay Press-Gazette, 1921 to present
Halas by Halas: The Autobiography of George Halas, with Gwen
    Morgan and Arthur Veysey
George Halas and the Chicago Bears, by George Vass
The Milwaukee Journal, 1933 to 1995
Milwaukee Journal Sentinel, 1995 to present
Racine Journal-News, 1921-1922
NCAA Football: The Official 1996 College Football Records Book
Notre Dame Football Press Guide, 1996
National Football League Record and Fact Book, 1936 to present
The NFL's Official Encyclopedic History of Professional Football
Packer Legends in Facts, by Eric Goska
The Official Encyclopedia of Football
The Sports Encyclopedia: Pro Football
The Baseball Encyclopedia

Index

Gary D'Amato

Gary D'Amato, a sports columnist and feature writer for the *Milwaukee Journal Sentinel*, has covered some of the most prestigious sporting events in the world. His assignments have included the Super Bowl, the Olympics, the Masters golf tournament, the Indianapolis 500, and an Evander Holyfield-Mike Tyson heavyweight championship fight. In 1996, D'Amato's story about Michael Johnson's triumph in the 200-meter dash at the Summer Olympics was judged one of the top five event stories of the year in the national Associated Press Sports Editors contest. D'Amato also has won an APSE award for best sports column; a Milwaukee Press Club award for best state sports story; and three Wisconsin Newspaper Association awards for sports writing and feature writing. In 1992, D'Amato won the Russ Catlin Award, a national honor, for the best auto racing story of the year. D'Amato was born in St. Francis, a suburb of Milwaukee, and was graduated from the University of Wisconsin-Whitewater. Prior to working for the *Journal Sentinel*, he covered sports for the *Freeport Journal-Standard,* the *Racine Journal Times,* and *The Milwaukee Journal*. He is the co-author of one other book: *The Packer Tapes*, published in 1995 by Prairie Oak Press.

Cliff Christl

Cliff Christl, an assistant sports editor for the *Milwaukee Journal Sentinel*, spent twelve years covering the Green Bay Packers in the 1970s and 1980s. He has been named sportswriter of the year in Wisconsin a record-matching five times by the National Sportscasters and Sportswriters Association. Twice in the last four years, Christl has placed in the top ten in the national Associated Press Sports Editors contest in the enterprise reporting category. He has won a Wisconsin Newspaper Association award for best state sports column and a Milwaukee Press Club award for best state sports story. The Wisconsin Newspaper Association also awarded him an honorable mention for investigative news reporting. Christl was born in Green Bay and was graduated from the University of Wisconsin-Oshkosh. Prior to working for the *Journal Sentinel*, he covered sports for the *Manitowoc Herald-Times, Green Bay Press-Gazette*, and *The Milwaukee Journal*. He is the co-author of two other books: *Sleepers, Busts & Franchise-Makers: The Story of the Pro Football Draft*; and *Bicycling Wisconsin.*

Don Pierson

Don Pierson, who wrote the foreword for the book, has covered pro football for the *Chicago Tribune* since 1969. He covered the Chicago Bears from 1972 to 1987, and the NFL at-large since 1988. In 1994, Pierson won the Dick McCann Award, presented at the Pro Football Hall of Fame for long and distinguished reporting of pro football.